FANTASY CITY

American cities have reinvented themselves, devastated by the impact of deindustrialization and government cutbacks. In *Fantasy City*, John Hannigan describes how cities have now come to represent themed fantasy experiences; the piers, factories and warehouses of the past have been replaced by the casinos, megaplex cinemas and themed restaurants. *Fantasy City* offers the first comprehensive account of how this new form of urban development has emerged and intensified and asks whether such areas of fantasy end up destroying communities or create new groupings of shared identities and experiences.

By offering provocative insights into urban development and by drawing on extensive material taken from a wide range of sources, John Hannigan has written the first comprehensive account of this new form of urban development. *Fantasy City* will therefore be essential reading for urban sociologists and students in geography, cultural studies and current affairs.

John Hannigan is Professor of Sociology at the University of Toronto. He is the author of *Environmental Sociology* also published by Routledge.

FANTASY CITY

Pleasure and profit in the postmodern
metropolis

John Hannigan

London and New York

First published 1998
by Routledge
11 New Fetter Lane, London EC4P 4EE

Simultaneously published in the USA and Canada
by Routledge
29 West 35th Street, New York, NY 10001

Routledge is an imprint of the Taylor & Francis Group

Reprinted 1999, 2000

© 1998 John Hannigan

Typeset in Goudy by Routledge
Printed and bound in Great Britain by Biddles Ltd, www.biddles.co.uk

British Library Cataloguing in Publication Data
A catalogue record for this book is available from the British Library

Library of Congress Cataloguing in Publication Data
Hannigan, John.
Fantasy city: pleasure and profit in the postmodern metropolis / John Hannigan.
p. cm.
Includes bibliographical references and index.
1. Cities and towns–United States. 2. City and town life–United States. 3. Sociology,
Urban–United States. I. Title.
HT123.H337   1998
307.76´0973–dc21   98–23774
CIP

ISBN 0–415–15097–3 (hbk)
ISBN 0–415–15098–1 (pbk)

FOR RUTH, OLIVIA, MAEVE, TIM AND T.J.

CONTENTS

ILLUSTRATIONS

Tables

Figures

PREFACE AND
ACKNOWLEDGEMENTS

Anyone who writes a book entirely about urban entertainment is assumed to be either a dedicated fan or an implacable ideological enemy. Alas, I fall into neither camp. Although I don't claim to be an amusement park aficionado, I fondly recall my experience as a child riding the giant roller coaster at Crystal Beach, at the time the longest wooden structure of its type in the world. I don't dream of attending fantasy baseball camps in Florida, yet I still take my glove to games at the Skydome and can boast of having seen batting legend Harmon Killebrew play as a Washington Senator (several times). I've never been to a Rolling Stones concert but I've seen Tom Jones perform at the MGM Grand in Las Vegas. What I will confess to, however, is a lifelong fascination with cities – their architecture, rhythms and subcultures. While I cannot claim to have worn out as many pairs of shoes as the 1920s pioneering urban sociologist Robert Park, I've nevertheless spent many hours exploring cities and their attractions around the world. And, as a veteran city-watcher, I am intrigued by the question of whether the themed entertainment destinations which I discuss in *Fantasy City* will create a new sense of urban vibrancy and vitality or, alternatively, will instill a safer, but duller version of metropolitan life.

Fantasy City began as a 1995 "Trend Report" in the journal *Current Sociology* on the nature of the postmodern city. My thanks to the editor Bob Brym for encouraging me to delve into this body of research. Kudos should also go to my editor at Routledge, Mari Shullaw, who gave the go-ahead for this project, so totally different from my previous book on the social construction of environmental problems. Although we had never met prior to my completing the first draft, Sharon Zukin nevertheless provided great encouragement for polishing the final manuscript of *Fantasy City*, through her written comments and her enthusiasm for the topic, conveyed over a lunch in Toronto's Eaton Center in August 1997. I would also like to thank Jeff McNair and Steve Rhys of Forrec Ltd. who gave up several hours from their hectic schedules to help me sort out hype from reality in the themed entertainment business. Of course, I am solely responsible for the specific interpretations to be found in this book.

Finally, as with my first book, my family helped immensely. Tim, our resident computer ace and pop guru, provided numerous free services from setting up the text and tables on the Mac to scanning in the boxed inserts. My multi-talented wife, Ruth, took many of the accompanying photographs and performed miracles as the photo editor on the other pictures. Her fascination with marketing in the entertainment business has been infectious and has led to many interesting and worthwhile discussions. The weekly arrival of the trade paper *Amusement Business* is always an event in our house. Thanks also to Maeve, Olivia and T.J. for their assurances that Dad was doing something "neat."

ABBREVIATIONS

APA	American Planning Association
AWZA	American Wilderness Zoo & Aquarium
BID	Business Improvement District
DDC	Disney Development Company
FEC	Family Entertainment Centre
IPO	Initial public offering
LBE	Location based entertainment
LBO	Leveraged buyout
MLB	Major League Baseball
NBA	National Basketball Association
NFL	National Football League
REIT	Real estate investment trust
RFP	Request for Proposals
SMSA	Standard Metropolitan Statistical Area
SFRA	San Francisco Redevelopment Agency
TEA	Themed Entertainment Association
TIF	Tax increment financing
UEC	Urban entertainment center
UED	Urban entertainment destination
ULI	Urban Land Institute
WEM	West Edmonton Mall

CHRONOLOGY OF KEY EVENTS

1933	The first drive-in movie theater opens in Camden, New Jersey.
1955	Disneyland opens in Anaheim, California.
1958	The Dodgers team move from Brooklyn, New York to Los Angeles.
1961	The Six Flags Over Texas theme park opens, the first one in the Six Flags chain.
1964	Freedomland USA theme park is unsuccessful.
1965	The State of Nevada allows the corporate ownership of gambling casinos.
1971	Peter Morton and Isaac Tigrett launch the Hard Rock Cafe in London, Great Britain.
1971	The Magic Kingdom, the first phase of Disney World, opens near Orlando, Florida.
1975	The Detroit Lions leave the downtown Tiger Stadium for the suburban Pontiac Silverdome.
1976	The State of New Jersey licenses Atlantic City as a gaming center.
1981	Faneuil Hall opens in Boston, which begins the start of the festival market place phenomenon.
1982	The Hard Rock Cafe chain arrives in the US, with the opening of its first Los Angeles restaurant.
1982	EPCOT opens in Florida
1985	The West Edmonton Mall is completed. It is the first shopping center of its kind to combine shopping and entertainment to a significant degree.
1989	Disney–MGM Studios opens in Florida.
1991	In New York, Robert Earl opens the first Planet Hollywood theme restaurant.
1991	The *Diamond Queen* is launched on the Mississippi River in Iowa. America's first modern-day riverboat casino, it initiates the start of legalized riverboat gambling in the US.

1992   Oriole Park at Camden Yards in Baltimore, Maryland is completed. This is the first of the neo-traditional ballparks located in American central city sites.

1993   Universal CityWalk opens in California.

1994   Seagram buys MCA for $5.7 billion.

1995   Disney purchases Capital Cities/ABC for $19 billion. The age of "synergies" is now in full swing.

1995   The 104-year-old Elitch Gardens opens its season at a new site in lower downtown Denver, the only US amusement park so far to relocate to a downtown site.

1996   NikeTown opens in Manhattan, launching a new chapter in retail theater.

1997   Disney opens the refurbished New Amsterdam Theater on 42nd Street in New York – the cornerstone of the much heralded 42nd Street Development Project.

1997   Ogden opens its first American Wilderness Experience at Ontario Mills Mall, forty miles east of Los Angeles, becoming the first of a new generation of simulated nature attractions in exurban shopping centers.

INTRODUCTION

On a bitterly cold winter's night in March 1997, thousands of local Toronto people turned out to celebrate the opening of the city's Planet Hollywood restaurant. At a closed-off intersection at the base of the CN Tower, a makeshift stage was erected, flanked by a set of giant speakers. After dark, Hollywood star Bruce Willis, accompanied by fellow celebrity investors Demi Moore and Sylvester Stallone, took to the stage where he and his rock band, The Accelerators, performed a brief set before retiring inside the restaurant to an inaugural party whose guests included actors Luke Perry and Tom Arnold, blues musician Jeff Healy and a sprinkling of players from the Toronto Raptors basketball team. By nine o'clock the street was quiet and the crowd had begun to wander off. The event lived on, however, in the prominent coverage it received in the local media over the next day, and again when rumors (unfounded) of a marital split between Willis and Moore briefly surfaced. Two weeks later with an estimated 15,000 fans in attendance, Willis and Arnold again, together with celebrity shareholder Arnold Schwarzenegger, movie stars Will Smith and Samuel L. Jackson, and rock musician Jon Bon Jovi, popped up in Vancouver to launch yet another Planet Hollywood restaurant. "We are bringing memorabilia from warehouses in Hollywood, the authentic stuff", Schwarzenegger said. "And we bring an incredible amount of celebrities" ("Stars draw throng" 1997).

The Planet Hollywood openings are part of a "new phase of entertaining consumption" (Warren 1993: 174) which is sweeping across urban landscapes worldwide. In its wake it is depositing an infrastructure of casinos, megaplex cinemas, themed restaurants, simulation theaters, interactive theme rides and virtual reality arcades which collectively promise to change the face of leisure in the postmodern metropolis. So far, we've only glimpsed the leading edge of this emerging "Fantasy City" but there is every indication that by the next millennium this will have become a global trend. In the late 1990s, nearly every major multinational entertainment company has established a development team to evaluate, plan and initiate urban entertainment destination (UED) projects. At least a dozen of the key real estate developers in North America have indicated that they will introduce projects which will feature significant entertainment components, either as a retail anchor or as a stand alone venue (Beyard and

1

Rubin 1995: 6). In the near future, major entertainment complexes are set to open on 42nd Street in New York, at Metreon in San Francisco, and on the site of a retired military base in Toronto. Stricter planning laws, more active city centers and less competitive retail markets have all contributed to a somewhat slower pace of UED development in Europe, but a trio of first generation projects – Centro in Oberhausen, Germany; Port Vell along the harbor in Barcelona, Spain; and Kinepolis in Brussels, Belgium – are on a comparable scale to their American cousins (Robinett and Camp 1997). The Asia-Pacific region is a major growth area for themed entertainment projects (see Chapter 9) as a pent-up demand for retail, entertainment and recreational activities fuels the construction of scores of theme parks, water parks and malls. China, for example, has embraced this new phenomenon with forty-one theme parks having opened over the last decade and many more planned, including one scheduled for a northern suburb of Beijing which promises, somewhat ominously, to simulate the blast of the nuclear bomb which destroyed Hiroshima ("Asians at play" 1996:48–9).

These developments are indicative of a new urban economy which has its roots in tourism, sports, culture and entertainment. In what may be a sign of things to come, a 1995 report by a business forecasting group at the University of California, Los Angeles, announced that for the first time the number of jobs in entertainment industries in the State of California surpassed those in the aerospace industry. In the Los Angeles area alone it is estimated that there are more than 4,400 firms who make their living out of the film business and 100,000 freelancers employed in the industry ("A busted flush" 1997: 26). Tourism remains a strong force in the local economy, producing an annual revenue of $7.2 billion; making it second only to business and management services as the LA region's largest industrial sector (Molotch 1996: 240). Next door in the State of Nevada, Las Vegas, the once and future entertainment capital of America, is booming. Between the years 1989–1999 it will have welcomed $16 billion worth of investments in entertainment related mega-projects. Taking its cue from these larger entertainment capitals, municipalities across Canada and the US have attempted to bolster local economies which have lost their manufacturing base by undertaking new development which blends sports, entertainment and retail. In Trenton, New Jersey's Roebling redevelopment area, formerly the site of a collection of aging steel and wire factories, a $45 million arena is to be built forming part of a triangle of new construction which includes: Waterfront Park, a minor-league baseball stadium; a $44 million hotel and conference center; and a renovated Trenton War memorial. "For Trenton to advance," Mercer County executive Robert D. Pranetti observed, "we had to find a niche in modern economic times . . . and the leisure-spending industry is probably among the fastest growing in an area in which older cities like this can be competitive" (Gabarine 1997).

Defining features

Fantasy City is bounded and defined by six central features. First, it is *theme-o-centric*, by which I mean that everything from individual entertainment venues to the image of the city itself conforms to a scripted theme, normally drawn from sports, history or popular entertainment. Sometimes, a single theme is used, for example, based around a blockbuster movie, a cartoon character or a country-music star. While at other times, "theme enhancement" is employed in which an ambience is created around a distinctive geographic locale, historical period or type of cultural activity. Within large-scale projects "multi-theming" is implemented in which the site is divided into a series of zones, each with its own thematic focus (Rubin *et al.* 1994: 64). Such theming is "singularly blind to context" (Adler 1995: 70), especially with relation to the surrounding neighborhood. While developers make some effort to tie the different elements of their projects together under an umbrella of motifs such as "old town" or "seaside," in fact, each restaurant, theater or shop is internally themed according to a standard formula which is "rolled out" across the globe.

Second, not only is Fantasy City themed but it is also aggressively *branded*. Urban entertainment destinations are not financed and marketed exclusively on the basis of their ability to deliver a high degree of consumer satisfaction and fun but also on their potential for selling licensed merchandise on site. Sometimes branded identities derive from the success of a location based entertainment (LBE) project, but in other instances they represent the imposition of pre-existing consumer and show business brands (such as Nike, Universal, Coca-Cola, ViaCom) on leisure sites in the expectation of creating a profitable "synergy." Another option is the rising popularity of "naming rights"; the sale of corporate names for sports stadiums and arenas and concert halls. While such public places as Grand Central Station or Piccadilly Circus are not up for grabs just yet, a kind of precedent was set recently when Continental Airlines became the first national corporate sponsor of New York's theater district, soon to be re-christened "Continental World" ("Coffee, tea or Broadway" 1997). Indeed, one indicator of the rapidly institutionalizing linkage between branding and UEDs may be seen in plans by the Themed Entertainment Association's Northeast Chapter to offer a fourteen week course through New York University's Stern School of Business titled, "Expanding Your Brand Through Location-Based Venues. "

Third, Fantasy City operates *day and night*, in the same spirit as the Nevada casinos. This reflects its intended market of "baby boomer" and "Generation X" adults in search of leisure, sociability and entertainment. In marked contrast to the traditional suburban shopping mall which shuts down by nine or ten o'clock at night, the developers of urban entertainment centers (UECs) actively encourage after-dark activities which range from themed night clubs (Billboard Live, Dave & Busters) to late-night entertainment "destinations" in tourist areas such as south Florida (Church Street Station, Coco Walk, Disney's Pleasure Island).

Fourth, Fantasy City is *modular*, mixing and matching an increasingly standard array of components in various configurations. Typically, an UED project will contain one or more themed restaurants (the Hard Rock Cafe, Planet Hollywood, the Rainforest Cafe), a megaplex cinema, an IMAX theater, record (HMV, Virgin, Tower) and book (Barnes & Noble, Borders) megastores, and some form of interactive, high-tech arcade complete with virtual reality games and ride simulators. Large, publicly sponsored projects might also include an aquarium, sport stadium and/or arena, live theater and a science museum. Paradoxically, the more cities seek to differentiate themselves on the basis of distinctive fantasy themes, the more they resemble one another with the same line-up of attractions.

Fifth, Fantasy City is *solipsistic*; isolated from surrounding neighborhoods physically, economically and culturally. As such, it is the epitome of what Christine Boyer (1993) has termed the "city of illusion" – a metropolis which ignores the reality of homelessness, unemployment, social injustice and crime, while eagerly transforming sites and channels of public expression into "promotional spaces." Despite some concessions towards minority hiring, job training and investment, too many UED projects stand apart from their neighbors. In this respect they emulate the experience of Atlantic City, where the glittering strip of casino-hotels along the Boardwalk stand in stark juxtaposition to a declining local community.

Finally, Fantasy City arguably is *postmodern* insomuch as it is constructed around technologies of simulation, virtual reality and the thrill of the spectacle. Without a doubt, a major inspiration has been the Disney model, not just because it has been widely imitated but also because a number of the Disney "imagineers" (designers) have migrated to other entertainment and real estate companies and projects where they bring their "Magic Kingdom" sensibility. Increasingly, as motion picture and amusement park technologies merge to produce a new generation of attractions, the space between authenticity and illusion recedes, creating the condition of "hyperreality" described by such postmodern writers as Umberto Eco and Jean Baudrillard. Furthermore, Fantasy City is postmodern insofar as it represents a "collage" (Dear 1995: 30) or "gigantic agglomeration" (Soja 1989: 246) of themed attractions, more closely connected to global commerce than to one another.

Two views

The advent of Fantasy City has not been without controversy. Proponents, largely located within the development and entertainment industries, see this as a key urban growth area of the future. One major promoter has been the Urban Land Institute (ULI), an education, research and lobbying organization which serves the real estate sector. Since March 1995, the ULI has sponsored an unprecedented four professional seminars dealing with the topic of developing UEDs, all of which have been oversubscribed, with attendance from both Canada and the US and abroad. In the fall of 1996, ULI launched *The E Zone*, a monthly newsletter for members which specializes in news about pending urban entertainment projects. Themed entertainment has been the subject of several workshops and sessions at the conventions of the International Council of Shopping Centers and was spotlighted at a three-day professional workshop co-produced by the Themed Entertainment Association (TEA) and the publishers of *TCI* (Theatre Crafts International) and *Lighting Dimensions* magazines. At the 1997 TiLE (Trends in Leisure and Entertainment) conference and trade show in Strasbourg, France, topics for discussion included "Urban Entertainment Real Estate"; "Theming in Entertainment and Dining"; and "Planetariums and Edutainment."

Also supportive are a number of local politicians, planners and economic development officers who view UEDs as the key to continued urban growth. Reacting to a just announced C\$2 billion development plan for a downtown site adjacent to the CN Tower which contains a significant entertainment component, Toronto mayor Barbara Hall endorsed the development as "an important part of the next century of this city" (Wong 1997). Similarly, Jimmie Sacco, general manager of Pittsburgh's Three Rivers Stadium, greeted news of a proposed \$1.5 billion sports/entertainment/retail/industrial renaissance plan targeted for both the downtown area and for its outlying counties, with the observation: "For this project to be approved would show that Pittsburgh is moving forward into the next century" (Waddell 1997: 13). In 1996, the New York Metro Chapter of the American Planning Association (APA) gave its top award to officials and civic groups who had backed the \$1.7 billion Times Square Redevelopment Project. This "Miracle on 42nd Street," as TIME magazine (Handy 1997) described it, includes renovations of the New Amsterdam and New Victory theaters as well as the requisite mix of themed restaurants, record and video superstores and virtual reality arcades.

Not every one, however, is as impressed as the APA. Opposition to the themed metropolis has come from academics, neighborhood activists and writers, all of whom decry the elitism and architectural phoniness of these new "landscapes of leisure." These views are epitomized in published volleys by two well-known American architectural critics, Ada Louise Huxtable and Paul Goldberger.

In her book *The Unreal America*,[1] based on a lecture she gave to the American Academy of Arts and Letters, Huxtable (1997a) launches a jeremiad against the architecture of Fantasy City on the grounds that it celebrates the fake over the real, thereby elevating surrogate experience and synthetic settings to a position of primacy. In Texas, for example, a movie-set Alamo has joined the genuine article as a popular tourist site, even outstripping the original because it is larger and more noticeable. On an extended tour through Ellis Island, once the gateway in New York's harbor for new immigrants to America,

Huxtable finds a huge disparity between the empty and decaying rooms in the unrestored buildings, which summon up ghosts of past inmates, and the restored portions with their clichéd commercial displays which evoke "something else" unconnected to a concern for the past. In today's fractured and deeply troubled society, she observes, we discard the harsh truths of history in favor of something which reassures and entertains (1997a: 31). This intrusion of commercialism into history results in a "hollow history" in which the surrogate version usually appears as little more than a "reduced and emptied-out idea."

In a contribution to an edited volume in honor of former New York mayor Robert Wagner, Paul Goldberger (1996) takes a different line of argument. Disneyfied landscapes such as South Street Seaport in New York or CityWalk in Universal City, California, represent what he terms "urbanoid environments" – sealed-off private environments purporting to be public places. As such, they contribute to the rise of the "private city" in which the disorganized reality of older streets and cities is replaced by a measured, controlled and organized kind of urban experience which is intimately linked to a fusion of consumerism, entertainment and popular culture. Such quasi-urban environments, he maintains, seek to provide all the energy, variety, visual stimulation and cultural opportunities of the real thing, while, at the same time, shutting out the problems that have come to accompany urban life, notably poverty and crime. In doing so, the new developments end up discouraging the mixing of different classes of people in order to make the city safe for the middle class. Goldberger laments this strategy, observing that it blurs the lines between city and suburb, with the former taking on certain characteristics more associated with the latter. Here, he drifts back towards Huxtable's thesis, maintaining that real cities are preferable to their urbanoid clones because they are more "authentic," by which he means that they possess elements of roughness, serendipity and creativity which are missing in the Disney-style version.

Huxtable and Goldberger do not categorically condemn everything to be found in Fantasy City. At the same time as Huxtable excoriates surrogate experience and synthetic settings, she praises the architecture of Las Vegas where she believes the "real fake" has been developed into an art form:

> Continuous, competitive frontages of moving light and color and constantly accelerating novelty lead to the gaming tables and hotels. The purpose is clear and the solution is dazzling; the result is completely and sublimely itself. The outrageously fake has developed its own indigenous style and life style to become a real place. This is an urban design frontier where extraordinary things are happening.
>
> (1997b: 40)

Similarly, Goldberger distinguishes between Disney, the company, which "has done so much to devalue authenticity in the new urban paradigm" and Disney's restoration of the New Amsterdam Theater in New York which is "really quite un-Disneyesque." "As the New Amsterdam is restored," he observes, "this will not be the invention of a make-believe past; it will be the reinvigoration of a very real one. This is the kind of remake of an urban icon that more cities need" (1996: 144).

Still, by and large both Huxtable and Goldberger remain pessimistic about the future of the theme park city, viewing it as a failed attempt to create a genuine urban form comparable to the great cities of the past.

The outline for *Fantasy City*

Over the following chapters, I will argue that Fantasy City is the end-product of a long-standing cultural contradiction in American society between the middle-class desire for experience and their parallel reluctance to take risks, especially those which involve contact with the "lower orders" in cities. The "merchants of leisure" who have piloted the urban entertainment industry since the late nineteenth century recognized this paradox early on and deliberately designed activities, venues and technologies which could be counted on to both dazzle and reassure. From time to time, however, they have lost their way, either running out of star dust or failing to adequately insulate their customers from the realities of the surrounding city. At these junctures, a succession of visionary entrepreneurs – Walt Disney, James Rouse, Steve Wynn – have emerged who have re-established the winning formula and put urban entertainment back on the map.

With the current rise of "urbanoid environments," to use Goldberger's term, a major initiative is once again underway to convert American downtown areas into glittering, protected playgrounds for middle-class consumers. Exciting as this promises to be, the meteor-like spread of urban entertainment centers, designer sports stadiums and gargantuan casino hotels inevitably raises a number of significant issues for the future growth of the postmodern metropolis Are fantasy cities the culmination of a long-term trend in which private space replaces public space? Do these new entertainment venues further entrench the gap between the haves and have-nots in the "dual city"? Are they the nuclei around which new downtown identities form or do they simply accelerate the destruction of local vernaculars and communities? And, finally, do they constitute thriving urban cauldrons out of which flows the elixir to reverse the decline of downtown areas or are they danger signs that the city itself is rapidly being transformed into a hyperreal consumer commodity? Together, these questions invoke four domains of moral meaning: polity, equity, authenticity and civility.

While for a long time urban historians have noted the "private" character of the American city (Warner 1968), it is feared that this attribute will be further exaggerated with the growth of Fantasy City. As I outline in Chapter 7, the majority of large-scale UED initiatives are created by public redevelopment agencies in joint business with private partners from the real estate and

7

entertainment industries. If we look to past experience, we can expect the private sector to dominate this relationship, thereby imprinting the themed environment with its attributes of exclusion, competition and commodity-led relationships (Fainstein 1994: 225–6). Ominously, in its first and most extensive foray into urban planning on non-company property, Disney consultants proposed (unsuccessfully) a redesign for the civic center in Seattle which would have made an admission fee inevitable (Warren 1994). While most public–private partnerships are unlikely to go so far as to charge taxpayers a fee to enter a city hall, none the less, it is important to consider how the boom in urban entertainment could sway the balance between public and private space in the future city.

Second, we must be prepared to judge how equitable these new themed developments are likely to be, both in terms of the audience they serve and with respect to the surrounding community. If these leisure sites are nothing more than high-tech playgrounds for tourists and suburban day-trippers, and have no discernible economic effect on the neighborhoods in which they are situated, then it can be argued that their benefits need to be re-evaluated, particularly from the perspective of public policy. "For whom are we saving the cities?" asks urban sociologist Gregory Squires (1989: 9); this is a fair question, especially since the festival market places, new sports arenas and stadiums, casinos, museums and aquariums and other similar projects are usually framed within the context of inner-city revitalization and underwritten by public subsidies.

Third, we need to grapple with the charge that these new themed entertainment projects are bogus because they are "inauthentic." At first glance, this seems to be purely an aesthetic issue, as much about taste as about anything else. The proliferation of simulated environments, from an Irish pub to a New York neighborhood, may strike some observers as déclassé – like plastic pink flamingoes or velvet paintings of Elvis – but this is not legitimate grounds for rejection. Similarly, the premise that the "authentic" can only be located within working-class job settings (steel mills, working ports), housing (cottages, tenements) or cultural activities (bingo, bowling, bars), whereas the rest is an example of "false consciousness," is a romantic notion (Fainstein 1994: 231–2). Still, this concern about authenticity is not without some grounds. As Susan Davis (1997) has demonstrated, the simulation of nature found at Sea World in San Diego is neither entirely accurate, nor is it completely lacking in ideological baggage. Instead, it's a carefully crafted version of the marine world which is meant both to humanize dolphins and other sea creatures and to make concern for them a badge of bourgeois status. With a new generation of nature-themed attractions about to appear (Ogden's American Wilderness Zoo & Aquarium at exurban super-malls in California, Arizona and Texas; Disney's Wilderness Lodge in Florida), it is important to assess how and with what intent the natural environment is depicted within these theme parks, as well as considering the social implications. Similarly, Goldberger's concern over "urbanoid environments" such as Universal's CityWalk is valid inasmuch as these quasi-places have the capacity to replace real streets and to preclude civic action wishing to keep community spaces alive.

Finally, we should consider the issue of whether current entertainment developments represent an existing new form of urban renewal or whether they are simply a case of cynical hucksterism. Once again, it is important here to separate matters out from the issue of "good taste." It is easy to equate civility with a certain lifestyle. In Celebration, Disney's recently opened new town in Florida, urbanity is defined as being able to walk downtown for a coffee cooler at Barnie's (Pollan 1997: 62) as opposed to having to drive to the mall for a surf 'n' turf dinner. While there's a lot to be said for a neighborhood which offers specialty coffee, cool jazz and the Sunday *New York Times*, in essence a vibrant urban experience constitutes more than this. Above all, an urban lifestyle is about choice and opportunity. In the lakeside neighborhood where I live with my family, coffee aficionados can patronize upmarket chains such as Starbucks, Second Cup and Timothy's; however, they can also hang out at the Roastery, whose proprietor has been known to show up at 6 a.m. with free thermoses of coffee for parents waiting in a queue to enroll their children in swimming lessons, or at Ritter's, whose walls display the work of local artists. It is important to consider whether the high-rent environs of Fantasy City can accommodate this type of variety and choice, or if the relentless drive for brand superiority, extension and "roll out" which characterizes theme park cities will impose a uniformity in which local initiative and identity is stifled.

I wish to begin with a retrospective look at the "golden age" of urban entertainment which shone brightly for three decades from 1895 to 1925. Some commentators have seen in this period the "unmediated experience of urbanity" (Goss 1996: 222) which has since disappeared, despite recent attempts to revive it. Dazzling as it must have been, nevertheless I maintain that it was not quite what it seemed. Deliberately constructed by a small cast of leisure merchants, the commercial culture which encompassed amusement parks, vaudeville halls, nightclubs, baseball stadiums, movie palaces and other leisure venues was, in fact, carefully regulated so as to reconcile the competing currents of democratic access and class control. In particular, I identify two key social constructions favored by the entertainment entrepreneurs of the time: "democracy's theater" and "the good-natured crowd" which together acted to create a public culture which appeared to be original, affordable and universal, even if it was not entirely any of these things.

By the 1950s, the neon lights had gone out and downtown areas were dying. In Chapter 2 I trace the decline of public entertainment during this period and its implications for downtown vitality and urban sociability. A quarter of a century later, urban entertainment made a remarkable, if not complete return, conveying the message that "Cities are fun." In Chapter 3 I document this come-back, starting in the 1970s with the building of downtown malls and festival market places and picking up steam in the 1990s with the boom in themed restaurants, special format theaters, virtual reality arcades, sports-entertainment complexes, gambling casinos and other components which make up Fantasy City.

What is the appeal of Fantasy City to postmodern consumers? In Chapter 4 I suggest four possibilities: the siren song of seductive technology; a new source of "cultural capital"; a prime provider of experiences which satisfy our desire for "riskless risks"; and a form of "affective ambience." I conclude by considering the implications of the emerging theme park city for the invention and testing of new identities and lifestyles, notably those related to gender and sexuality.

How should we account for the rise of Fantasy City in the final decade of the twentieth century? In Chapter 5 I attribute this to the convergence of three major corporate trends in the 1990s: the increasing dominance of rational techniques of production (the "McDonaldization" of the market place), the proliferation of themed environments, and the elevation of "synergies" as a key logic in the entertainment and development industries. This has given rise to a further convergence of four consumer activity systems – shopping, entertainment, dining, and education and culture – producing three new hybrids: shopertainment, eatertainment and edutainment.

Who is behind these new landscapes of pleasure? In Chapter 6 I profile the emerging nexus between a brace of large-scale real estate developers, many of whom are survivors of the economic downturn of the early 1990s, and the world's most influential entertainment companies: Disney, Universal, Sony, Warner Bros., Sega. In particular, I outline the risk factors which constrain each of the four major private players (corporate financiers, real estate developers, entertainment companies, retail/entertainment operators) involved in building Fantasy City and the strategies which they employ in order to manage these risks and coordinate their efforts.

What has been the role of elected politicians, city planners and public agencies in the creation of Fantasy City? In Chapter 7 I examine the public–private partnerships which support this new generation of downtown developments and assess the financial benefits and costs to the community of these arrangements. In particular, sports stadiums and arenas have been identified as a special trouble spot, siphoning off large sums of tax dollars while offering limited returns. Drawing on recent research by Mark Rosentraub and others, I offer an assessment of the economics of these professional sports facilities and the problems which surround them.

If one city could be said to represent the successful development of fantasy cities, that city would be Las Vegas. Once regarded as a seedy mixture of neon, glitter, blackjack and organized crime, Vegas today is a booming entertainment center which has aimed its sights at family vacationers by providing an infrastructure of amusement parks, magic shows and themed hotels. In Chapter 8 I profile the "New Las Vegas" and compare its economic miracle to the rapidly expanding but frequently troubled gaming industry which in its wake has churned up riverboat gambling, native-run casinos, and start and stop expansion in Atlantic City.

While a large part of *Fantasy City* focuses exclusively on the odyssey of urban entertainment in twentieth-century America, the "leisure revolution" has recently spread offshore. Nowhere is this more striking than on the Asia-Pacific Rim where two decades of economic prosperity has produced a tidal wave of new urban theme parks, resort hotels, multiplex cinemas and even ice rinks. In Chapter 9 I trace the rise of the booming themed entertainment industry in Australia, China, Indonesia, Malaysia, Singapore and other nation states in the region, contrasting its form and function with that of the North American. This provides an especially pertinent example with which to examine the penetration of multinational capitalism into Asia and its attendant cultural impacts.

In Chapter 10 *Fantasy City* concludes by looking at the impact of the new urban entertainment economy on the future of cities. Will it become, as Soja (1996) fears, a defining feature of the social construction of urban life, accelerating the destruction of local vernaculars and identities and destroying what limited degree of public, democratic space remains in the postmodern metropolis? Or is it the Rosetta Stone of urban revitalization, unlocking the secret code of how to bring people back to the city center in order to discover a new form of civic sociability? Much depends, I argue, on cities themselves. Urban policy-makers need to be proactive rather than reactive, they need to become full collaborative partners with the private sector rather than supplicants who enter into flawed and costly development deals. And of equal importance, they must not fail to recognize and accommodate the cultural diversity in the community in favor of a generic model of UED development which is only destined to succeed in a handful of tourist-rich cities.

Part I

GOING OUT AND STAYING IN

In 1987, Randall Duell, one of the pioneers of entertainment theming, was interviewed by the *Amusement Park Journal*. Duell, known as the "dean of amusement park architects," had been an art director at MGM Studios for a quarter of a century, working on such classic films as *Singing in the Rain* with Gene Kelly before turning to park design. The theme park business, Duell observed, is all about how to combine entertainment and commercial value. Unlike in real cities, visitors should "never look down an open street," there should always be another attraction around the corner to draw people in and make them want to stay longer (Ruben 1987: 9).

For over a century, leisure merchants in the US, Canada, Australia and elsewhere have attempted to marry entertainment and commerce in order to create "something of interest on the street," as Duell calls it. Like the quintessential roller coaster, urban entertainment has continuously looped the loop, rising to thrilling heights and then plunging back down. In part, this has reflected increases in leisure time, breakthroughs in new engineering technology or the fluctuating state of the economy. But, as I will argue in the first section of this book, it has also been closely tied to the odyssey of the American middle class as it has traveled in and out of the central city in search of prosperity, security and fun. I begin my account of this journey on New Year's Eve 1904, on the cusp of the "golden age" of popular urban entertainment in America.

Figure 1.1 "Shooting the Chutes": Scarboro Beach Amusement Park, 1907.
Source: Courtesy of City of Toronto Archives, The James Collection (no. 162).

1

"AT PRICES ALL CAN AFFORD"

The "golden age" of popular urban entertainment in America

In 1904, the Times Building, situated in the heart of the rapidly developing Times Square district of Manhattan, New York, was completed. In celebration, *New York Times* owner Adolph Ochs orchestrated a New Years Eve party on a scale not previously seen in America's largest metropolis.

At dusk, the streets around Times Square were crowded, and by nine o'clock the Square itself was jammed with partygoers. By ten o'clock, every restaurant on Upper Broadway was full and fashionably dressed men and women were being turned away, despite, in some cases, the offer of substantial sums of money to the doormen. At eleven o'clock, Fanciulli's Concert Band, featured performers at the 1904 St Louis World's Fair, filed into a makeshift bandstand along 43rd Street and started up a program which lasted into the small hours of the morning. "Broadway," the *Times* correspondent marveled, "seemed the thoroughfare to which all faces were turned and about every man, woman and child who put foot upon the Street at one time or another during the evening visited Times Square."

On the stroke of midnight, a cluster of fireworks was launched 1,000 feet into the air illuminating the sky. A deafening shout rose up from the crowd accompanied by an ear-splitting blast from hundreds of party horns. This was echoed by the sound of factory, locomotive and steamship whistles welcoming in 1905. "Never was a New Year's Eve more joyously celebrated."[1]

The year 1905 was an early peak in what has come to be regarded as the "golden age" of popular urban entertainment in America. In the thirty-five years between 1895 and 1930, city life was transformed by the emergence of a new infrastructure of commercialized leisure: amusement parks, theaters, nightclubs and cabarets, baseball stadiums, ballrooms, burlesque houses, storefront nickelodeons and grand movie palaces. For the first time, historian David Nasaw observes, "the city was becoming as much a place of play as a place of work" (1993:9).

If you had traveled back in time a quarter century from this New Year's Eve celebration, you would have found a very different city and society. Rather than an apparent sense of common good fellowship, the world of leisure and entertainment in the nation's urban precincts reflected a class structure which had calcified after the Civil War. "The differences between mid-nineteenth century urban theaters," muses cultural historian Robert Snyder, "increasingly expressed the social differences between New Yorkers, with drama and opera houses for the rich, cheap Bowery theaters for the poor, and foreign-language theaters for immigrants" (1989:5).

America's newly emerging industrial élite, having made their fortune from steel, railroads and banking, were anxious to create institutions and a lifestyle which would publicly proclaim their patrician taste and culture. One expression of this was the establishment of exclusive social clubs,[2] from the downtown sanctuaries of Boston and New York where the members discussed politics, literature, science and technology over sumptuous meals, to the élite hunting and fishing associations which were the one indulgence the straight-laced "iron-makers" of Pittsburgh allowed themselves. The leading citizens in American cities further displayed their rank by financing a series of cultural institutions: the Boston Museum of Fine Arts (1870), the Metropolitan Museum of Art (1870), the Metropolitan Opera Company (1880). Less morally uplifting but also part of upper-class culture were the private gambling casinos, horse racing and college football games.

At the opposite end of the social spectrum was the leisure world of the industrial working class which revolved around two established institutions: the saloon and the cheap variety theater. In addition, popular amusements included restaurants, lecture halls and fraternal lodges, beer halls, billiard parlors, bowling alleys, picnic groves and pleasure gardens. Most of these were stratified by gender, being the sole preserve of men. Excluded from this "homosocial" network of leisure institutions, working-class women had a more circumscribed set of activities which largely centered round the family, church and neighborhood (Peiss 1986).

Virtual recluses from the recreational scene, the "respectable" middle-class shunned both the leisure pursuits of the élite and those of the working class. Instead, middle-class life was patterned by a reverence for quiet seclusion and privacy. It did, however, allow for family outings to libraries, concerts and travelogues and musicals sponsored by church-affiliated associations such as the YMCA (Nasaw 1993: 15).

Very few leisure and entertainment activities crossed class barriers. Some sporting events – trotting races, boating regattas – attracted a mixed crowd, but even then the more affluent patrons were careful to maintain their social distance from the "rabble" (Rosenzweig 1983: 68). Museums, the pride of the ruling class, were generally deemed "educational" and therefore acceptable places for the middle class to visit. On occasion the definition of what constituted a museum was stretched to include "freak shows" which had more in common with P.T. Barnum's circus than with the halls of learning. For the most part, however, it could be said that there was no public entertainment zone which spanned the social length of American society.

The commercialization of leisure

By the end of the nineteenth century, however, the situation had radically altered as a new commercial culture centered around leisure and entertainment established itself in urban areas. Its growth can be explained by a number of factors: more leisure time for workers; rising incomes; an expanding white-collar sector which included a considerable percentage of women; advances in technology, notably the electrification of street lights, trolley lines and advertising billboards; the growth of banks and financial institutions and the emergence of new sources of capital.

Merchants of leisure

Of particular note was the emergence of a cohort of entertainment entrepreneurs who had the vision and ability to raise capital in order to build an infrastructure of entertainment. Some of these "merchants of leisure" had made their fortune in other businesses, bringing money and know-how to the burgeoning public amusements industry. Marcus Loew, whose movie theater empire began with chains of nickelodeons and vaudeville houses had previously been a furrier, as had Adolph Zuker, a nickelodeon owner who formed Famous Players in 1912. Horace Bigelow, the "Great Amusement Caterer" of Worcester, Massachusetts, was already a wealthy boot and shoe manufacturer when he decided to transfer the techniques of mass production and vertical and horizontal integration to leisure-related enterprises (Rosenzweig 1983: 173). Henry Davis, who became Pittsburgh's leading vaudeville czar and who is generally credited with opening the first storefront nickelodeon theater there, was a high-profile real estate speculator who was the principal in purchases and sales of $2.5 million worth of downtown Pittsburgh property in 1905.[3]

Other merchants of leisure funded their entertainment ventures by soliciting funds from outside backers, some more respectable than others. Frederic A. Thompson and Elmer S. Dundy found the money to build Luna Park, Coney Island and the New York Hippodrome thanks to the United States Realty Company, a firm controlled by John W. "Bet a Million" Gates. Gates' ventures into stock manipulation and trust-busting inspired the turn-of-the-century "robber barons" J. Pierpoint Morgan to warn that "the man cannot be entrusted with property" and Andrew Carnegie to declare "he's a broken-down gambler" (Wendt and Kogan 1948:10–11). The Shubert Brothers, whose Shubert Theatrical Corporation dominated legitimate theater venues in America up until the 1950s, were initially funded by George Cox, a saloonkeeper and real estate mogul who was the Republican boss of Cincinatti, and by Joseph L. Rhinock, a Kentucky congressman who had extensive race track interests and real estate holdings (Stagg 1968).

From 1906 onwards, a new, richer source of capital emerged in the form of investment banks such as Lehman Brothers and Goldman Sachs. Not only did they raise capital for mass market retailers such as Sears, Roebuck and Company but they also embraced the entertainment business, financing a variety of projects: theaters, electrical sign advertisements and even RKO (Radio-Victor-Keith Orpheum) one of the first full-service entertainment firms. Together with other brokers of the new corporate industrial order – public relations men and government information agents – for the first time these investment bankers created a national consumer market for the "culture of desire" that spun out across the country from urban entertainment districts such as Times Square (Leach 1991).

By the 1920s financing had expanded from the more adventuresome investment banks to financial houses of high standing such as Manufacturers Trust Company and the National Bank of Commerce. Thus, a prospectus prepared by the investment house of Halsey, Stuart & Co. in 1927[4] notes that "approximately $200,000 in motion picture securities have been financed through Wall and La Salle streets in the last twenty-four months."

Creating a public culture

These new leisure merchants recognized early on the necessity of creating a public culture which was attractive, non-threatening and affordable in order to lure as wide a cross-section of society as possible. Vaudeville impresarios, for example, sought to actively reverse the fragmentation created by race, class, gender and ethnicity by pioneering a form of entertainment which would bring together people who expressed profoundly different ways of thinking and behaving. (Snyder 1989).

To do so required a sleight of hand worthy of a skilled illusionist. Increasingly, working people had money and free time but as a group on their own, they were seen as neither a reliable market nor one which was particularly profitable. The middle classes represented a more desirable clientele but, as we will see, they were deeply nervous of the blue-collar crowds which they believed were prone to drunkenness and rowdyism. In order to attract the former market without losing the latter, leisure entrepreneurs needed to convince less affluent patrons that they were being transported to magical realms (the amusement park, the movie palaces) beyond the orbit of everyday constraints of class and gender, and at the same time reassure bourgeois pleasure-seekers that these new public amusements were safe and physically and morally "clean." To pull off this seemingly impossible task the merchants of leisure successfully constructed and marketed two concepts: "democracy's theater" and the "good-natured crowd."

Democracy's theater

In a 1907 editorial in the trade magazine *Moving Picture World*, W. Stephen Bush rhapsodized that "the moving picture theater is not confined to any class or clique. The millionaire and the clerk, the laborer and the capitalist sit side by side and both find equal enjoyment in the pictures".[5] Similar comments were made in relation to amusement parks. Coney Island was depicted in the popular magazines of the day as "a mingling of individuals of all ranks and classes, college and factory workers dining next to each other, the disregarding of character or station, equality being taken for granted joyfully" (Weinstein 1992: 2). From 1900 to 1920, concludes Judith Adams, a present-day chronicler of the amusement park industry, Coney Island and other parks reflected the increased "democratic character" of society where "people of all classes, including the vast immigrant population could mingle with little regard for the strict social distinctions or mores of the time" (1991: 63). Baseball, fast becoming the most popular spectator sport at the turn of the century, also came to be regarded as symbolic of the democratic character of the emerging commercial culture. In his history of Shibe Park in Philadelphia, the first concrete and steel stadium to be built in America, Bruce Kuklick speculates that baseball "may have assisted in creating a mass democracy, eventually bringing social groups together." One way this occurred, he suggests, is by popularizing so-called working-class attributes – informality, physical intimacy and the mixing of the sexes – among non-working-class baseball fans (1991: 47).

Are these commentators correct, did "democacy's theater" prevail? Not exactly. It's true that some leisure merchants attempted to project the idea that their facilities were open to everyone. In an advertisement for the soon-to-be-opened New York Hippodrome, promoters Thompson and Dundy proclaim themselves "Purveyors of Amusement for the Masses at Prices All Can Afford," especially noting the availability of 1,500 seats in the Family Circle for twenty-five cents each.[6] Motion picture kings, Balaban and Katz, explain in a 1925 issue of their *Magazine* that in their elaborate new movie palaces they had not "attempted to establish financial class distinctions, or to divide our auditoriums by means of reserved sections which seem to be more desirable and exclusive [because] *the American people don't like this distinction.*"[7]

Yet, at the same time, there is evidence to suggest that the lower strata of society were only admitted grudgingly to many of the new public amusement venues, and, as soon as it was financially feasible, were once again excluded. Movie entrepreneurs, for example, tested out the nickelodeon concept (i.e. five-cent storefront theaters) on less wealthy patrons, but soon abandoned them for a more selective middle-class audience who had a greater discretionary income and more leisure time (Gomery 1992: 29). Movie exhibitors, including those who were engaged in a rags-to-riches climb out of the ethnic slums, continually complained in trade journals, personal correspondence and Congressional testimony that nickelodeon audiences as a group were an albatross because they lacked "class" (Merritt 1976: 65–6).

Film scholars have expended some effort in using city and business directories to map out the growth of nickelodeons and movie theaters between 1905 and 1915 in various American urban locales. For the most part, their data suggest little evidence of any inclination to concentrate in working-class neighborhoods. Merritt (1976) discovered that Boston nickelodeons were located along busy main streets both downtown and in the surrounding residential communities of Dorchester, Roxbury, Cambridge, Sommerville, Newton, Belmont and Watertown. "No instance has been found," he claims, "of a Boston movie theater opening between 1910 and 1914 in an area that could be described as a working-class community – Castle Square, the North End, the South End or North Roxbury" (p. 78).

Allen (1982) presents a detailed analysis of the location of motion picture exhibitors in Manhattan between 1906 and 1912. While few theaters were located in exclusively middle- and upper-class neighborhoods, neither were they found in the poorest areas. Rather, the major groupings of theaters were in traditional entertainment districts such as the Bowery and Union Square or in stable, high-density, ethnic neighborhoods such as Little Italy and Jewish Harlem.

From 1907, more and more entrepreneurs began to move away from storefront nickelodeons towards more elaborate and spacious middle-class theaters with mixed programs of film and vaudeville and, not incidentally, with higher prices. This did not eliminate working-class audiences but did limit their frequency of attendance.

But what of other venues beside movie theaters? Some – cabarets, roof-top theaters, restaurants with dance floors – traditionally had always been beyond the reach of the working class. Other venues deliberately discouraged grass-roots patronage. Professional baseball clubs restricted the number of bleacher seats; kept ticket prices high; and scheduled games on weekday afternoons ensuring that the bulk of the fans would be professional, white-collar workers and self-employed business operators. The only manual workers who attended ball games were artisans who enjoyed the Saturday half-day off, or those whose work schedules gave them free time in the mid-afternoon, i.e. butchers, bakers, city workers. It wasn't until the 1920s, when a rising standard of living, the cheap cost of tickets, Sunday ball and the introduction of night baseball made working-class attendance more possible, did baseball become an increasingly lower-class sport (Riess 1989).

In her research which looked at department stores which were in operation during the year 1932, Jeanne Lawrence (1992) concluded that rather than being expressions of democratic culture where women from all walks of life could learn about merchandise and "being American," as historians such as Gunter Barth and Daniel Boorstin have suggested, it makes more sense to locate a hierarchy of stores within the urban environment. The same can be said for movie theaters and other entertainment venues of this era. Until the arrival of the big downtown movie palaces in the 1920s, seamstresses and socialites rarely rubbed shoulders under the same roof at the same time; the latter group tended to see feature films at converted vaudeville houses or at legitimate theaters, while the former went to single-reel features at lower cost neighborhood houses (Nasaw 1993: 221). Even Coney Island was stratified with working people

20

heading for Steeplechase Park while the urban middle-classes favored Luna Park or Dreamland.

"Democracy's theater" certainly did not extend to the African-American population. Although African-Americans represented a potentially large market for urban public amusements, Jim Crow laws and practices in the South and widespread prejudice and discrimination elsewhere served to keep them out. If they were allowed admittance, it was almost always in a segregated context. Whites-only theaters were sometimes opened to black patrons, but they were normally consigned to the upper balcony and admitted through a separate entrance. Amusement parks were little better; one survey of the "Recreational Facilities of the Negro," published in 1928, reported that two-thirds of the amusement parks surveyed practiced segregation while, in the South, various idiosyncratic arrangements were made including admitting blacks on "off days" and the building of separate "pleasure resorts" (Washington 1928. Cited in Nasaw 1993: 92).

The only entertainment venues where one was likely to find a mixed audience were the jazz clubs and cabarets which operated in some of the larger Northern cities. Particularly of note were the "black and tan" cabarets in Chicago. In his book, *Autobiography of Black Chicago*, Dempsey Travis recalls how the lively nightlife in 1940s Harlem, where "downtown white folks came uptown nightly to slum, get high and sometimes fly," reminded him of the action at the cabarets on the South Side of Chicago during the 1920s and 1930s (1981: 112). Not suprisingly, these black and tan clubs eventually caught the attention of white, middle-class reformers outraged by what they perceived as interracial immorality (Grossman 1989).

Was "democracy's theater," then, a notable social accomplishment? Some contemporary historians have embraced the notion, seeing it as part of a broader trend toward democratization in American life. Although he is careful to point out that interclass conflicts in Worcester, Massachusetts had not vanished, Rosenzweig nevertheless concludes that Worcester's middle-class, by sharing their leisure time in movie houses with blue-collar patrons, were now less likely to condemn working-class amusements as they had done in the past (1983: 226). In a feminist critique, Peiss (1986: 186) detects a significant shift from a restrictive "homosocial" culture to a "heterosocial" one in which working-class women found a space to pursue social experimentation, personal freedom and unsupervised fun beyond the reach of neighborhood and familial control. Nasaw is less inclined to believe that the intermingling of the classes at commercial amusement venues had any lasting effect, however, he does suggest that "going out" provided a momentary escape, not just from one's class or ethnic group, but from a society differentiated along these lines to "an alternative and more 'liberated' way of being socially human" (1993: 46).

However, when all things are considered, the notion of "democracy's theater" appears to have been somewhat of a phantom. While it is true that by 1930, with the notable exception of race, the urban entertainment scene had opened up considerably to all who could afford it, this was scarcely a corrective to the deeply embedded problems of race, class, gender and ethnicity which continued to persist. As Snyder (1989) observes, the new commercialized entertainment culture was limited in its ability to help those marginal to American life:

> Three cheers for vaudeville? No, its shortcomings were too pronounced for that. . . . Vaudeville never treated blacks as well as it treated whites, and in its own way it portrayed women as sex objects in a way ever more problematic than had been the case in the nineteenth century. . . . The conflicts between Jewish and Irish New Yorkers in the thirties and forties, and all of the city's racial tensions that endure to this day all testify to the limits of integration through popular culture.
>
> (1989: 160–1)

"Democracy's theater" can be seen instead as a carefully constructed conceit which allowed shop clerks and factory workers to imagine they were being offered entry into middle-class life "on a new basis, outside traditional forms and proscriptions" (Kasson 1978: 108). This was, of course, patently untrue. When, for example, amusement parks such as Coney Island took on a more proletarian character, the middle-class fled never to return. Nevertheless, the leisure merchants at the turn of the twentieth century succeeded in promoting this construct together with the related notion of "the good-natured crowd."

The good-natured crowd

From looking at historical accounts, it seems apparent that the American middle classes at the tail-end of the nineteenth century feared the outbreak of disorder among working-class crowds. In Worcester, for example, "people of refined tastes and sensitive nerves" frequently fled to the countryside over the Fourth of July weekend to escape the noise, drinking and boisterous behavior which accompanied popular celebrations.[8] Not that one could always blame them! The behaviour of working-class audiences and crowds frequently threatened to tip over from lively to violent. Patrons in the gallery in vaudeville theaters and burlesque houses were often rowdy: whistling, hand-clapping and bombarding orchestra and audience members below with debris. They could also be harsh if they took a dislike to a celebrity: Kuklick recounts how a mini-mob chased Detroit Tigers baseball star Ty Cobb, who was widely despised for his tendency to "spike" opposing players on the basepaths, through the streets of North Philadelphia. Cobb avoided certain injury only by hopping on to a passing trolley car.[9]

So as to reassure potential middle-class patrons, leisure entrepreneurs took a number of drastic and extraordinary steps. Amusement parks were fenced off, entry was controlled and security was emphasized. In a typical example from a

1914 advertising brochure, Kennywood amusement park in Pittsburgh reassured respectable patrons that "courteous uniformed police are always present to suppress the slightest semblance of disorder" (Jaques 1982: 22). Movie theater owners in the 1920s hired small armies of ushers and uniformed attendants to maintain the appearance of order, and some even went so far as to claim that the air in the theater was fresh and constantly replaced in order to eliminate clothing and body odors, presumably one of the "dangers" of sitting in the same venue as less affluent movie-goers (Nasaw 1993: 234–5).

An important addendum to this was the portrayal of blue-collar audiences as benign: good-natured, earthy, sometimes boisterous, but never ugly or violent. The media were especially concerned with the issue of crowd order and control. For example, the New York Times coverage of Coney Island celebrations on Decoration Day 1905 proclaims the record-breaking crowd of 250,000 as "Huge, Happy, Orderly" in its headline, and later goes on to write that they were"quiet, orderly but out for fun nevertheless".[10] For a chapter in his book on live theater, Going Out, Nasaw borrows the phrase, "The Best Smelling Crowd in the World," from Edwin Slosson, a turn-of-the-century journalist. By this it is implied that audiences were not only inclusive rather than snobbish but they were also on their best behavior.[11] Even on their own turf, working-class crowds were depicted as possessing a unique blend of cheekiness and good cheer as can be seen in the events of the Physical Culture Show (see below).

The Physical Culture Show

During the early years of the twentieth century, an annual event of note at Madison Square Garden in New York was the Mammoth Physical Exhibition or Physical Culture Show. Promoted by its founder Bernard McFadden as an effort to "show how the spread of physical culture has improved the human body," it was a peculiar mix of various athletic contests and male and female models who stood on pedestals and paraded their physiques.

In 1905, the Physical Culture Show caught the attention of moral crusader Anthony Comstock and his Society for the Suppression of Vice who laid charges against several Show officials for distributing "obscene" posters advertising the event. The arrests generated considerable publicity and on the night of the show 20,000 mainly working-class patrons showed up. Fifteen thousand people were admitted, but the rest were excluded when the Fire Inspector ordered the police to close the doors to the arena.

Although the "mob" outside struggled to get near the entrance, those inside were described by the New York Times as "orderly" and "a good natured crowd." As it happened, the show itself was rather tame with the most lively action occurring in the stands.

The star performer was a feisty red-haired female usher who became the focus of the crowd's attention.

Patrons who didn't have coupons were yanked out of their seats to the cheers of the audience in the galleries. On one occasion, the usher attempted to discipline six men who were perched on the back of their seats. "Sit down," she roared, and when they failed to do so, she jerked one after another into their chairs and threatened to throw them out into the street if they didn't behave. "Who is she?" called out someone in the gallery and the crowd below retorted, "Anthony Comstock" (the well-known American moral crusader).

Similarly, the crowd had a good time poking fun at the contestants who were ostentatiously posed as figures from Greek and Roman mythology. When a large-chested man in tights posed as "Ajax Defying the Lightning," a young woman in one of the arena boxes exclaimed in a shrill voice, "I wonder if it eats beans?," causing Ajax to nearly come tumbling off his pedestal.

Source: "Comstock takes hand in Physical Culture Show."
New York Times, 6 October 1905, p. 9;
"20,000 in a crush at the beauty show."
New York Times, 10 October 1905, p. 9.

Amusement entrepreneurs produced a constant stream of public relations material designed to reassure the middle class that both the shows and the intended audiences were beyond reproach and suitable for families. Operators of amusement parks, for example, successfully distanced themselves from the gambling, drunkenness and prostitution which had formerly been associated with these facilities. At Coney Island, only soft drinks were sold, performers were warned to restrict their use of vulgar language, attractions were designed specifically for women and children, and the parks themselves were enclosed and admission fees were charged (Weinstein 1992–3: 128–9). B.F. Keith, who with his partner Edward F. Albee became the reigning czars of vaudeville, not only banned alcohol and smoking from his theaters and insisted on hats being removed during the performance, but he also requested that patrons refrain from foot-stamping, pounding their canes and talking loudly (Snyder 1989: 32). This insistence on "clean" shows was summed up by L.H. Ramsey, proprietor of the 450 seat Hippodrome vaudeville theater in Lexington, Kentucky, who confided to a reporter in November 1909:

There is but one salvation for any vaudeville house in this community, that is, give a show at all times to which any mother feels perfectly safe in sending her girl, knowing that she will neither see nor hear anything tending to the suggestive of ill.[12]

Inventing a new commercial vernacular

One source of the present reverence for this "golden age" of popular entertainment is a unique vernacular which is said to have originated in New York and rippled across the continent. This "culture of pastiche" (Taylor 1988) is evident in a number of places: vaudeville, the penny-press, Coney Island, the music of Tin-Pan alley. Integrating elements of New York street experience into the newly emerging commercial culture, it created a popular idiom which dominated for half-a-century, shaping a wide variety of entertainment products: Broadway musicals, films, stand-up comedy, tabloid newspapers and television variety shows. Many of the well-loved icons of show business – George Burns, Milton Berle, Groucho Marx, Jack Benny – were steeped in this vernacular and they have left a rich legacy for today's stars. Among various examples, we can see echoes of this in the routines of *The Muppet Show*, in the stage show of pop diva and actress Bette Midler, and in movies starring such diverse performers as Barbra Streisand and Rodney Dangerfield. This style of performance could be said to constitute the American equivalent of the British music hall tradition, which has had a wide-ranging influence, from the Beatles to the late comedian Benny Hill.

As Peiss (1986: 187) has noted, the genius of the promoters and entrepreneurs from this era was in the way they were able to scour New York's dance halls, variety theaters and street culture, identify fads and fashions and then transform them into safe, controllable activities that could be sold to all sections of society, in night clubs, amusement parks and the movies. It was, William Taylor reflects, a remarkable achievement, creating "an arena" where "all could find genuine, if partial, representation of their experiences" at the same time as deflecting periodic challenges by middle-class reformers such as Anthony Comstock who "saw street life or anything deriving from it as representing various ugly forces of subversion" (1988: 113).

In the music world, one of the most important changes was the shift from the sweetly sentimental ballads of the nineteenth century to songs which borrowed the syncopation and rhythm of traditional African-American music. Over time, Tin-Pan alley lyricists also began to appropriate ethnic and racial accents and vocabulary. Irving Berlin's classic song, "Puttin' On the Ritz," for example, celebrates the promenade on Lennox Avenue in Harlem, inventing a unique linguistic mix of black slang and refined diction and allusion (Furie 1991: 204). In a similar fashion, a new "Broadway slang" was invented by celebrated authors and journalists Damon Runyon, Ring Lardner and Walter Winchell. Many of these words and phrases – fan, flop, wow 'em, payoff, turkey, phoney, cinch, squeal, crash the gate, wash-out – are still familiar today (Taylor 1991b: 214). So too are some well-known stereotypes which can be traced back to these writers, notably, the "tough on the outside soft on the inside" gamblers, gangsters and molls sentimentalized by Damon Runyon in *Guys and Dolls* and since immortalized in countless Hollywood movies.

It is possible, of course, to challenge whether the experiences of those whose music, language and lives were the inspiration for this cultural pastiche were served fairly by this reformulation. In the same way in which contemporary critics question the integrity of white rappers or of Paul Simon's incorporation of African and Brazilian rhythms into his music, not all cultural observers celebrate the creative borrowing of the tin-pan alley songsmiths, charging that it did not truly and adequately represent the lives of those groups from whom the music forms and language were appropriated.

Furthermore, some historians have suggested that the substantial success of these leisure merchants in creating a wide-ranging and popular commercial culture may have pre-empted the emergence of a separate, politically adversarial working-class culture. It should be noted, however, that the "saloon" culture which thrived among many urban working-class populations prior to the commercialization of popular amusements was not overtly political, although it occurred within the context of the ethnic group and neighborhood of the participants.

Whatever the case, the culture of pastiche which was invented during this "golden age" remains an important yardstick with which to measure the contribution of today's Fantasy City. And, further, it poses the question of whether urban entertainment districts centered around motion simulators, Disney musicals and themed restaurants evoke an element of neighborhood or street experience, or, for that matter, *any* experience at all.

This is not to say that this earlier time was free from the tide of inauthentic images and simulated experiences which pervade today's theme parks. As Alan Bryman (1995) has demonstrated, the Disneyesque principle of "time-space compression" – in which time and space become both condensed and confused – was firmly established in a number of entertainment venues during the "golden age," most notably the Midway at the 1893 World's Columbian Exhibition and Thompson and Dundy's Luna Park at Coney Island (see "Inspired Lunacy" p. 27). To this can be added the Hippodrome extravaganzas, "lobster palaces,"[13] summertime roof gardens and the fantastical movie palaces of the 1920s and 1930s. In short, the scarlet letter of "postmodernism" can be affixed to the architecture and attractions of the "golden age" just as it has been to today's theme park city.

Inspired lunacy: The genius of Frederic Thompson

Frederic A. Thompson was one of the great show business geniuses of the early twentieth century, an entrepreneur who symbolized the energy and vision of those who established the "golden age" of public amusements.

After serving as an architect's apprentice, Thompson drifted from job to job – steel and iron working, mining, engineering and journalism – taking from each knowledge which he would later combine in a matchless fashion. By the turn of the century, he had discovered a considerable talent for designing midway amusements at world's fairs and other exposi- tions. His most conspicuous achievement was a fantasy ride titled "Trip to the Moon," which had its début at the Pan–American Exposition in Buffalo, New York in 1901. More than simply a carnival ride, "Trip to the Moon" was a participatory fantasy experience. After experiencing the sensation of flying to the moon, patrons were then transformed into extraterrestial tourists: shopping, viewing a "Moon Calf" and sampling green cheese.

After a year of recreating the "Trip to the Moon" at Coney Island's Steeplechase Park, Thompson, together with his business partner and fellow showman Elmer S. "Skip" Dundy, founded his own Coney Island attraction – Luna Park. Luna Park was billed as an "electric city by the sea," its lavish, ornamental fantasy architecture was lit up at night by an unprecedented 250,000 electric bulbs. Themed areas included an Eskimo village, the canals of Venice and a Japanese garden. Thompson and Dundy supplemented these displays with live entertainment shows, the most spectacular of which were disaster spectacles: "Fire and Flames," in which a four-storey apartment building was burnt down; re-creations of the the Johnstown (1889) and Galveston (1900) floods; and the eruption of Mount Vesuvius, including the destruction of a replica Pompeii. Luna Park was an instant success, drawing a record-breaking 245,000 patrons on the Fourth of July weekend 1903.

With Luna Park's established, Thompson revived an idea which had preoccupied him – the building of a "hippodrome" in the heart of Manhattan. Inspired by the large department stores which were beginning to dominate the retail trade in American cities, Thompson believed the magic formula to be low ticket prices, a large seating capacity and a brand of entertainment which would mix vaudeville, the circus and grand opera.

The Hippodrome opened in April 1905 to widespread acclaim. It boasted a state-of-the-art technical system which used concentric runways, electrically powered hydraulic lifts (which could raise a portion of the stage 8 feet in the air), and a 14-feet deep water tank which could accommodate a range of displays, from aquatic ballet to the staging of a historical sea battle. It seated 5,200 people, presented fourteen shows a week, and had a cast of 1,000 performers (give or take a few horses and elephants). To top it off, the stage was twelve times larger than a standard Broadway theater.

The Hippodrome's four-hour premiere bill – "A Yankee Circus on Mars" and "Andersonville" (a Civil War pageant) – met with overwhelming popular and critical success. "Not in Paris or London is there anything to equal the Hippodrome!" exalted the *New York American*, while *Variety* announced that, by the third week in May, New Yorkers had succumbed to "Hippritis fever."

One year later, Thompson and Dundy lost the Hippodrome to John W. "Bet a Million" Gates and other investors at the US Realty Company but not before they had staged several more memorable extravaganzas, the most noteworthy was an aquatic tableau vivant, "The Court of the Golden Fountains," in which a golden ship layered with tiers of costumed showgirls lay moored among illuminated mussels and electric bullrushes while live swans navigated the incandescent pool and a cloud of white doves flew down from the peak of the Hippodrome's domed ceiling.

In many respects, Frederic Thompson could be described as the Walt Disney of his time. His combination of magical boyishness, technical virtuousity and a keen sense of showmanship meant that he marketed fantasy on a scale equalled only perhaps by P.T. Barnum.

Source: Adams (1991); Kasson (1978); Register (1991);
Van Hoogstraten (1991);
"The Hippodrome," *New York Times*, 21 May 1905, p. 5;
"Show of the Week," *Variety*, 16 December 1905, p. 8.

Nevertheless, synthetic as it might have been, it is this cultural pastiche which singles out the "golden age" of public entertainment as an era which we remember as urbane, culturally rich and shamelessly nostalgic. As Brooks McNamara has observed, in our fantasies the Broadway impresarios George M. Cohan and Florenz Ziegfeld "dine endlessly at Sardi's on some type of perpetual opening night" while, outside, "Runyonesque characters loiter in Shubert Alley beneath a forest of neon signs advertising the *Follies* of nineteen-something-or-another" (1991: 178).

A golden age?

In *The City Builders*, her anatomy of the real estate boom of the 1980s, Susan Fainstein (1994: 228–33) challenges the tendency of post-structuralist urban critics to base their argument on two central assumptions: (i) that the city once nurtured a greater degree of social diversity than it does today; (ii) that during an earlier period there was a greater degree of authenticity. Such claims, Fainstein points out, are suspect, based more on nostalgia than on fact. In a similar scenario to that of the gated communities of the 1990s,[14] groups who were considered socially unacceptable were kept out of the better areas of the city through the enforcement of vagrancy laws, through a panoply of exclusionary laws pertaining especially to people of color, and by granting police a free hand in the maintenance of social order. As for the idea that a "golden past" once existed in which urban form "expressed an authentic relationship with the forces of production and reproduction," Fainstein argues that there is little basis for this supposition; most major urban structures were, in fact, bastardized re-creations, and as such, rife with historical inaccuracies.

Many of the same arguments can be made in assessing whether the "golden age" which prospered at the beginning of this century has since become "lost." As I have argued in this chapter, the belief that city-dwellers exclusive of race, class and gender came together at amusement parks, movie palaces and sports stadiums without restriction is an exaggeration. While there is significant evidence of barriers being broken down, especially when compared to the immediate post-Civil War era, nevertheless, the twin concepts of "democracy's theater" and "the good-natured crowd" were illusionary. Instead, public entertainment venues continued to be socially stratified, both formally and informally.

At the same time, there is little evidence to suggest that the "golden age" was any more "authentic" than the Fantasy City of today. I concede that to some people the "electric city by the sea" at Luna Park or the electric bullrushes which illuminated the Hippodrome may seem preferable to the electrical parade of cartoon characters which light up the sky at Disneyland every night. However, it is difficult to see how either reflects the underlying economic and social processes of their respective eras. If anything, we celebrate the fantasy architecture and culture of the earlier era because it was *more* extravagantly dreamlike and fantastical than today's creations which seem deliberately formulaic (with Las Vegas perhaps the exception).

Fabricated or not, the surge of commercialized leisure during the first decades of this century did invigorate city life to an extent which has yet to be duplicated. It was a time of wealth for downtown areas, with most cities having an entertainment district of some note. While there may not have always been "Laughter and Liberty Galore" as the title of Nasaw's (1993) chapter on dance halls, ballrooms and cabarets suggests, going out meant something more glamorous and exciting than today's shopping trip to the mall.

Inevitably, perhaps, it couldn't last. By the 1930s, signs of decline were beginning to become obvious. Amusement parks had begun a journey down a long path of decline. Vaudeville and live theater had given way to burlesque and cheap "B" movies. By 1931, 42nd Street in New York had become a working-class male domain dominated by a "rough trade" in male prostitution. After the Depression, the Times Square district filled up with an increasing number of sailors and soldiers, and, to accommodate them, unemployed young men from the economically devastated cities of Pennsylvania, Massachusetts, New York and the industrial South (Chauncey 1991: 322). Where before there had been lobster palaces and cabarets, now there were cheap dance halls, chop suey joints and dime museums specializing in "freaks. " Historians have offered various explanations for this decline ranging from the effects of the stock market crash and the constraints imposed by Prohibition, to the greed of big entertainment promoters who sought to capture a larger, less discriminating audience. Whatever the cause, the illusion of the "good natured crowd" which had played a major role in sustaining downtown entertainment areas a decade earlier had shattered and, with the dawning of the age of suburbia after the Second World War, entertainment districts in America's cities would soon face their most serious crisis.

Figure 2.1 "Eyeing the past": a drive-in movie theater in the 1960s.
Source: Photo by Doug Griffin, courtesy of Ted Cowan. Reprinted with permission from The Toronto Star Syndicate.

2

DON'T GO OUT TONIGHT

Suburbanization, crime and the decline of sociability

On 25 June 1955, a New York institution, the roof garden which crowned the Astor Theatre in Manhattan, was closed to be replaced by a series of penthouse offices.[1] Just three weeks later, on 17 July, Disneyland Park opened its gates in Anaheim, California. In tandem, these two events represent a microcosm of the forces which were to drastically alter the pattern of urban commercial culture over the next twenty-five years. Once the leading purveyors of popular culture, entertainment zones in city centers fell on hard times, losing their clientele to the new medium of television, to a host of outdoor leisure-time activities and to new suburban and exurban theme parks, movie theaters and shopping malls. Urban downtown areas became synonymous with images of physical blight, vice and escalating crime, prompting suburban commuters to stay away. By 1967, as inner-city riots swept across Detroit, Newark and Los Angeles, according to one Gallup poll less than one in five (22 percent) of Americans desired to live in a city (Peter 1967).

With the exception of a few large metropolitan centers – New York, Chicago, San Francisco – increasingly there was little to draw tourists or suburban day-trippers to the downtown area. According to retail sales volume figures released by the US Bureau of the Census in 1961, one in four of America's 109 major central business districts reported lower dollar sales volumes in 1958 compared to figures for 1948. Especially large declines were reported in Detroit (27 percent), Los Angeles (19 percent), Milwaukee (16 percent) and St Louis (13 percent) (Sigafoos 1962: 25). Hit the hardest were the non-merchandising facilities – the performing arts, sports attractions, historic sites, amusement parks, restaurants and convention centers – in medium- and small-sized cities such as Akron, Ohio; Gary, Indiana; and Newark, New Jersey, which were neither buttressed by tourism nor reinvigorated by new waves of immigration (Kornblum and Williams 1978: 76). Appearing on a late-night television talk show, novelist Kurt Vonnegut delivered a stinging epitaph for his home community of Indianapolis, Indiana which he described as a "cemetery with lights that came to life one day a year for the Indianapolis 500 auto race" (Rosentraub 1997: 211). In his appraisal of the "emerging city" in 1962, urban sociologist Scott Greer (1962) concluded that, while there was little danger of the central city becoming a ghost town, nevertheless the suburban areas would continue to act as a magnet for the metropolitan population since it represented a better match in terms of lifestyle and household needs.

The decline of urban entertainment areas

Anthony Downs and his associates at the Brookings Institution in Washington, DC have identified "forty theories of urban decline" which they have proposed in order to explain the falling population and employment experienced by many US cities during the 1960s and 1970s. These forty theories, they conclude, can be condensed into six groups: (i) *disamenity avoidance theories*: people and/or businesses leave the city for the suburbs so as to avoid negative factors such as crime and high energy costs; (ii) *tax avoidance theories*: tax burdens are lower in the suburbs than in central cities; (iii) *positive upgrading theories*: suburbs provide a better standard of living and a wider range of amenities; (iv) *economic evolution theories*: suburbanization is a natural stage in the evolution of the city, optimally combining activities and their locations; (v) *biased policy theories*: government policies influencing investment, housing and economic activity favor suburbs over central cities; (vi) *demographic trend theories*: population growth or migration trends have a negative impact on central cities (Bradbury *et al.* 1981). In attempting to explain the decline of urban entertainment areas from the 1950s to the 1970s, these six "theories" can be further reduced to three explanations: demographic and lifestyle changes, competition/substitution and disamenity/avoidance.

Demographic and lifestyle changes

The story of the post-Second World War baby boom is by now well known. On the return of the troops in 1945, North American cities faced a serious housing shortage, as few new units had been completed during the Depression and war years. Many couples temporarily moved in with their parents in the central city but longed for a place of their own. This need for one's own place was exacerbated by the delay in having children due to the war. Bolstered by various government subsidies, low-cost mortgages and tax breaks, the construction industry embarked on a suburban building spree, offering new, larger houses with recreation rooms and fenced back yards at affordable prices. For example, in 1954, Levitt Homes offered its "Rancher" home in Levittown, New Jersey with no downpayment necessary, $10 closing costs and low monthly payments (Palen 1992: 190).

With such deals on offer as this, it comes as no surprise that suburban growth outstripped central city expansion. By 1950, the suburban growth rate in the US was ten times that of the central cities and, four years later, an estimated nine million Americans had moved to the suburbs (Jackson 1985: 238). In city after city, the suburban percentage of the SMSA (Standard Metropolitan Statistical Area) grew rapidly and steadily. From 1950 to 1970, for example, the suburban percentage of the SMSA for Detroit increased from 38.7 to 64.0 percent; in Philadelphia from 30.1 to 51.8 percent; and in Minneapolis-St Paul from 27.6 to 59.0 percent (Choldin 1985: 238).

Demographic change and suburban residence brought a dramatic shift in people's lifestyle. Cultural observers of suburban life usually depict this as a shift away from "going out" towards one of "staying in." Various factors are cited as contributing to this new attitude toward leisure: the constraints imposed by having to look after young children; the necessity of having to drive as opposed to being able to "step out"; a new-found pride in home ownership; and the rise of television ownership. Writing in 1958, Robert C. Wood made the observation that what was striking in the lives of most suburban residents was their decision to turn their backs on urban culture and experience, and instead restrict their interest and associations to the immediate neighborhood (1958: 107–8). When David Popenoe conducted a three-year in-depth study of life in Levittown, Pennsylvania in the early 1970s, he concluded that recreation in the working-class suburb was "mostly a private activity of home and yard," situated around the backyard, the recreation room and the television set (1977: 134–5). Suburban residential neighborhoods, observes urban historian Kenneth Jackson, "have become a mass of small private islands; with the backyard functioning as a wholesome, family-oriented, and reclusive place" (1985: 280).

Yet, paradoxically, Americans were also taking to the outdoors as never before. In 1963, Conrad Wirth (1963), director of the National Park Service, reported that in the previous year the number of visitors to parks and other areas administered by his agency reached an all-time high of 88,457,000. Also in 1963, the National Swimming Pool Institute calculated that swimming had climbed to third place behind driving and walking as the most popular outdoor recreational activity in the country,[2] a trend evident both in the building boom in public municipal pools and in the explosive growth of smaller backyard residential installations. In 1960, *Life* magazine reported that Americans were expected to spend $250 million on private swimming pools, two-thirds of which were backyard pools purchased by families with modest incomes.[3]

Clearly, this new demand for outdoor recreation was being fueled by something more than just the baby boom and the shift to the suburbs. In a 1953 feature report on the "Leisured Masses," *Business Week* situated these changes in the context of the workplace. The leisure boom, it pointed out, reflected a number of longer term trends which had accelerated after the Second World War: shorter working hours, longer weekends, paid vacations and a growing retirement population. Some employees, notably in the garment and printing trades, in construction, the rubber industry and office workers, had seen their 40-hour week reduced to 35 hours. The Saturday half-day, eliminated for some occupations at the turn of the century but reinstated during the war, was now gone for good. Paid vacations of three weeks or more became a standard feature of many labor contracts.[4]

As a consequence of this boom in new leisure activities, traditional forms of urban entertainment – movies, theater, spectator sports – suffered a drop in attendance. In a commentary in the trade paper, the *Hollywood Reporter*, movie producer Darryl F. Zanuck made the distinction between *recreation* – an activity which you participate in – and *entertainment* – something others provide for you. By the early 1950s, Zanuck concluded, the public was shifting to a more participation-minded mode, as evidenced by increased involvement in a wide selection of outdoor recreational activities.[5] Zanuck may not have been aware of them, but US Department of Commerce figures for 1952 offered a convincing illustration of his thesis: total expenditure on flowers, seeds and potted plants for that year was $836 million, a figure which rapidly approached the sale of movie tickets ($1.1 billion).[6] As the decade progressed, motion picture receipts steadily declined as a percentage of total recreation expenditures: from 12 percent in 1950 to 6 percent in 1959 and as low as 3 percent by 1969.[7] Indeed, if we subtract admissions to drive-in theaters, cinema receipts dip even lower. Americans, it seemed, had better things to do than go downtown to the movies.

Competition: From drive-ins to Disneyland

It may seem surprising that the American leisure merchants didn't follow their markets and immediately relocate their operations to the suburbs. In the 1970s, for example, Australian cinemas had moved outwards and soon outnumbered downtown movie theaters by six to one. As well, retail merchants grasped on to this and set up shop in thousands of newly built suburban malls. Eventually, the shift to the American suburbs did happen, but first movie exhibitors, the backbone of the public entertainment business, faced a significant legal and regulatory hurdle.

In 1949 Paramount Pictures along with several other major Hollywood motion picture studios were convicted of anti-trust violations. As part of the divorcement decree imposed by the US Supreme Court, film exhibiting units were split off from the production and distribution arms. Unable to draw directly on capital from the parent company, theater chains could ill afford to undertake a new building campaign in the suburbs. Furthermore, the consent decree in the Paramount case stipulated that the major chains – Loew's, Inc., Paramount, RKO, 20th Century-Fox and Warner Bros. – could not acquire new theaters unless they pleaded before the Southern District of Manhattan Court on a case by case basis. This was an expensive and time-consuming process since they faced stiff opposition from attorneys representing the Federal Department of Justice. In such cases, the court was not sympathetic; it was impossible, for example, to exchange the closing of a downtown movie palace for the purchase of one in the suburbs (Gomery 1992: 89).

This situation gave rise to a new competitor: the drive-in theater ("Ozoners", see below). With a minimum of land improvement required and very little risk involved, the construction of "ozoners" took off in the 1950s, representing the "quickest and cheapest solution to the problem of theatre construction (Belton 1992: 76). By the early 1960s there were approximately 6,000 drive-ins throughout the US and one in five admissions sold was to a drive-in.[8] Nor was this trend restricted to the US: both Canada and Australia established their own drive-in circuits, with the latter having approximately the same number of ozoners per capita as in the US.[9]

With the major chains effectively neutralized, drive-in ownership became more widely dispersed than conventional in-town theaters.[10] Many were operated by local "mom and pop" owners, very much the same case as the early days of the nickelodeon era. A few independent chains, notably General Cinema and Durwood Entertainment (later American Multi-Cinema), eventually vaulted from drive-in ownership to prosperity with multiplex theaters in shopping malls in the 1970s and megaplexes in the UEDs of the 1990s.

Some cultural commentators have awarded drive-ins 1950s icon status and, in the process, have somewhat romanticized them. However, one aspect of this unique form of movie-going is worth noting. With most ozoners operating beyond the reach of corporate ownership and control, this left plenty of room for individual initiative and experimentation. As John Belton (1992: 78) has observed, some entrepreneurs, perhaps inspired by Walt Disney, even created entertainment complexes around their drive-ins – incorporating everything from a roller-skating rink (Dillsbury, Pennsylvania) to a miniature railroad which traveled through a diamond mine populated by shovel- and pick-wielding mechanical elves (Houston's Sharpstown drive-in). Unlike some small-time amusement businesses that later grew into big theme parks (for example, Knott's Berry Farm in Orange County, California), ozoner entertainment areas were usually no more than an adjunct to the show. Nevertheless, they did exhibit a degree of local creative input and control which regrettably disappeared with the ascendancy of shopping center multiplexes in the 1970s and 1980s.

"Ozoners"

Looking back at suburban American life post-Second World War, nothing seems more emblematic than the drive-in theater, or as it was nicknamed, the "ozoner" (see Segrave 1992: 18).

Drive-ins had in fact been in existence since June 1933, when Richard Hollingshead Jnr, a sales manager of an auto accessories firm and an erstwhile inventor, opened the Automobile Movie Theatre in Camden, New Jersey. After a slow start, construction of new theaters began to boom, rising from just over a 100 in 1945 to 3,000 by 1954. Ozoners were a product of their time. Suburban baby boomers, burdened by the demands of commuting and child-care and enamored with their automobiles, flocked to drive-ins because they were cheap (especially once "one-fee-per-car" admissions became popular), convenient and informal. Teenagers with nowhere else to go for privacy parked in the back rows.

Almost from the beginning, drive-in theaters provided a host of "extras," partly for promotional purposes but mainly to round out an evening of fun, since long summer days together with daylight saving time necessitated late starts to screening the films. Attractions included children's playgrounds, dance contests, fireworks, picnic areas and golf driving ranges. Some ozoners even offered a laundry service. Drive-in operators heavily promoted their snack bars which in some cases offered a full dinner. Similar to the "tail-gating parties" which are increasingly popular at National Football League (NFL) games today (see Chapter 10), some drive-ins encouraged patrons to arrive early and to dine around barbecue pits or in an outdoor patio area.

Drive-in theaters had to endure a host of technical problems. The screen was dull compared to indoor theaters; the sound quality of the in-car speakers was tinny; and fog, cold, rain and insects were a constant annoyance. For many years, the major film studios denied drive-ins first-run films, reserving these for indoor theatres. The ozoner industry regarded the invention of a "daylight screen" as their Holy Grail, allowing them to improve the quality of light and to extend their show times; unfortunately, despite a series of promised breakthroughs, this never came about.

By the late 1960s, drive-in growth had begun to stall and a decade later it entered into serious decline. As suburban real estate prices soared, the land on which drive-ins stood became too valuable to devote to a seasonal activity. New competition from multiplex cinemas in shopping malls and, later, from cable television and video, eroded ozoner profits. Changes in demographics and family structure further undermined the customer base. By 1990, there were less than a 1,000 drive-ins remaining in the US. A year later, the "Route 35 Drive-In" turned out its lights in favor of a twelve-screen, indoor multiplex, leaving New Jersey, the birthplace of the ozoner, without a single drive-in.

Source: Jonas and Nissenson (1994); Rood (1994); Segrave (1992).

Downtown entertainment venues not only faced competition from drive-ins, and later, movie theaters located in regional malls, but with the building of Disneyland in Southern California, they were pitched against the new phenomenon of theme parks located beyond the urban fringe.

Suburban fun parks, had, of course, always existed, many of them continuations of the turn-of-the-century "trolley parks." Most became defunct over the years, but a few – Kennywood on the edge of Pittsburgh, Cedar Point in Sandusky, Ohio, Conneaut Lake Park in western Pennsylvania – were blessed with good management and money for constant improvements and have survived up to the present day. By contrast, almost all the amusement parks closer to the city centers went out of business by the end of the 1970s.

Scores of books and articles have been written addressing the question of why Walt Disney, against all odds, succeeded with a new theme park in the 1950s. Industry veterans whom Disney consulted assured him that it was impossible to operate an amusement park without one or more blockbuster thrill rides such as a giant roller coaster. Disney, of course, proved them wrong. Probably the most convincing explanation is Disney's cross-merchandising of television, toys and live entertainment. This synergy was first realized through the "Davy Crockett" phenomenon. Not only was *Davy Crockett* the first mini-series on television, but sales of his raccoon-skin cap were wildly popular and Americans flocked to Disneyland where Crockett lived on in "Adventureland." Bob Hope, renowned not just as an actor and a comedian but also as a shrewd real estate investor, was one of the first to recognize the genius of the Disney formula. In the mid-1960s, Hope and his advisers considered a plan to develop a 400-acre amusement park with a wild-West theme; a key element in Hope's project (which never came to fruition) was promotion through intensive television tie-ins, as Walt had done with Disneyland.[11]

However, success for the new theme parks was by no means automatic. Up until the opening of Six Flags Over Texas in 1961, all the Disney clone parks had so far failed, with some never even reaching opening day. In August, 1960, *Life* ran an effusive cover story on the "boom" in amusement parks. The article described "bigger-than-ever audiences this summer" and a "surge in customers." Of the big new parks in the US – Disneyland, Freedomland (New York), Africa USA (Florida), Fort Dells (Wisconsin) – half were said to have adopted the theme park pattern. Despite a few disastrous failures, *Life* pronounced the "fun spot" industry on the move, with 1959 figures totaling $2 billion in receipts, an increase of $250 million from the previous year. Attendance as well jumped by a whopping 50 million people.[12]

Yet, most of these new-style fun parks failed within a short period of time. Various reasons have been suggested for this: underfunding, poor maintenance, a lack of media support, an incomplete infrastructure. The most spectacular failure was Freedomland (see "Freedomland USA," p. 40), which was seeking refinancing at the same time as *Life* was praising it as "the latest, largest and most elaborate theme park." Other failures included Magic Mountain in Denver (scheduled to open in 1958, but didn't); Pleasure Island in Boston (opened in 1959, it failed as a theme park and consequently was downsized, becoming a small, traditional amusement park); and Pacific Ocean Park in Santa Monica, California (opened in 1958, it closed due to bankruptcy a decade later).

Freedomland USA: The failure of an urban theme park

Freedomland USA opened 19 June 1960. It was the first major theme park to be built after Disneyland. Located in the north-east Bronx, half an hour from Manhattan, its 2.5 acres were laid out in the shape of a map of the United States, echoing its emphasis on American history. Freedomland was intended as the "Disneyland of the East," however, its inspiration derived more from Dreamland, the third park within turn-of-the-century Coney Island. Eschewing thrill rides, it sought to be both educational and entertaining, offering such re-creations as a fishing village, the Chicago fire and a Santa Fe train robbery.

By all rights Freedomland should have been a winning attraction. Its creator was C.V. Wood Jnr, one of Walt Disney's planning associates in the design of the Anaheim theme park, and it also had creative input from Randall Duell, who went on to become the dean of amusement park designers. With the decline of Coney Island, it had little competition in the largest urban region in the US. On opening day, it was overrun by 60,000 patrons, twice the expected number. Yet, from the outset, Freedomland courted disaster.

As seems to be the case with most amusement park failures, Freedomland suffered from underfinancing. This was evident on opening day when only half the park was completed. With the failure of a public stock offering, the enterprise fell into a quagmire of debt, including a series of construction lines totaling nearly $4 million. William Zeckendorf, whose firm Webb & Knapp was one of New York's most prestigious real estate developers, tried to salvage the project by undertaking a series of refinancing moves, including selling some of his hotels to provide working capital. A year after it had opened, the park added $3 million worth of standard amusement rides and scaled down its historical and educational attractions. This only had the effect of generating a breach of contract suit from one of its exhibitors, a paint manufacturer, Benjamin Moore & Co., who made the accusation that family recreation and entertainment delivered with "dignity and propriety" had been replaced by commonplace and vulgar entertainment which pandered to "teenage jazz enthusiasts."

By 16 September 1964, the losses could no longer be sustained and a petition for bankruptcy was filed. With only $734,000 from admissions in the 1964 summer season, Freedomland's owners attributed its troubles to competition from the World's Fair which was being held on the other side of New York, but clearly its difficulties had been present since the beginning. Theme park construction didn't stop with the closure of Freedomland but, as the *Wall Street Journal* advised a year later, developers needed to approach the field with a greater sense of care and caution, sticking to the successful formula worked out by the Six Flags chain in Texas, which they later replicated in Georgia and Missouri. Implicit in Freedomland's decline was another lesson, however: stay away from the city. "No urban park," amusement park chronicler Judith Adams observes, "has been able to guarantee the safety, cleanliness and order essential to a successful family attraction."

Source: Adams (1991); Jaques (1981); Kyriazi (1976);
"Freedomland is sued for changing character,"
New York Times, 5 September 1962, p.44;
"Freedomland asks court to help in solving its financial troubles,"
New York Times, 1 July 1964, p.45;
"Petition for bankruptcy filed,"
New York Times, 16 September 1964, p. 45.

With the success of Six Flags Over Texas in 1961 and a second park in the chain, Six Flags Over Georgia, near Atlanta, six years later, the tide had begun to turn. When Disney World opened in Florida in 1971, themed entertainment came of age and, for the first time, the entertainment venues of the central city were facing a serious challenge.

While they may differ in their content, Six Flags and Disney have followed more or less the same formula: an exurban location beyond the reach of public transport; a single admission price; cleanliness; attention to maintenance and safety; staff recruited from young people of high-school and college age (as against the old-style "carny" worker); half-a-dozen themed sections or areas each with a specific motif but loosely connected to a unifying idea; non-stop sensual bombardment and state-of-the-art technical virtuosity. Together, these requirements insure a "safe, controlled leisure environment, cloistered by distance and barriers from the fearful, chaotic, and generally decaying city" (Adams 1991: 109).

There is no way of knowing for certain to what extent drive-ins, theme parks and other amusement innovations of the 1950s and 1960s poached audiences from central city entertainment venues. It may be the case that few patrons of these new attractions would have chosen to go into the city for pleasure. On balance, evidence from the early 1950s suggests that outdoor theaters did not steal large numbers of customers from indoor theatres, with each attracting a different audience. In 1954, for example, attendance at indoor theaters was actually *higher* during the summer months when one would expect competition from the ozoners to be at its strongest. One survey in 1950 indicated that drive-ins drew just 15 percent of the customers of indoor theaters.[13] Nevertheless, throughout this period indoor film distributors consistently blamed drive-ins for the decline in their attendance figures and for the closure of downtown first-run theaters; especially complaining about the ozoner practices of free admission for children and a flat-rate per car admission.

In addition, there is no evidence to suggest that patrons of the new Disney-style theme parks would have flocked to Coney Island-style parks within the city limits if given no other choice. Indeed, Judith Adams (1991) argues that the steady decline in attendance at traditional locations began as early as 1921, and by the 1950s, relatively few middle-class patrons wished to share these venues with their new clientele of blacks, rural poor whites, Hispanics and other under-privileged groups who had begun to settle the inner city in increasing numbers. Even if the middle classes wished to go, the lack of parking facilities was a powerful disincentive for a suburban population increasingly dependent on their cars.

In *Chicago* magazine, Morry Roth (1976) noted that big name entertainment was flourishing in suburban nightclubs while downtown Chicago clubs – the Empire Room, Mister Kelly's and the Chez Paree – were foundering. Roth concluded that this was largely a practical matter: suburban establishments such as Condesa del Mar in Alsip and the Sabre Room in Hickory Hills successfully followed a standard formula of cheap labor, plentiful parking, accessibility and a feeling of safety.

Ultimately, the direct impact of new competition from drive-in theaters, theme parks and other entertainment venues situated beyond the city limits seemed to vary by place and time. Smaller and medium-sized cities were hit harder than large metropolitan areas because they lacked downtown neighbor-hoods whose residents continued to patronize entertainment facilities. Thus, even as the flight to the suburbs was proceeding, a July 1950 Gallup poll found that in cities with a population of 10,000–100,000, drive-ins captured 19 percent of all movie patrons, compared to only 6 percent for cities over 500,000.[14]

Furthermore, during this period the larger more cosmopolitan cities were not scaling down their cultural features; rather, they too exhibited new competitive currents. For example, in the early 1950s the theatrical world in New York was revitalized by the resurgence of the off-Broadway scene. In November 1953, fifty off-Broadway productions were running, twice the number than on Broadway. Nearly a decade later, theater historian Julia Price observed that off-Broadway productions were "attracting more and more out-of-towners, people who want to be intellectually stimulated but who nevertheless prefer a comfortable house" (1962: 119–22). By contrast, the "Great White Way" was heading toward "The Broadway Malady of 1963," with losses totaling 5 to 7 million dollars in 1962 (Bermel 1963: 56).

With the approach of the 1970s, urban entertainment began to change. In the suburbs, drive-ins were in decline and were replaced by hundreds of new multiplex theatres, built within the precincts of shopping malls which were being erected at a record pace. These served neither the serious movie-goer nor the family seeking a fun night out, but rather shoppers looking for a bargain matinee (Belton 1992: 214). What they found within these multiplexes, film scholar Douglas Gomery has observed, "proved as far from the golden days of the movie palace as one could imagine" (1992: 99–100). Entombed in concrete "screening rooms" with small screens, overpowered by Dolby sound systems, the loud volume of which penetrated the thin walls between adjoining auditoria, and distracted by spilled popcorn, sticky floors and other indicators of minimal upkeep, patrons of mall multiplexes were victims of the new, cost-driven economics of film exhibition.

Disincentives: Race, crime and the central city

Perhaps more than any other factor, social historians have pointed to the fear of the central city as being responsible for the decline of downtown movie palaces and other popular amusement venues. Whether this fear of crime was based on fact or fiction soon became irrelevant, Nasaw (1993: 249) observes, since the results were the same: a dwindling number of pleasure seekers and an ever greater perception of cities as dangerous places to be. As a result, the central city leisure areas acquired a litany of ills: unchecked physical blight, the spread of pornography and commercial sex, the closure of movie theaters and ancillary businesses, for example, restaurants, coffee shops and record stores (Kornblum and Williams 1978: 75).

Within this self-fulfilling prophecy, crime and race were closely linked. In a test of their "theories of urban decline," Anthony Downs and his associates at the Brookings Institution constructed indexes of distress for cities and SMSAs which ranked American cities from worst to least worst. When they analyzed the magnitude of "white flight" from the city centers, racial concentration played a major correlative factor, more than the increase in violent crime (Bradbury et al. 1982). This was further reinforced by the extensive television coverage of the urban riots in the late 1960s which depicted the inner city as a battle zone and wasteland.

Detroit

No American city highlights this process more than Detroit, Michigan. The "Motor City," had always displayed a tough side but it was also rich in sports, entertainment and cultural institutions. In the 1940s, the Paradise Theater played host to a stream of famous performers: Duke Ellington, Dizzy Gillespie, Billie Holiday, Lionel Hampton. Later, jazz and blues clubs flourished in the downtown area. The Detroit Red Wings hockey team won three Stanley Cup championships (1952, 1954 and 1955), while the Detroit Tigers were perennial contenders for the American League baseball title.

Despite its blue-collar status, Detroit had a vibrant arts scene. I remember crossing the border from Windsor, Canada with my father on multiple occasions in the 1950s to visit the Detroit Institute of Arts or to attend a concert at the Edsel Ford Auditorium by the Detroit Symphony Orchestra under its much respected conductor Paul Pare. In 1963, the Fisher Theater opened downtown in a remodeled motion picture house; my mother still has fond memories of seeing a production there of Tennessee William's *Night of the Iguana* starring Bette Davis. Even as late as 1965, a charity benefit starring black entertainers Sammy Davis Jnr and Dick Gregory, and backed by auto company officials, grossed $40,000, at the time a record for a single performance.[15]

Yet throughout this period Detroit was undergoing major demographic and sociological changes. Drawn by the booming auto industry, Southern migrants poured into the city swelling the black population from 300,000 in 1950 to 660,000 in 1970. At the end of the Second World War, Detroit was a mainly white city. However by the end of the 1960s, African-Americans made up just under half (44.5 percent), rising to 56 percent in 1975. At the same time, whites were fleeing to the suburbs in record numbers resulting in an overall population decrease (20 percent between 1950 and 1976) and a devastated tax base. In his autobiography, *Hard Stuff*, former Detroit mayor Coleman Young notes that, in a reversal of social history in which people have traditionally followed employment opportunities, in the 1950s and 1960s the jobs followed the people out to the suburbs, resulting in inner-city unemployment rates of over 20 percent (Young and Wheeler 1994: 151).

Two events book-ended this exodus to the suburbs. In 1954, Hudson's, the commercial anchor of Woodward Avenue, built its Northland store on vacant land just beyond the city's northern boundary in what was billed at the time as the largest regional shopping center in the world. And, in 1975 the Detroit Lions, a long-time National Football League franchise, escaped Tiger Stadium in downtown Detroit for the Pontiac Silverdome twenty miles away.[16]

By 1961, a *TIME* cover story carried the caption "Detroit in Decline." The magazine noted the city's high unemployment, the exodus of the middle class to the suburbs and the blight that was "creeping like a fungus through many of Detroit's proud old neighborhoods."[17] Inner-city neighborhoods were especially victimized by the urban highway craze of the 1950s and 1960s. As the home of auto manufacturing, Detroit embraced highway construction and took full advantage of the Federal Highway Act of 1956 which encouraged freeway network expansion. The majority of these new freeways ended up converging in the downtown area, dividing and destroying many of the city's ethnic neighborhoods; by 1970 alone an estimated 20,400 homes had been demolished for freeway construction.

Then, in 1967, the city experienced what may well be the worst civil disorder to befall an American city in the twentieth century. By the time the riot was over, there were 43 deaths, over a thousand injuries, 2,500 burnt-out stores and more than 2,000 arrests. Television coverage of the Detroit Riot was extensive and, at times, overheated. Within the city, news crews covered the riot on a 24-hour basis while outside the media depicted Detroit as "a city in ashes" (Fine 1989: 358).

In the aftermath of the riot, the white exodus to the suburbs escalated reaching a high of 80,000 people in 1968. Furthermore, in the years following the disturbance Detroit lost 110,000 jobs (Young 1994: 180). Not surprisingly, any residual appeal that the downtown entertainment may have had was lost. Windsor residents, many of whom had stood along the Canadian side of the Detroit River and watched the flames from the burning buildings during the riot, no longer crossed over the border for an evening out. Rather, the reverse occurred with suburban pleasure-seekers enjoying dinner and a floor-show at the Elmwood Casino, the Top Hat, the Metropole and other Windsor supper clubs which offered big-name entertainment.

By the 1970s, the streets of downtown Detroit routinely emptied after dark. According to one commentator:

> At night only a handful of whites can be seen in the downtown theaters. The restaurants which are busy during the day do a minimum of business at night, with few exceptions; many are quietly folding, as are the nightclubs. Detroit streets are so deserted after dusk that the city appears to be a ghost town – like Washington, DC; the nation's capital.
>
> (Widick 1989: 210)

Only two of the downtown movie palaces which had been erected in the years 1916–1928 remained in the once flourishing Grand Circus Park theater district, the Adams and the Plaza, and they were given over to what Jerry Herron (1993) has termed the "postmodern splatter movie": such as *Commando*, *Nightmare on Elm Street Part Two* and *The Dead Zone*. A legal ruling in the mid-1970s that overturned the monopoly rights of the old downtown movie houses to first-run films rang the death knell for these theaters since suburban patrons were more likely to choose the convenience and safety of venue in a nearby mall. As historian John Bukowczyk (1989: 40–1) sadly notes, the 1950s experience of traveling to downtown Detroit to see a first-run film or a special production such as a widescreen Cinerama spectacular, in a richly ornate movie-house atmosphere, followed by a trip to Sanders Ice Cream Parlour on Woodward Avenue, is now a thing of the past, "increasingly remote from our contemporary experience."

Detroit may constitute the worst case scenario but throughout this period many other American cities saw a marked decline in traditional entertainment venues in part, at least, because of increasing urban crime and racial tension. The latter was further escalated when the emerging Civil Rights Movement began to challenge long-established racist policies and rules of exclusion by which proprietors of public amusement facilities kept them exclusively for the use of the white middle class.

One of the first post-war protests focused on Euclid Beach Park,[18] located on the southern shore of Lake Erie, eight miles from the center of Cleveland. Once known as the "grand dame" of Ohio amusement parks, Euclid Beach first opened in 1895 as a pleasure resort, and later became famous for its dance pavilion where such bands as the Lawrence Welk Orchestra appeared regularly. It was also noted for its park police who consistently took a vigorous stand against drinking and rowdyism. The Euclid Park slogan was "Nothing to Depress or Demoralize" and they took strong measures to ensure this was the case.

In 1946, an inter-racial task force composed of activists from the American Youth for Democracy, the United Negroes and Allied Veterans of America, and the National Negro Congress visited Euclid Park and were summarily evicted. Subsequently, Harris C. Shannon, the park manager, told a local newspaper that the long-standing ban on black participation in "close contact activities" did not constitute discrimination but rather was a "business necessity"; it was cheaper, he claimed, to face a few discrimination suits than to lose the business of its white patrons.

A series of escalating clashes between park police and protesters from veteran and civil-rights groups culminated in several violent confrontations in August and September 1946 in which a black transit worker was attacked and beaten by a park policeman, and an off-duty black police officer who attempted to intervene on behalf of an inter-racial group from CORE (Congress of Racial Equality) was shot in the leg with his own revolver. As a consequence, City Council passed legislation providing for the licensing of amusement parks and giving it the power to revoke a license on evidence of racial discrimination. Euclid Park partially circumvented this, however, by operating its dance pavilion as a private dance club.

Euclid Beach Park endured until 1969 when escalating competition from Cedar Point and Geauga Lake, both within an hour's drive, combined with the appearance of a number of juvenile gangs who were attracted by the park's open-gate policy which allowed anyone on to the grounds free of charge, drove away most of its customers. A similar scenario unfolded at other amusement parks which were accessible to inner-city populations.[19]

In the mid-1950s, Olympic Parc in Irvington, New Jersey, founded in 1887, was desegregated by civil rights protesters. By the mid-1960s, it had become a hang-out for gangs of urban youths from nearby Newark and was the site in May 1965 of a riot in which the participants spread out into neighboring residential areas, smashing windows and vandalizing property. That year, Olympic Parc was closed and the land sold to urban developers. Riverview Park in Chicago became the site of racial and gang conflicts and persistent vandalism, causing Chicago pleasure-seekers to stay away from its rough, dangerous atmosphere. Pacific Ocean Park, on the border between Los Angeles and Santa Monica, and made famous as a midway site by various 1960s television dramas, closed in 1967 when a shift to a pay one price policy "let many undesirables onto the premises," thus driving away many patrons (Surface 1983: 43).

The closing of these amusement parks cannot be blamed entirely on their growing reputation for rowdyism and violence; the owners too were culpable insomuch as they let the premises go to seed, unwilling to put money into improvements either because they were financially distressed or because they saw greater value in selling the land for real estate development purposes.

During this period, downtown sports stadiums also began to leave the precincts of the central city. In the mid-1960s, the Chicago White Sox, one of baseball's classic teams, came close to leaving town because its fans were nervous about traveling to Comiskey Park, adjacent to the city's "black belt" (Riess 1989: 248). In 1970, the Philadelphia Phillies moved out of Shibe Park (Connie Mack Stadium), its home for sixty years; Phillies owner Bob Carpenter believed that white baseball fans would no longer come to an "undesirable" neighborhood to see a game. The stabbing of a fan in the process of buying a ticket for the final game, seemed to underscore Carpenter's fears (Kuklick 1991: 181). Similarly, the "Cavs," Cleveland's new NBA franchise remained for only four years in the Cleveland Arena, an aging downtown facility. In 1974, the team shifted to the Richfield Coliseum, a suburban entertainment venue located between the Cleveland and Akron–Canton metropolitan areas. The Cavs' move, Rosentraub observes, "was part of a nationwide trend; many teams sought to follow their wealthier fans to the suburbs to avoid the conflicts and tensions that were dominating so many of America's urban centers" (1997: 254).

In 1958, in a move which even today haunts New York politicians, the beloved "Bums" of Brooklyn became the Los Angeles Dodgers; and the New York Giants baseball team also headed west, settling in San Francisco. In 1963, the Washington Senators left Griffith Stadium in the increasingly crime-ridden Washington, DC for Bloomington, Minnesota, a suburb of Minneapolis. These new venues, Nasaw observes, were "far from their home neighborhoods, far indeed, from any type of neighborhood" (1993: 252), situated on major highways, inaccessible by mass transit and surrounded by acres of undeveloped land that could readily be converted into parking lots.

In the mid-1960s, Walt Disney Productions was engaged in serious discussions with the Civic Center Redevelopment Corporation about the possibility of building a Midwestern version of Disneyland Park in downtown St Louis, Missouri. The four-storey entertainment center, to have been located in a multi-level building on a 2.5 acre super-block site at the Riverfront urban renewal project, would have been framed by the city's new sports stadium and the "Gateway Arch," a 630-foot structure on the banks of the Mississippi River. The deal fell apart in July 1965 when civic officials balked at Disney's insistence that the city completely finance the $30–$50 million cost of the project, turning over all future profits to Disney Productions once the capital costs were repaid. It was felt that the facility was too small and that the environment (an urban renewal area) was unlikely to meet the target of 25,000 or more visitors a day needed to make the plan financially feasible.[20] Disney himself, deep in preparation for the New York's World Fair and rumored to be about to embark on a new venture in Florida, wasn't inclined to pursue the project any further.

In retrospect, St Louis civic officials probably made the right decision, at least from a business point of view. Indoor amusement parks were a new concept in 1965, twenty years ahead of their time. In the 1970s, two major indoor parks, The World of Sid and Marty Krofft – a $14 million indoor high-rise amusement park in the Omni International Complex in Atlanta, Georgia – and the $40 million Old Chicago Park, built adjacent to a 7-acre retail shopping area in a Chicago suburb, both failed, the former after only five months of operation. While it is true that both of these projects were underfinanced, it is by no means certain that the Disney name could have rescued the St Louis Park, especially after the opening of Six Flags over Mid-America in Eureka, Missouri, forty miles west of St Louis in the foothills of the Ozarks.

Still, a Midwestern Disneyland in downtown St Louis would have been a tremendous symbolic gesture of faith at a time when inner cities were rapidly losing their appeal as venues for public entertainment. As it was, St Louis opted instead to purchase the Spanish pavilion at the 1964 New York World's Fair and move it to a site on the banks of the Mississippi, a decision which made about as much historical sense as the relocation of London Bridge to Lake Havasu, Arizona or the ocean liner *Queen Elizabeth* to the Delaware river in Philadelphia. As for Walt Disney Productions, within months of axing the St Louis concept, it announced that it would be building "Disneyland East" in the swamps of central Florida.

Figure 3.1 "The vast picture show": Famous Players' Silver City Riverport multiplex cinema in Richmond, British Columbia.
Source: Courtesy of Christopher Grabowski.

3

"CITIES ARE FUN"

Entertainment returns to the city center

As Americans prepared to enjoy the final days of summer 1981, they were greeted with a surprising message on the 24 August cover of *TIME* magazine: "Cities Are Fun." The article celebrated the new pride and vitality which had come to US cities, as symbolized by the transformation of Baltimore's "Inner Harbor" from a 250-acre wasteland of disused wharves, markets, warehouses and railroad yards into a retail/entertainment wonderland full of "jams and jollity" (Demarest 1981). Fourteen years after the urban riots had devastated inner-city neighborhoods in Cleveland, Detroit, Los Angeles and other major cities, downtown appeared to be making a comeback.

In formulating strategies designed to return downtown areas to prominence, urban planners, civic leaders and real estate developers learnt several lessons. First, the building of office towers and department stores was not in itself sufficient to re-energize a city center. Workers in high-rise office buildings might shop downtown during their lunch break, but come six o'clock most of them returned to the suburbs, leaving the downtown core a ghost town. Second, it was unwise to choose locations which required large-scale urban renewal. Such projects had boomeranged in the 1950s and 1960s, provoking protest by those who sought to rescue inner-city precincts from the often senseless and indiscriminate path of the bulldozers. Instead, it made strategic sense to build in lightly populated areas, for example, along the waterfront or in derelict warehouses and railroad stations. Third, successful urban revitalization required innovative partnerships between the public and private sectors. This necessitated a type of role reversal wherein city leaders became more proactive and entrepreneurial while developers learned to navigate the shoals of municipal politics. Finally, it was perceived that the task of creating a vibrant downtown required heavy investment in flagship destination projects: such as convention centers, aquariums, professional sports complexes, casinos, museums, redeveloped waterfronts and entertainment districts (Brown and Laumer 1995: 47). If out-of-town day-trippers were to be drawn back into the city center, particularly after dark and on weekends, they had to have somewhere to go which was exciting, safe and not available in the suburbs. Flagship projects came to be valued both as a way of establishing confidence among nervous investors and developers and as a marketing tool with which to change perceptions of down-town from images of "dereliction, emptiness and crime" to those of "quality, entertainment and festivity" (Fitzsimmons 1995: 26).

A moveable feast: Festival markets and inner-city redevelopment in the 1970s

At the start of the 1970s, downtown development was not viewed as an attrac-tive proposition. Prospective developers faced a long list of obstacles: rigid building codes, bureaucratic red tape, difficulties in assembling land, continuing fallout from the neighborhood destroying urban renewal projects of the 1950s and 1960s. Added to this was the inability to line up support from major retail tenants who feared city center developments would be plagued by crime and drive away customers. Most developers, if the thought ever occurred to them, "looked at downtown and still saw a quagmire" (Frieden and Sagalyn 1989: 84).

How, then, did the metamorphosis occur in which politicians, planners and builders suddenly discovered the right formula for downtown renewal?

In the canon of orthodox planning, the favored view is that a new set of public–private partnerships began to emerge in the 1970s, reaching its zenith in the urban regeneration effort of 1980s. The key players were a small number of "maverick" developers (Victor Gruen, Ernest Hahn, James Rouse), "messiah" mayors (Donald Schaefer, Baltimore; Kevin White, Boston; Richard Caliguiri, Pittsburgh) and entrepreneurial public managers (Gerald Trimble, Pasadena and San Diego; John Clise, Seattle). Together they overcame the seemingly insur-mountable barriers erected by conservative mortgage lenders, shrinking federal subsidies, obsessive preservationists and narrow-minded neighborhood opponents.

This hagiographic version is best summarized in the rise to fame of James Rouse. In 1972, Rouse, best-known theretofore as the builder of the first enclosed shopping mall in the US and of the racially integrated new town of Columbia, Maryland, was approached by Boston architect Benjamin Thompson regarding the development of a retail complex on the site of the historic Quincy Market. Jolted by the riots of the 1960s and convinced that the suburban dream was starting to fade, Rouse believed that the task of working for the recovery of America's cities "should be transcending in our lives and businesses" (Rouse 1984: 22). Deftly negotiating the shoals of Boston politics, Rouse and Thompson transformed the old market into Faneuil Hall Marketplace. Combining a design rich in historical associations with a Disney-style mainte-nance system, Faneuil Hall Marketplace was an instant success, drawing 10 million visitors in its first year; a figure equal to that of the gate count at Disneyland (Frieden and Sagalyn 1989: 7).

Rouse dared to break the cardinal rule of retail merchandising by initially restricting the number of institutional chain-store tenants in favor of small, independent shopkeepers who had limited resources but interesting products.

The "most creative economic feature of this market success story," rhapsodized urban commentator Roberta Brandes Gratz (1989: 324–5), was a fleet of forty-three pushcarts (barrows) which were added just before opening day so as to create an illusion of greater commercial activity. These were subsequently made a permanent feature as they proved to be so popular.

Rouse replicated his success with Harborplace in Baltimore, and, later, in New York (South Street Seaport), Milwaukee (Grand Avenue), St Louis (Union Station), Miami (Bayside) and Honolulu (Aloha Tower). Described by the journal *Planning* (May 1985) as "the Robin Hood of real estate," Rouse's name took on a generic meaning, with people talking in admiring terms of the "Rouse-ification" of cities.

The festival market place formula differed from the traditional shopping mall in several respects. Whereas malls were designed as "lobster traps" with an anchor at either end – usually a large department store such as Sears or J.C. Penney – festival malls were different. Not only did they lack dominant anchors, but they favored an eclectic mix of specialty shops over a roster of chain stores. Waterside,[1] a Rouse-designed waterfront market place in Norfolk, Virginia modeled on Baltimore's Harborplace, sought to keep its retail emphasis dynamic by limiting the rental period for retail kiosks to six months at a time and for pushcarts, only a few weeks. This was the reverse of the standard shopping mall where the emphasis was on stability and consistency. As well, festival markets highlighted eating and entertainment as much as shopping. Image was important and they were unified by historic and/or architectural themes. Rather than a general customer base, they aimed at a specialized target market: affluent, educated, young adults (Robertson 1995: 432).

Rouse may be considered a modern-day urban Robin Hood among mainstream planners, but critical opinion is divided within architectural and social science circles. One of the most vocal opponents of the Rouse-style public–private partnerships is Marc Levine, a professor of History and Urban Affairs at the University of Wisconsin, Milwaukee and a former economic policy advisor to Massachusetts senator Ted Kennedy. Levine makes the charge that Rouse-ification is in fact a "tale of two cities": pockets of revitalization surrounded by areas of extreme poverty (1989: 25). Boston and Baltimore, both success stories of the 1970s, exhibit this pattern, their redeveloped downtown areas constituting "islands of renewal in a sea of decay" (Berry 1985: 69).

Levine is particularly concerned with the isolation of downtown redevelopment projects from the economy of surrounding neighborhoods. For one thing, there is relatively little economic spillover to local shops and businesses from mega-projects such as the festival market places. Tourists and other visitors rarely venture beyond the confines of these flagship developments, leaving neighborhood merchants, in many cases, worse off than before. Nor are they fertile sources of employment. Jobs that do become available for local people are usually at entry level, paying substantially less than former manufacturing positions which have shifted to the suburbs or offshore. Furthermore, these job opportunities are more often than not dead-ends: rarely do they lead to middle-income management positions which instead go to suburban commuters. The optimistic claims about the "trickle-down effects" of city-center development projects which inform public pronouncements are thus over exaggerated.

Levine demonstrates his criticisms through an empirical analysis of Baltimore, whose Inner Harbor project, together with the surge of additional private investment in the waterfront area which it unleashed, made it a template for urban revitalization in the 1980s. While acknowledging that certain ripple effects did occur, none the less Levine argues that the ripples failed to reach most of Baltimore's neighborhoods. For example, in the decade 1970–1979, the proportion of city neighborhoods with a high concentration of poor residents increased from 9.7 percent (1970) to 16.6 percent (1980). Most of these impoverished neighborhoods were predominantly black. Suburbanites appeared to have captured the lion's share of well-paid professional and managerial jobs created by downtown developments. Levine poses the question: "for whom is Baltimore's Metrocenter being revitalized"? The answer, he suggests, is high-income, out-of-town tourists and a new urban gentry: young professionals living in three gentrifying neighborhoods adjacent to Inner Harbor – Federal Hill, Fells Point and Ridgely's Delight – (Levine 1987). Thus, projects such as Harborplace have helped Baltimore to become the archetype of the 1980s "dual city," a city of haves and have-nots.

Festival market places have also been criticized on aesthetic and philosophical grounds. The accusation is that Rouse and his disciples have tried too hard to create a unified historical experience in areas which retain only residues or fragments of a distant past. In doing so, they have "so conflated geographical space and historical time that the actual uniqueness of place and content have been completely erased" (Boyer 1992: 200). Oil City, a 1980s urban redevelopment built on the site of a decayed industrial district in Syracuse, New York, typically reflected all the contradictory elements of the festival market place, combining a disjointed repertoire of historical themes and artifacts – the hub of an old waterwheel from the closed salt works, a 100-year-old carousel rescued from a defunct amusement park in western New York State and a statue of Benjamin Franklin (Roberts and Schein 1993).

Furthermore, critics complain that festival markets are too similar in their design and content and thus virtually interchangeable. As a consequence, local landscapes are decommissioned in favor of a single generic model. This is the important first step, they warn, in the emergence of "clone cities" (Law 1992: 605), each with its requisite waterfront development, festival market place, convention center, science museum and aquarium. In the early 1980s, Sharon Zukin (1982: 78) argued that what was being created was a national, middle-class culture as represented by a coast-to-coast chain of red-brick shopping centers with their standardized assortment of gourmet and ethnic food shops, crafts boutiques, bookstores, crêpe or oyster bars.

Finally, critics question the ideological integrity of the festival market place.

The historical tableaux presented in these Rouse-ified projects is tainted, it is claimed, because they fail to present an "authentic" sense of place and time. By "authentic," what they usually mean is a narrative of the experience of "working people." Thus, Christine Boyer condemns the staging of the past as portrayed in New York's South Street Seaport on the grounds that it ignores the "poverty that led the seamen to indenture themselves[2] in favor of a nostalgic panegyric to "travel and adventure, exotic commodities and trade" (1992: 199–200). Likewise, Jon Goss (1996: 229) castigates a giant 268-foot historical mural painted on the inside wall of a terminal shed at Aloha Tower for making heroes of the merchant-financiers and politicians who promoted the early development of Honolulu, while not depicting the thousands of Asian immigrants who labored on plantations and on the waterfront, and who organized themselves against oppressive conditions.

Some academic commentators are also offended at the overtly commercial flavor of festival market places. Such developments, complains economic geographer David Harvey, constitute landscapes of and for consumption in the same manner as Disney theme parks. Within their environs, the world of commodities "could be celebrated under tight security surveillance and control." In Baltimore, for example, the architecture of function which had previously dominated the city, was replaced by "an architecture of play and pleasure, of spectacle and commodification, emphasizing fiction and fantasy" (Harvey 1991: 60). Especially of concern is what architectural historian Margaret Crawford (1992) has termed the "principle of adjacent attraction," by which the boundaries of commerce and culture are indelibly blurred. The idea is that consumers are drawn in through the nostalgic appeal of quasi-historical architecture and attractions, whose attributes are then transferred psychologically to the items for sale in the gift shops and boutiques. Not only is thematized history and geography used to sell everything from posters to fudge, but these consumer items end up as stand-ins for real-life travel and experience (Sorkin 1992a: 216).

Downtown cultural revitalization 1980s style

Despite these caveats, by the 1980s a new formula for downtown revitalization had come to be widely accepted. As desirable as festival market places still appeared to many economically distressed cities, by themselves they were insufficient to ensure a steady flow of visitors to the city center. And they were not the moneymakers that at first they seemed to be. For one thing, they cost three times as much as conventional shopping centers to build (on a square foot basis) yet they attracted one-third of the consumer spending. Put simply, this means a festival market place needs nine times the customers in order to match the profitability of a shopping center (Millspaugh 1995). Stand-alone festival market places, then, despite their bright public image, were rarely able to fully support the capital cost of initial development. Furthermore, they began to face competition from a new generation of mega-malls which contained their own themed attractions. Consequently, festival market places needed to be supplemented by a standard repertoire of "special activity generators" – convention centers, sports arenas and stadiums, casinos, arts and entertainment complexes – large facilities capable of attracting both tourists and day-trippers from the suburbs and the surrounding metropolitan region (Robertson 1995: 433). In combination, these constituted a "structured urban revitalization package" (Law 1993) which could be aggressively marketed as part of a city's re-imaging efforts.

Cultural districts

In the 1970s, shopping and dining were the dual engines which drove the commercial regeneration of downtown areas. Culture and entertainment, by contrast, were important in creating a sense of occasion and excitement but were not in and of themselves considered the end destination or a direct source of income.

To generate publicity for Harborplace in Baltimore, the Rouse Company created a series of special entertainment events, including concerts, boat shows, and Christmas festivals. According to a study by Rouse in the early 1980s, 54 percent of people who came to shop and spend money at Harborplace came downtown either because of these festivals or because of their general perception that Baltimore was a "festival city" (Hillman 1984: 99). Writing in a newsletter for downtown development executives, Mary Gornto, an organizer of the "Riverfest" in Wilmington, North Carolina, offered this sage advice:

> Myriad plans have been designed by both private and public sectors to revitalize downtowns. Although necessary aspects of revitalization, such techniques as facade renovation, sophisticated financial packaging and street improvements do not always assure success. Rather, these efforts must be aggressively marketed to create interest and commitment to any revitalization program. The public must be "sold" the attitude that downtown *is* an exciting place in which to shop, work, live and invest.
>
> (1981: 10)

In addition to food and special events, Gornto recommends a continuous schedule of entertainment – ballet, band concerts, madrigal singers, jugglers, magicians – in order to assure that there will always be "something to see and enjoy" whenever people arrive at the urban festival (ibid.: 11).

Eventually, however, some city planners set out to give culture a more central and autonomous role in the urban regeneration process. One strategy which proved popular in the 1980s was to deliberately establish cultural, arts, or entertainment districts – geographical areas which provided accommodation and work opportunities for actors, musicians, dancers, film-makers and the like. Such districts act to encourage urban revitalization in three interrelated ways:

(i) through the residential development of lofts and other premises formerly given over to industrial use; (ii) through the symbiotic development of new retail projects which help to offset the pull of suburban malls and super-centers; and (iii) through the creation of a night-time economy in areas which are all but deserted after dusk (Wynne 1992: 19).

Cultural arts districts were established during the 1980s across the US. It took five years of lobbying before Tuscon, Arizona's art district received its first year of funding in 1988; in St Paul, Minneapolis' twin city, a local coalition established thirty artists' studio homes in a five-storey converted shoe factory in Lowertown, the city's arts district. In Dallas, Texas, a 60-acre parcel of land near the Dallas Museum of art was dedicated to "cultural facilities expansion" (Clay 1994). The inspiration for these initiatives was the creation of an artists' district in downtown Manhattan in the early 1970s. In this case, the city passed a series of zoning resolutions and building code alterations enabling artists to rent manufacturing lofts in Soho and later in TriBeCa, for combined living and studio use .[3]

Another approach was to build mixed-use centers in which the cultural components were equal to the commercial, residential and retail aspects. The Yerba Buena Center, an 87-acre development in San Francisco adjacent to the Moscone Convention Center and opened in stages between 1993 and 1995, is a leading example. Projects like the Yerba Buena Center are said to recognize that shopping in itself has begun to pale as a primary reason for going downtown, and that other incentives are necessary (Fleissing 1984: 90). Mixed-use centers which include cultural components are especially appealing because they attract both public (federal grants for the arts, tax advantages) and private (corporate donations) subsidies, thus reducing the share which developers need to contribute (Whitt 1988: 60). For example, the Denver Center for the Performing Arts, a four-building complex connected by a glass galleria, pooled city resources and those from the Helen Bonfils and Frederick Bonfils Foundations and incorporated these with funds raised through a municipal bond issue.[4]

As part of this cultural revitalization, some of the classic theaters from the "golden age" of urban entertainment were miraculously rescued from the wreckers' ball and restored, constituting the nucleus of a revitalized theater district.

In 1921–22, under the patronage of the New York theater impresario Marcus Loew, a planned entertainment district, Playhouse Square, was built at the downtown end of Euclid Avenue in Cleveland, Ohio. The centerpiece of the Square was a group of four vaudeville and motion picture palaces: the Allon, Ohio, Palace and State theaters. By 1969, all four theaters had closed and two, the State and the Ohio, faced demolition.

In 1970, however, a non-profit group dedicated to saving Playhouse Square obtained a reprieve and with the support of the Junior League created a cabaret in the lobby of the State theater. Its first major production, the musical revue

"Jacques Brel is Alive and Well and Living in Paris," ran for two years making it the longest-running show in Cleveland theater history. In 1973, a foundation was created to raise funds and to carry out the restoration, operation and management of the theaters. Drawing on a combination of private and public funding sources, the State, Ohio and Palace theaters were leased and renovated and became the home of ballet, opera and large-scale musical productions. The revival of Playhouse Square as a performing arts center was the largest project of this type in the US in the 1980s and, according to a 1988 study, it brought $15 million to the Cleveland economy each year.[5]

Similar restorations, albeit on a lesser scale, were undertaken across America throughout the 1980s. In Detroit, where efforts at urban revitalization have generally faltered, a local pizza chain magnate and sports team owner, Mike Illitch, purchased the Fox Theater and restored it in an effort to revive the defunct Woodward Avenue entertainment district.[6] Voters in Portland, Oregon approved a $19 million general obligation bond issue to construct a performing arts complex, with the balance of the finance coming from private sources. The centerpiece of this project is the renovation of the historic Paramount Theater into a first-class concert hall, home to the Oregon Symphony.[7] In a similar fashion, encouraged by the restoration of the defunct Saenger movie theater into a live performance venue, New Orleans undertook to return the Orpheum Theater to its former glory, and made it the permanent home of the New Orleans Symphony. As part of a wave of downtown development catalyzed by Richmond Renaissance, a bi-racial, public–private partnership active in New Orleans in the early 1980s, an abandoned Loew's theater was transformed in 1983 into the 2,000 seat Virginia Center for the Performing Arts (Reinhard 1984). Under the auspices of the City Center Redevelopment Corporation of St Louis, Missouri, the "fabulous" Fox Theater (4,500 seats) was renovated, as was a former movie house (2,800 seats) which became home to the St Louis Symphony Orchestra (Ward 1984). In one of the largest projects from this era, the Beaux Arts Theater, the one remaining classical auditorium in downtown Honolulu, was finally reopened in May 1996 after a decade of work. The center-piece of the Hawaii Theater Center, it is considered a key element in the redevelopment of a section of Honolulu's Chinatown district. Seeded by a $500,000 donation from a private citizen, the $21 million restoration was partially bankrolled with public funds (Weathersby 1996).

According to a report produced by the Harvard University Business School (1984), there are a number of key factors in ensuring the success of downtown cultural revitalization projects such as those which I have just listed. First, a dense network of ties needs to be established between major social, political, business and special interest groups in the community, as the projects are too large to be carried out by any one group alone. Second, the organizing vehicle needs to take the form of a non-profit organization, since this permits donations from private foundations which are legally constrained so as only to be able to contribute to non-profit groups. Third, positive media coverage is vital in creating public interest in and maintaining the momentum for the developing projects. Fourth, the hiring of a prestigious outside consulting firm is important in building legitimacy and attracting attention. Consultants' reports are crucial in attracting additional, high-profile board members, winning the support of key civic groups and municipal officials, attracting media attention and raising funds. Fifth, cultural rehabilitation projects need to be linked to other ongoing redevelopment projects, such as festival market places, office complexes and retail malls. Otherwise, these projects will seem isolated and will be more difficult to justify and fund. Finally, a crisis such as the imminent threat of demolition faced by the two theaters in Cleveland's Playhouse Square can help to generate media attention and funding support.

Not all of the cultural activity which reinvigorated downtown areas during this period was the direct result of strategic initiatives undertaken by public–private partnerships. In some cases, city center locations were co-opted by marginal groups who converted them to spaces of pleasure and cultural opposition. For example, the Loisada neighborhood on the Lower East Side of New York nurtured a spicy stew of cultural expression in the period between the mid-1970s and early 1980s in which the main ingredient was a Puerto Rican poetry movement known as the Nuyorican Poets Experience. During this era, a network of magazines, music festivals, cafés, community centers and organizations nourished an outpouring of literature, mural painting, photography, experimental theater, movies, music and dance, all of which explored an alternative sensibility to the dominant Anglo culture (see Maffi 1994). Such pockets of creative resistance, however, tend to face a constant pressure towards gentrification: the more they become celebrated as artistic hangouts, the more they end up functioning as the "shock troops of neighborhood reinvestment," opening up the area to more middle- and upper-middle class landscapes of consumption (Smith et al. 1994).

Disney comes to town: The new entertainment economy

Despite the charges of some critics that festival market places and other urban revitalization projects of the 1970s and 1980s had "brought Disney to the city," in fact, Disney and other entertainment-based companies, initially were not very eager to establish a new beachhead in America's downtown areas. As we have seen, Disney briefly flirted with the notion of building a theme park in St Louis in the 1960s but withdrew when it became clear that the city was not prepared to accept all the financial risk. In a later initiative, Disney "imagineers" were involved in a project to redesign the civic center in Seattle, Washington but residents parted company when their plans were deemed inappropriate (see Warren 1994). Within the Disney Company itself, it was felt that the establishment of new urban theme parks might detract from attendance at Disneyland and Disney World, even if these were built in cities which were a considerable distance away from Florida or California. As Michael Rubin, a

Philadelphia development consultant who has been at the forefront of the urban entertainment business, told a 1995 industry seminar, "ten years ago, it would have been unimaginable for Disney to be at 42nd Street and yet Disney is there now leading a major revitalization" (Rubin 1995). By the start of the 1990s, however, attitudes were changing.

Technological breakthroughs, most of which had their origins in the motion picture industry, meant that sophisticated special effects could be compressed in time and space; making them more amenable to downtown sites where land was at a premium. One of the first examples of this miniaturization was Doug Trumbull's patented technology which combined 35mm film with a flight simulator to create movie rides. Trumbull, who had designed the special effects for a number of futuristic Hollywood movies, such as *Blade Runner, 2001: A Space Odyssey* and *Close Encounters of the Third Kind*, first introduced the concept with the "Tour of the Universe" ride at Toronto's CN Tower in 1985, and, five years later, he created the "Back to the Future" ride for MCA/Universal Studios. By 1993, he had miniaturized his simulator theater into a fifteen-seat modular unit that could fit into a 30-foot-by-30-foot space that is less than 15 feet high. That same year, Iwerks Entertainment, a competitor, developed a high-technology entertainment environment called Cinetropolis which took up only 50,000 square feet of space. Cinetropolis had its debut in 1994 at the Foxwoods Casino in Connecticut (Rubin *et al.* 1994: 61). Motion simulator rides and theaters are at the cutting edge of this technology today, but they are only a starting point. For Disney, Universal and other theme park operators, the glittering prize is the ability to "downscale" theme park experiences, recreating in a $5–$20 million venue the essence of what they now produce in a $200 million complex. Already, IMAX Corporation, the pioneer of large-format movie technology, has brought to market the new SR projection system which is small enough to fit into multiplex cinemas and yet costs two-thirds less to build than a conventional IMAX theater. This system is designed to bring the technology to smaller urban markets with a population base as low as 500,000, compared to conventional IMAX theaters, which need a population of one million or more (Enchin 1997).

At the same time as these technological breakthroughs were occurring, a new "entertainment economy" was gathering momentum both in America and abroad. In a 1994 cover story, *Business Week* noted that more than $13 billion in big entertainment projects – theme parks, theaters, casinos and ballparks – were in the pipeline in the US with many more to come (Grover *et al.* 1994: 60). Not all these projects were designated for downtown areas but, in contrast to the recent past, many were. This new entertainment economy is fueled by several broad socio-economic trends.

Demographically, the baby boom generation has now reached middle age and can afford to indulge itself in such consumer luxuries as large screen televisions and vacation jaunts to Orlando or Las Vegas. In 1993, according to data gathered by the US Commerce Department, American consumers spent a total of $341 billion on recreation and entertainment, including $28 billion on gambling, $14 billion on amusement parks and other commercial participant amusements and $12 billion on spectator sports and other live entertainment. This is $71 billion more than was spent on public and private education in the United States. Significantly, the figures for these two categories were roughly equal in 1980 (Grover *et al.* 1994: 60; Landler 1994: 66). Buttressing these "boomer" dollars is the rising entertainment spending by the so-called "Generation X": the generation born in the 1960s who are now entering their thirties. Together, the "boomers" and "Xers" are regarded as the backbone for these new and sophisticated forms of entertainment that are conveniently located in urban settings.

Flush with discretionary income, middle-class consumers are at the same time leading increasingly hectic lives with less rather than more leisure time (Hochschild 1997; Schor 1991). One consequence of this is a shift away from long summer vacations to other travel alternatives, notably extended weekend retreats and short holiday visits to urban centers within several hours by air of one's home. This "localization of leisure" (Rubin and Gorman 1993) has helped to create a rising demand for urban location-based entertainment facilities not only in tourist centers such as southern Florida, but also in places which formerly would not have been on the tourist agenda: Baltimore, Cleveland, Pittsburgh. While there is some difference of opinion, urban entertainment developers and operators usually estimate that visitors will stay somewhere between two to five hours as compared to a stay of several days at a theme park. Economic success, therefore, depends on the nurturing of a strong regional market where customers make repeated "leisure safaris" into the city center.

Even in the heartland of America, a place not considered a tourist mecca, big-time entertainment complexes are being established. Branson, a small town in south-west rural Missouri near the Arkansas state line, has become a popular destination for tourists with a yen for country and western music. With thirty-four theaters, many owned by the country music stars who perform there, a theme park (Silver Dollar City) and an "Elvis-o-Rama" exhibit, Branson draws over five-million visitors each year. River Bluff Landing, a recently announced $300 million project in Sevierville, Tennessee includes three theaters, a freshwater and saltwater aquarium, a restaurant, two hotels and a boardwalk (Hackett 1996).

The resurgence of urban entertainment has benefited from a recent escalation of "convergences" or "synergies" within and among the communications, entertainment, retail and real estate development industries.

In a series of mergers and takeovers which stunned financial analysts in the mid-1990s, Walt Disney acquired Capital Cities/ABC in 1995 for $19 billion, thereby becoming an owner of one of the original three television networks; Viacom bought Paramount Communications Inc. and, with it, Blockbuster Entertainment in 1994 for a combined $17.4 billion giving it control of a variety of entertainment properties: video rentals, a movie studio, a book publisher and MTV, the music video channel; and Seagram, the Canadian liquor and orange juice giant, bought MCA for $5.7 billion thereby acquiring a movie studio, a theme park and a theater chain. Most of these transactions were based on the premise (now under some critical fire) that growth would follow if companies controlled both programming and distribution (Landro 1996).

Even where the players kept their separate identities, an unprecedented series of alliances were formed. Sega, the video game czar of the early 1990s, joined forces with Universal and Dream Works SKG in a venture to design and build more than 100 high-tech urban entertainment centers by the millennium. Sony Corporation, the Japanese electronics conglomerate signed a multi-pronged three-year pact with specialty format film company IMAX which included the construction of two new theaters in San Francisco and Berlin, as well as an extended lease on the instantly successful Sony–IMAX theater at Lincoln Square in Manhattan.

But, as the decade of the 1990s unfolded, it became increasingly clear that all was not well with suburban shopping centers and regional malls. After twenty years of constant expansion, suburban retailing had become oversaturated leading to consumer fatigue. As industry researcher Quentin Davis has observed "Shop 'til you drop" has progressed to "malled to death." [8] At the same time, the problems of the inner city that suburbanites thought they had left behind – traffic congestion, high costs, crime – had begun to migrate to the suburbs. By the end of 1992, *Fortune* magazine felt compelled to warn its readers that US suburbs were "under siege," the victim of a wave of carjackings, muggings and parking-lot robberies (Farnham 1992). Nor were the "edge cities" – clusters of malls, office developments and entertainment complexes that rise in the rural residential area around the suburbs – exempt. Revisiting some of the edge cities on which he had first reported for *The Atlantic Monthly* in 1986, Charles Lockwood (1994) found that many shopping malls were losing their best retail tenants and suffering vacancies, in the same way that downtown shopping districts had been replaced some years earlier. To make matters worse, juvenile gangs in Detroit, Houston, Los Angeles and other metropolitan areas had begun to invade shopping malls, causing mall managers to invoke a series of tough security measures, notably curfews for teenagers. Increasingly weary and fearful, shoppers began to look for other options.

One choice was to abandon nearby shopping centers for "big box" stores (Home Depot, Staples, Computer City). In the decade since they first appeared on the exurban landscape, superstores have risen to $550 billion in annual sales, one-third of the total retail revenue in the US (Panek 1997: 66). Other popular alternatives have included power centers, factory outlet malls and mega-malls located beyond the pull of the city. Another option was to return downtown. To attract a new clientele from the suburbs, downtown merchants and developers began to turn to the concept of "shopertainment" (see Chapter 4) in which retail and entertainment are combined in new ways. As we have seen, the festival market places of the 1980s were one attempt to inject a greater entertainment component into the shopping experience. By the 1990s, however, there was a growing recognition that rather than constituting an ancillary element entertainment itself should be the central focus.

In this rapidly evolving business climate, entertainment and commercial activity became complementary and mutually supportive of land uses in downtown renewal projects. Carl Weisbrod (1995), a public planner in New York relates how the concept of an "entertainment destination" along 42nd Street went from being no more than an afterthought in the 1970s to a primary anchor which drove the entire redevelopment project in the 1990s. Originally seen as a dead space between the merchandise mart and office buildings planned for the eastern terminus and the hotel which was slated to be built at the western end, the once derelict theaters are now the site of a super-block which includes major projects to be built by Disney, Livent and Madame Tussaud's. Once again, it had become an "entertainment street." As evidence, Weisbrod cites the example of Morgan Stanley, the investment bank, which considered buying a building in Times Square in the 1980s but withdrew because it balked at having to put up a "supersign," as mandated by the public planners. Five years later, Morgan Stanley reconsidered, not only buying the building on Broadway between 47th and 48th Streets but also agreeing to put up the largest supersign in the area, a giant information display featuring two 44-foot high barrel-shaped maps highlighting the cities where the company has offices and, above these, three 140-foot long electronic stocktickers which transmit information in "real time" (Dunlap 1995).

So far, urban entertainment destination projects are not as prolific as downtown malls or festival market places. None the less, there is a rapidly accelerating interest in these developments in both the private and public sectors. Between March 1995 and June 1996 the number of city-led initiatives in the urban entertainment development field rose from five to thirty-one, with an additional twenty-seven projects under active consideration. During this same period, the number of themed restaurant concepts jumped from nine to thirty-two (Serino 1996: 26). If and when a critical mass of these projects are up and running, the growth rate should speed up even further.

Part II

LANDSCAPES OF PLEASURE

One of the most frequently cited characteristics of the contemporary city is its role as a center of consumption, a place in which advertising, shopping and entertainment are incorporated into every aspect of urban life (Thrift 1993: 230–1). As outlined in Chapter 1, this is not as recent as some postmodern theorists would has us believe, but, nevertheless, consumption has become a major urban preoccupation.

How then are we to interpret the consumer experience in Fantasy City? Is it technologically driven? Is it solely about status and identity? Is it a matter of embracing desire or encasing it in a prophylactic of vicarious experience? Is the theme park city the furthest point in the rationalization of modern society or is it part and parcel of the postmodern backlash against the iron cage of efficiency and organizational control? Are the pleasure-scapes in Fantasy City liminal sites where we can escape the social bonds of everyday life or are they a forerunner of what society might look like at the beginning of the next millennium?

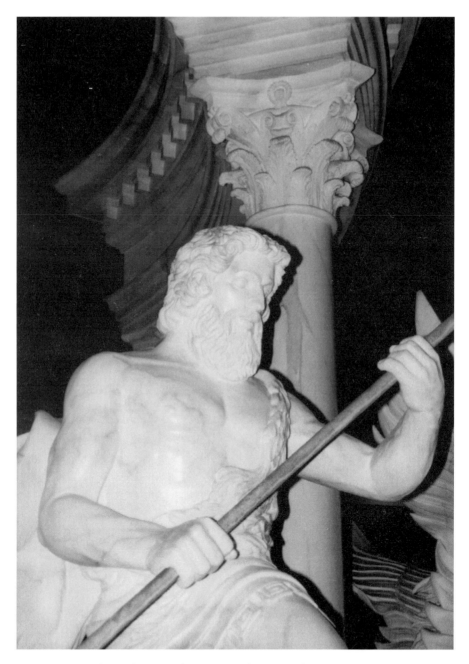

Figure 4.1 "Poseidon at the Festival Fountain": The Forum Shops at
Caesar's Palace, Las Vegas.

Source: Ruth Hannigan.

4

"SANITIZED RAZZMATAZZ"

Technology, simulated experience and the culture of consumption

In 1996, the *New York Times* published a story about two competing impresarios, Bobby Reynolds, owner of the International Circus Museum, and Dick D. Zigun, the proprietor of Coney Island USA, and their attempts to breathe new life into the legendary corner of West 12th Avenue and Surf Avenue at Coney Island. Among other things, the two sideshow operators disagreed on whether or not to provide seating for customers: Reynolds preferred a standing-room only policy while Zigun insisted that "post-modern people prefer to sit" (Martin 1996). Whether Zigun is correct in his assessment of contemporary Coney Island patrons is debatable, but it serves to remind us of the wider question of how the emergence of Fantasy City relates to a late twentieth-century consumer culture which has been frequently described as "postmodern".

The "postmodern consumer" is commonly depicted as elusive: a free soul who darts in and out of arenas of consumption which are fluid and non-totalizing. He/she eschews loyalty to brands while constructing individual identity from multiple images and symbols; subverting the market rather than being seduced by it. Instead of going along with the American Dream, as previous generations had done, postmodern consumers are said to be unabashed hedonists, living for the thrill of the spectacle without feeling the necessity to relate such fragmented moments to a large direction of progress (Firat and Venkatesh 1995).

Once we climb down from abstract theoretical discourse to the level of everyday life, however, the postmodern consumer is more difficult to define. Perhaps we can see flashes in the channel-hopping music video devotee; in the fans of the gender-bending Chicago Bulls basketball celebrity Dennis Rodman whose persona changes as frequently as his hair color; or in the postmodern tourist who regards the travel experience as "merely a series of games with multiple texts and no single authentic experience" (Lash and Urry 1994: 275–6). Even closer to the mark is the contemporary religious consumer who is like a shopper in a "supernatural marketplace," picking and choosing from conventional organized religion as well as from other alternative forms of spirituality (Bibby 1987).

The question we must ask is, do consumers in Fantasy City fit this profile?

Clearly, they inhabit an environment awash with postmodern signs, symbols and spectacles. Almost by definition, a trip to an urban entertainment destination promises immersion in the historical, the exotic or the futuristic. The festival market places of the 1970s and 1980s were premised on the notion of "authentic reproduction": evoking a sense of collective nostalgia through upmarket produce markets, craft-dominated specialty shops and gingerbread architecture. The fantasy cities of the 1990s also make this feigned genuflection to history and nostalgia, but equally they are eager to exploit what the art historian and cultural critic Robert Hughes (1996) calls "America's now psychotic cult of celebrity." When a Swiss guest staying at our house appeared one morning at the breakfast table wearing a faded Planet Hollywood, Las Vegas T-shirt, I asked her if she had seen any celebrities at the restaurant. "Only Andre Agassi [the tennis star]," she replied sadly, as though the dining experience had been a bit of a let down. More and more, it seems, the success of our urban encounters and experiences are determined on the basis of collective associations with celebrities, particularly Hollywood ones.

Seductive technology

As Max Frankel (1997) has suggested, it's not Mickey's *message* that brings the crowds to Disney World but rather the gadgetry with which the "imagineers" charm, frighten, delight and transport visitors to the Florida theme park. Technology itself, Frankel suggests, is our theater, endlessly seductive no matter how high the price. If we accept this view, the theme park city is destined to succeed because it offers technological treats not available on home computers or television screens. "Welcome to the Next Level of Entertainment," shouts the print ad heralding the opening of the first Playdium in Canada, a 30,000 square foot interactive entertainment center which boasts over 180 multi-sensory games plus an IMAX "Ridefilm" simulator.

Not that our love affair with technology is a particularly new phenomenon. But, as Mike Featherstone (1995) notes, the techniques for producing illusion and spectacles in the postmodern consumer culture have become more refined:

> There's a good deal of difference in technical capacity between the simulator of a trans-Siberian railway journey in which one sits in a carriage and looks through the window at a canvas of the landscape unfolding at the 1890 Paris Exposition[1] and the latest Disney World simulator "rides" in the sophistication of the detail achieved (through animatronics, sound, film, holograms, smell etc.) and the capacity to achieve a complete sense of immersion in the experience.
>
> (Featherstone 1995: 77)

While it is true that turn of the century audiences such as those who attended the Paris Exposition were more naïve and therefore more easily seduced by a less sophisticated technology, it also seems to be the case, Featherstone observes, that today's leisure-seekers are a different breed. That is, in the postmodern consumer culture we can readily "switch codes," participating in a simulated experience and then stepping back and examining the techniques whereby the illusion is achieved. In fact, frequently this is encouraged. Audiences at performances of Andrew Lloyd Webber's *Cats*, the "first real tourist musical" (Marks 1997: 4), routinely go up to the stage at intermission to examine the fantastical trash-heap set. At the Disney Institution in Orlando, one can enroll in mini-courses titled "Painting Illusions" and "Imagineer It" which reveal the process behind the Disney "magic." On an architecture tour, another course at the Institute, students are taken around the Disney compound and shown how various effects are achieved. For example, the sound of crickets outside the Wilderness Lodge hotel is piped through speakers set in the ground (which are turned off at bedtime) and the decayed marble sign outside the Hollywood Hotel attraction at the Disney MGM Studios is in fact made from Styrofoam pitted with hair spray. The Lodge is deliberately concealed from approaching visitors so as to create the illusion of isolation; even the guide rails along the road are purely decorative (the terrain is flat), but are meant to evoke a sense of the Pacific north-west (Sharkey 1997).

In all of this, Featherstone, notes, there is little sense of nostalgic loss; visitors seem to be able to embrace the fantasy at the same time as being able to appreciate the technological wizardry. The same can be said of science-fiction movies and television shows, like the *Star Trek* series for example, which generate a huge amount of spin-offs such as technical manuals, spaceship models, "the making of" documentaries and so forth, most of which seem to act as further encouragement to the thousands of "Trekkies" and sci-fi fans.

Cultural capital

Fantasy City's other source of appeal is that it opens up a new vein of what the French social theorist Pierre Bourdieu (1984) calls "cultural capital" – cultural resources which can be employed in order to give us an advantage in our dealings with others. In the context of Fantasy City, this is summed up by the increasingly popular, if clichéd, phrase, "been there, done that"; or as 'Fergie' (The Duchess of York) aptly expressed it: "Been there, done that, got the T-shirt" (Kaufman 1996). This projects a sense of blasé world-weariness and sophistication which strikes to the heart of the importance of branding. What's at stake is not just technological seduction but the bestowal of status. It is no accident that the profit core of themed restaurants and attractions is not from food, drink or the rides, but is generated instead from its logo-imprinted souvenir merchandise – acting as a passport stamp which confirms that the tourist has come and gone.

This "passportization of experience" is in evidence among participants in sports and leisure experiences. At Expo '67 in Montreal, it was considered a mark of distinction to have collected an imprint in your "passport" from popular attractions such as the Czech Pavilion. "Caravan," the multicultural festival which runs for several weeks in June in Toronto, has used this passport system for a long time. One popular activity among the athletes at the Olympic Games is collecting and swapping pins from participating nations. The Hard Rock Cafe chain has cleverly taken up this ritual, with customers and servers buying and trading pins from the different Hard Rock outlets around the world.

In the mid-1990s, my wife Ruth, who produces live music shows for children's entertainer Lenny Graf, did a promotional tie-in for a local radio station at the Mall of America in Bloomington. So as to project a "cool" image for Graf, she bought him a leather jacket with the "Planet Hollywood, Mall of America" logo. The jacket has since proved a hit with audiences and has been incorporated into the show. Its appeal can be seen as twofold: leather jackets are more expensive than souvenir T-shirts or baseball caps; but they are also regarded as "passports," proclaiming not only that you have been somewhere interesting but that you have consumed a highly-rated experience.

Working incognito for ten weeks as an assistant in a sports shop in a north England town, researcher Steven Miles (1996) observed that name-brand training shoes endorsed by high-profile sports stars constituted a significant source of "common cultural capital" for adolescent customers. It wasn't the brand *per se* that held the appeal, but rather, it was the adoption of particular styles which allowed teenagers a low-key way of stating their individuality within a conformist society. Although they freely admitted that the many popular "retro" styles of shoes lacked comfort, peer pressure meant they choose fashion over function. Although this will come as no surprise to those of us who have accompanied a teenager on a shopping trip, Miles does make an important point, however, when he argues that the purchasing behavior of young shoppers goes against the postmodernist profile of the consumer as independently constructing an identity from the extensive menu of options in the market place.

Fantasy City provides yet another level and source of cultural capital beyond sports knowledge (Erickson 1996) and fashion (Miles 1996) in its conscience combining of sports, restaurants, entertainment and high-tech experiences. What is significant is not so much the role of consumption in helping to assert status and identity but the fact that consumption is increasingly occurring within the context of programmed leisure experiences. As we approach the millennium, the global merchants of leisure, the architects of Fantasy City, are creating a new kind of consumer who feels "entitled" to a constant and technologically dazzling level of amusement (Christiansen and Brinkerhoff-Jacobs 1995: 94), and who effortlessly incorporates entertainment experiences into their repertoire of cultural capital. Thus, "been there, done that" (and having the trademarked souvenir to prove it) replaces the traditional "buy it and flaunt it" consumptive strategies of the past.

The "riskless risk"

Fantasy City is at the apex of what the American cultural commentator Russell Nye (1981) has termed "riskless risk." This, Nye explains, refers to being able to take chances that are in fact not really chances. The British sociologist, Chris Rojek, uses a related concept, "the recurrence of reassurance," to describe the way in which many contemporary leisure and tourist attractions are calculated so as to package our fantasy experiences within a safe, reassuring and predictable environment. Thus we "visit the old Tuscon Wild West town in Arizona and the Sheriff always kills the bandits for us; we go to the Disney island where pirates threaten to attack us but we always avoid their clutches; Freddie terrorizes us on Elm Street but he is always repulsed" (1993: 205).

Nowhere is this more evident than in the current transformation of Times Square, New York. When I first visited the area in the late 1960s, it was on its way to becoming the "sleaziest block in America" (as *Rolling Stone* magazine described it in 1981). Immortalized in such movies as *Midnight Cowboy* and *Taxi Driver*, over the years it had been taken over by peep shows, x-rated movie theaters, pornographic book stores and cheap restaurants specializing in leathery steaks. In its current and future rejuvenation as an urban theme park, Times Square will be cleaner, safer, and the kind of place where parents can take their children. As the Disney and Livent flags are raised over 42nd Street, the urban landscape will quickly come to be dominated by what *New York Times* architecture critic Herbert Muschamp (1995a) calls, "sanitized razzmatazz." For better or worse, what's likely to disappear is a sense of urban danger, deviance or desire, all of which were present in generous portions in the 1960s when I was first there.

The "riskless risk" so evident in the themed environments of Fantasy City is part of a wider trend in which various foreign cultures and domestic subcultures are appropriated, disemboweled and then marketed as safe, sanitized versions of the original. Indeed, Fantasy City can deliver faux versions of almost everything, from jazz clubs to runaway elevators. Why go to New York to experience life in the Big Apple when you can go to the New York New York casino in Las Vegas? Or if you want the reverse, venture forth to the "E Walk" on 42nd Street in Gotham where you will be able to experience the glitter of Nevada's casinos at "Vegas," a theme restaurant due to open in 1998 which includes non-stop live entertainment and Las Vegas-style buffets (but which are unlikely to be at Las Vegas prices).

Few, if any, among the clientele for these attractions have the desire to embrace the actual risks posed by inner-city life, any more than Disney World patrons want to encounter the dangers of a genuine jungle cruise with its disease-bearing mosquitoes and monsoon floods (A. Wilson 1991: 162). In fact, if Ulrich Beck (1992) is correct in his assertion that in the contemporary "risk society" we are increasingly subject to an escalating barrage of global-generated risks over which we have little control, then such mildly exciting but essentially harmless activities as virtual reality skiing, or skydiving the Grand Canyon in IMAX 3-D, may provide just the right measure of "reassurance," as Rojek (1993) terms it. Paradoxically, as entertainment technology becomes more sophisticated, we will come to expect a heightened degree of reality which at some point will approach the real thing ("actual reality," perhaps).

Fantasy City taps into a growing global market for "experiences" which would otherwise be unattainable by virtue of geography, cost or historical disappearance. In an insightful essay on the marketing of nature in the Sea World theme parks, Susan Davis (1995: 209) observes that the operators, Busch Entertainment, have designed an advertising campaign which promises viewers the chance to become explorers, journeying to "spectacularly inaccessible, invisible or little-known places" without venturing far from home. With its blend of seemingly unrelated fragments of time and place, Sea World patrons are tempted to vicariously experience: "a penguin-packed Antarctic ice flow, a Polynesian atoll seething with sharks, a forbidden reef infested with moray eels, the rugged stretch of the Pacific Northwest coast, a ghostly sea bottom in the Bermuda Triangle." In Japan, theme parks with a travel motif are currently in vogue. Without the need to venture abroad, Japanese visitors can experience shish kebabs and belly dancing (Turkish Culture Village), cobblestones and sauerkraut (Glucks Kingdom), sheep chasing (Yamaguchi New Zealand Village) and an antique organ pavilion (Canadian World). These "simulated enclaves of ethnicity" epitomize riskless risk: the parks do away with perceived travel nuisances such as paperwork, jet lag, crowded flights, foreign languages, and, most of all, crime (Talmadge 1996).

Yet, one cannot help but suspect that underlying this brave new virtual risk-modulated world there is a sense of regret. In *Blue Sky Dream*, a memoir of growing up the son of a fighter pilot turned aerospace engineer in California's Silicon Valley in the 1950s and 1960s, David Beers (1996) conveys an ambivalent sense of longing for an earlier time when experiences were seemingly larger and more real. This is epitomized in his visit to a high-tech video emporium where he buys a fantasy "experience" of eight minutes in a flight simulator for $12.75. "A virtual pilot rather than an actual one," Beers emerges from this ride with a "rueful sense of diminishment; as if this journey into space is a pale imitation of the recent past when American astronauts were cultural heroes" (Cooper 1996). In such a way, Fantasy City can dazzle us with its "realism" and three-dimensional wizardry, but nevertheless, it ultimately leaves us with the sensation that "virtual travel" is less risky than, say, a trip to the seashore or even venturing forth into the surrounding urban neighborhood.

At the epicenter of its appeal is the promise that Fantasy City will provide middle-class residents with a measure of urban experience in what is essentially a suburban context. As Paul Goldberger (1996: 136–7) has noted, visitors to the "private city" clearly want to have the best of both worlds, embracing the benefits of traditional cities – energy, variety, visual stimulation, cultural opportunities, the fruits of a consumerist culture – without exposing themselves to the problems that accompany urban life: poverty, crime, racial conflict. Not that this is an entirely new quest. As I outlined in Chapter 1, the urban bourgeoisie at the beginning of the twentieth century had a remarkably similar mindset, leading the leisure merchants of the day to devise ingenious strategies to induce them to visit the movie palaces, vaudeville houses and amusement parks without feeling threatened. Goldberger calls the faux market places of the postmodern city "urbanoid environments." Like "factoids" – pseudo-events pretending to be real news – urbanoid environments attempt to satisfy our cravings for physical proximity to others in a shared place but they do so in "an entertaining, sealed-off private environment" (ibid.: 140–1). Thus, the good news is that the urban impulse is alive and well but the bad news is that it is trapped in an alien body that, like the zombie-like creatures in *Invasion of the Body Snatchers*, looks the same but somehow isn't.

In the conclusion to his article, Goldberger raises another point which is important in relating fantasy cities to the culture of consumption. Disneyesque landscapes, such as the festival market place of South Street Seaport, are filled with consumers of culture, he observes, but not with those who make and shape it. In this aspect, they differ from districts of the city which are spontaneously colonized by culture producers. O'Connor and Wynne (1993) have identified two such redeveloped areas in the city center of Manchester in Great Britain – "Madchester" and the "Gay Village" – which they describe as spaces of pleasure and cultural production/consumption not anticipated or created by the planners and property developers.

There are various reasons why areas such as these two examples are an anathema to the corporate architects of Fantasy City. First and foremost is the issue of who's in charge. As I will discuss in Chapter 5, theme park cities tend to be cast in the "McDonaldization" model which follows the principles of efficiency, calculability, predictability and control. Since the self-reflexive cultural spaces of areas such as those described by O'Connor and Wynne are not subject to corporate dictates, they are viewed as too risky as potential sources for investment.

At the same time, these urban destinations are often magnets for tourists and suburban visitors looking for some excitement beyond the programmed variety available in Disney-style compounds. Cognizant of this, city planners and commercial operators are continually looking for ways to turn this to their advantage. In the 1960s, hippie havens such as the East Village in New York, Haight Ashbury in San Francisco and Yorkville in Toronto became a featured attraction on bus tours of the cities. In the case of Yorkville, it wasn't long before the chic cafés and Gucci–Pucci shops moved in, making it the most expensive shopping and dining area of the city. Even the areas cited by O'Connor and Wynne have felt this pressure. For example, the "Gay Village" was co-opted into the promotional image of the city as a symbol of Manchester's new creativity and vitality, a development which was greeted with ambivalence by Village residents.

While we haven't yet reached the point where visitors to the UEDs in Fantasy City are invited to experience simulated ghettoes, skid rows and bohemian districts populated by animatronic characters, there is nevertheless a constant pressure toward assimilating and sanitizing the alternative side to city life. One of the most popular Broadway musicals in 1996 was *Rent*, a rock musical which relocated the libretto for Puccini's opera, *La Bohème*, to the world of drugs, squatters and AIDS in Manhattan's Lower East Side. Tourists could purchase souvenir baseball caps and T-shirts in the lobby or go to Bloomingdale's department store which opened a boutique selling clothes inspired by the show. The Nederlander Theater where *Rent* relocated to after its initial success in a smaller venue, was described by *New York Times* critic Michiko Kakutani as Disneyfied – the "perfect symbol of the new cleaned-up Times Square: so bourgeois and wholesome it has had to import faux dirt" (1996: 16).

In the meantime, tourist buses carrying European and Japanese tourists set off on Sunday mornings to the black churches in Harlem to watch gospel choirs performing, transforming the area into "somewhat of an ecclesiastical theme park." Patricia Williams, an African-American law professor at Columbia University, compares the tours to a "safari." "All that's missing," she quips, "is the hats" (Bruni 1996). In another example of "city life as performance," a troop of Manhattan's most talented street performers – singers, dancers, comedians and even a multi-media artist and a unicyclist – were exported to the 1,000-seat theater at the New York New York Hotel & Casino situated along the Strip in Las Vegas, where they performed *MADhattan*, a 90-minute variety show, set decorated by graffiti artists (Melvin 1997).

"Affective ambience"

Finally, the entertainment venues in Fantasy City provide a form of "affective ambience" (Maffesoli 1996: 11) which is perfectly suited to the collective mood of the 1990s. Quasi-streets such as those found in Universal's CityWalk in California, may be inauthentic but they provide comfortable and convenient "sites of social centrality where people can interact lightly in crowds without too much hinging on the outcome" (Glennie and Thrift 1996: 235). As such, they redress one of the gaps of life in the suburbs.

Suburban neighborhoods (or at least the middle-class ones of the 1950s and 1960s) were frequently depicted as sociable places, especially in comparison to urban communities. Yet, much of this social life was practiced within *private* settings – backyards, pools, recreation rooms – and demanded a relatively high degree of personal commitment. At the same time, public settings such as giant supermarkets were designed to provide convenience and efficiency rather than social interaction. By contrast, life in an inner-city neighborhood or streetcar suburb provided a better balance between privacy and sociability. You may not have known your neighbors intimately, but it was possible to develop a comfort-

74

able, if limited set of social relationships simply by walking up and down the street each evening to buy milk or ice cream and stopping for a few minutes to chat with those sitting on their front porches or watering their gardens.

As Goldberger (1996: 141) has noted, Americans are now less inclined to satisfy their craving for physical proximity to others in a shared place on traditional streets, but it doesn't mean that this desire has been totally discarded. The urbanoid environments of Fantasy City provide a workable compromise, furnishing a "carnivalesque" -style atmosphere without demanding too much in the way of personal commitment or risk (Glennie and Thrift 1996: 234).

Although it has a reputation for being soulless, Las Vegas, surprisingly, provides an excellent setting for this mix of festivity and social interaction. Whether gathered round staged spectacles (the pirate battle at Treasure Island, the volcano eruption in front of the Mirage, the light and sound extravaganza of the Freemont Street Experience) or waiting in line at bargain buffets, people are inclined to talk. They discuss the relative merits of different hotels; how many times they've been to Las Vegas before; which shows are worth the money. And, sometimes, about themselves. Unlike cruise ships or resort hotels where one runs the risk of becoming attached to new "best friends," these interactions are brief and limited, but more frequent than one might expect.

Perhaps significantly, the theme parks and other venues in Fantasy City are beginning to aggressively market special holiday celebrations, in particular Hallowe'en. At Universal Studios, Florida, the park's creative division stages an annual seventeen-night event titled, "Hallowe'en Horror Nights." It includes a trio of haunted houses; the Crypt Keeper's Festival of the Dead Parade; the Midway of the Bizarre; and "Welcome to My Nightmare," a musical revue hosted by the "devil. " In 1996, Madison Square Garden in New York launched its Hallowe'en promotion called, "Madison Scare Garden" which runs for ten days in October. Sponsored by American Express, the arena is reconfigured into a 40,000 square foot "attic" featuring six main attractions, including the Caretakers Office and Fright Control Center, Haunted Theater and Freak Show and Pirate Jack's Patch O' Pumpkins (Melvin 1996d). In Toronto, "Screemers," a themed Hallowe'en attraction staged at the Canadian National Exhibition (CNE) grounds has become a fixture every October. In Berlin, Massachusetts, approximately 150,000 visitors each October pay from $15.50 to $18.50 each to enter "Spookyworld" which bills itself as "America's Horror Theme Park." Once inside, they can choose from eight attractions including a haunted hay ride, the Chamber of Horrors, Cirque Macabre and the Phantom Mine Shaft. "Spookyworld" has its own rating system, a five-skull "horrificness" scale, which is meant to help parents choose the most appropriate experience for their children (Melvin 1996b). At the Santa Cruz Beach Boardwalk in California, the "Terror on the Beach" attraction includes a twenty-one-room haunted house, surrounded by face painters, side-show performances, illusion shows, a walk-through cemetery, a giant labyrinth, make-up demonstrations, air-brush tattoos and warm apple cider (O'Brien 1997c).

In one of the most controversial staged Hallowe'en events, the Abundant Life Christian Center, an Assemblies of God church in Arvada, Colorado, charge $6 for a thirty-minute trip through "Hell House." "Part Dante, part Disney," the tour leads teenage visitors through a series of rooms in which "morality" tableaux are staged, such as the funeral of a homosexual who has died of AIDS, a young woman having an abortion, a girl's demise after mixing drugs and alcohol, in addition there are drunk-driving and suicide rooms. The trip through Hell ends with a sudden appearance by an angel who guides visitors to the Heaven room in which soft music plays and the scent of pot-pourri wafts through the air. In its opening eight nights, "Hell House" drew 4,500 visitors (Verhovek 1996).

While such themed events are unlikely to replace neighborhood trick or treating, they are clearly gaining in popularity. In 1996, both the Florida and New York events were sold out. Universal, in particular, sees an opportunity to become closely associated with Hallowe'en in the same way as Macy's, Gimbel's and Hudson's once did through their Thanksgiving Day parades. The Crypt Keeper's Parade is promoted by head writer Jason Surrell as "a great addition to Universal's Hallowe'en mythology" (O'Brien 1996d). As such, it has added another dimension to the ever-widening commercialization[2] of Hallowe'en, a holiday which now even has its own industry magazine, appropriately called Selling Hallowe'en (Schmidt 1995: 302).

As if marketing an already established holiday wasn't enough, Disney have gone one step further with their staging of a parade linked solely to the release of one of their movies. "Disney's Hercules Electrical Parade," which rolled along an 1.8 mile route in midtown Manhattan on 14 June 1997, could be nicknamed "The Night the Lights Went Out in Gotham," since the city agreed for streetlights to be turned off as the parade passed, and the 5,000 businesses along 42nd Street and Fifth Avenue were encouraged to follow suit. In contrast to special occasions such as the St Patrick's Day parade (New York, Boston) or the Caribbana parade (Toronto), both of which celebrate ethnic cultures, the "Hercules Electrical Parade," notes Ralph Destino, chairman of the Fifth Avenue Business Improvement District (BID), is purely commercial, with "no historic constituency in the city" (Purdy 1997).

Gender, lifestyle and identity

At the turn of the twentieth century amusement venues such as Coney Island performed an important role for working women. For the first time women were able to escape the "homosocial" networks of leisure institutions and enjoy "heterosocial" ones in which they had the space to experiment with new social identities (Peiss 1986). It is difficult to see how today's themed attractions could duplicate this feat. Indeed, most theme parks today, and their urban clones, continue to be biased toward the conventional family model, thus precluding any chance of gender-based experimentation. Furthermore, many of the venues in Fantasy City celebrate machismo and male fantasies, not so much in an overt sexual manner (the exception being, of course, Las Vegas), but in the glorification of fighter pilots, Western gunfighters, warring pirates and action figures (Gottdiener 1997: 136).

Gender has also been linked to the political economy of the theme park city. Elizabeth Wilson (1991: 25) has identified both the modern metropolis and its postmodern successor with a "masculine approach" of "intervention and mastery" as against a more feminine method of "appreciation and immersion," much in the same way that "eco-feminists" claim that women are more innately and sensitively attuned to nature than are men. The evidence for this assertion, however, is at best indirect. On the one hand, most of the large-scale real estate developers, merchant bankers and heads of entertainment conglomerates continue to be men. On the other hand, some key executives who are involved in strategic and operational planning for new urban entertainment projects are women – Joyce Storm (Sony), Cindy Aylward (IMAX), Rebecca Robertson (42nd Street Development Corporation) –. In their public presentations, at the very least, there seems to be little difference between these women and their male counterparts when considering UED developments.

Some cultural theorists, notably Morris (1988) and Glennie and Thrift (1996), have argued that postmodern shopping environments not only provide a kind of easy sociability but they have also become low-risk "proving grounds" for new identities and lifestyles, in particular those which are related to gender and sexuality. Thus, 14-year-olds can go to the mall and experiment with a range of styles and fashions which, among other things, may include nose and navel rings, tattoos, dyed hair and ripped jeans. It's still too premature to know whether the venues in Fantasy City will provide a similar milieu for this low-risk identity renegotiation. Unlike shopping malls which don't charge for entry, access to many of the commercial spaces in Fantasy City cost money, thereby filtering out "mall rats" (people who hang round the malls). Most of these entry-fee spaces are not aimed at teenagers but at affluent baby boomers and "Generation Xers. "

Other writers, notably O'Connor and Wynne (1993), see the once rigid grip of hegemonic élites in society rapidly slipping in the postmodern city, opening up an increasing number of "self-reflexive" spaces. In such spaces, they assert, local vernaculars "do not helplessly give way to the power-soaked, market-based landscapes" (Hannigan 1995: 164) and commercial cultures which dominate elsewhere in Fantasy City. Wilson (1991: 7–8) makes a similar claim, arguing that postmodern urban settings are ripe for the development of subversive, carnivalesque sites in which new sexual options emerge for women. In general, this seems to mean the flowering of lesbian culture. However, as Savage and Warde (1993: 118) have noted this view tends to be somewhat "romantic." For one thing, the emphasis on fashion and appearance can be viewed as restrictive, with the pressure to develop rigid sexual identities increasing rather than diminishing. Furthermore, such liminal sites can spawn activities such as pornography and prostitution which "reinforce and sustain patriarchal sexuality." Of course, most urban entertainment destinations are set up so as to exclude unconventional activity of this type. Thus, visitors to Orlando may get to choose between Disney and Universal but there are few real cultural choices available outside of the "commodity fairyland" (Fjellman 1992) which dominates the theme park environment of South Florida, and, increasingly, cities themselves.

Memory has become one terrain of contestation here, representing both a resource and a grammar in the process by which new performative identities are invented and tried out in public places. In his critical analysis of landscapes of memory in Old Pasadena, a five-block stretch of redeveloped, gentrified downtown near Los Angeles, Dickinson (1997) depicts postmodern consumers, young and old, as wandering up and down streets, alleys and squares in search of a lifestyle and identity. With no overwhelming consensus on how the past is to be used in building a new identity, or even *which past* is to be privileged in doing so, different groups of social actors actively contest the meaning of nostalgia and authenticity. Dickinson describes the ongoing conflict between the Expresso Bar, whose teenage customers favor black jeans, baggy T-shirts and Doc Martens shoes and identify with "the *real* Old Pasadena" – those parts of the downtown area as yet untouched by urban renewal – and the more affluent, upmarket customers of the Jumpin' Java Joints – new European-style coffee bars with a more genteel, Old World ambience.

To paraphrase Sharon Zukin (1995:47), whose past is it? And whose city?

Figure 5.1 "World's biggest Coca-Cola bottle": The Showcase, Las Vegas.
Source: Ruth Hannigan.

5

SHOPERTAINMENT, EATERTAINMENT, EDUTAINMENT

Synergies and syntheses in the themed environment

While it is possible to find individual elements of Fantasy City in earlier times, notably in the "golden age" at the turn of the twentieth century, it is the convergence of three major trends in the 1990s which has led to the emergence of the contemporary theme park city. These are: (i) an increasing dominance of rational techniques of production (i.e. the "McDonaldization" of the market place); (ii) the proliferation of themed environments; (iii) and the elevation of "synergies" of form, content and structure as a key business strategy.

The "McDonaldization" of the market place

In his book, *The McDonaldization of Society*, sociologist George Ritzer (1993) argues that we have increasingly moved toward a rationalized society which adheres to the principles of the fast food restaurant. Four pillars support the immensely successful McDonald's operational model: efficiency, calculability, predictability and control. That is, McDonald's, and similar establishments, offer service which is rapid, emphasizes products that can be easily calculated, counted and quantified (a "Big Mac," a "Whopper"), holds few suprises, and, by substituting non-human for human technology, exerts a maximum degree of organizational control over both customers and employees. Among the type of businesses which follow this formula are theme parks, shopping malls, professional sports venues and tourist resorts.

Theme parks such as Disneyland, Disney World and Busch Gardens offer "a world of predictable, almost surreal orderliness" (Ritzer 1993: 92) which depend on a sophisticated infrastructure of efficient people-moving mechanisms. As Alan Bryman (1995: 119–20) has observed, one reason for the presence of audio-animatronic figures (i.e. talking robots) everywhere in Disney parks, is that they are consistent and, therefore, predictable, compared to flesh and blood staff. Furthermore, in return for the assurance of safety and certainty, theme park visitors surrender an extraordinary degree of control, both in terms of freedom of movement and freedom of imagination. The Disney parks are not somewhere you go to explore, as individualized itineraries disrupt the standard-ized visitor flows which are central to their smooth and efficient operation. It could be argued that Walt Disney, rather than Ray Kroc (the founder of McDonald's), first pioneered the rational model described in *The McDonalization of Society*, although Ritzer counters that the fast food model is a more useful template to use because it reaches a wider cross-section of consumers on a daily basis.

Shopping malls as well, exert considerable control over both their customers and their retail tenants. Shopkeepers are subject to innumerable rules and regu-lations including the approval of their location, design and even name (Ritzer 1993: 111). Shoppers, especially young ones, are tightly regulated in terms of what they may or may not do. Included in the latter is anything which is judged by the management to be "disruptive" behaviour, for example, loitering, pick-eting or protesting. In contrast to traditional commercial streets, the unpredictabilities of the weather are eliminated. Similarly, the illusion of safety from crime is created through the omnipresence of closed-circuit television cameras, private security guards and other such measures.

Standardization is also frequently the case with professional sporting events. In baseball, artificial turf, domed roofs and alike, symmetrical stadium designs are brought together so as to eliminate the possibility of rain-outs, bad hops of the ball, fan interference and other inconsistencies. (Although the newer generation of neo-traditional baseball fields have reinstated some elements which were discarded during the 1970s and 1980s.) Some venues, for instance Toronto's Skydome, have even rationalized food service during games and other events by bringing in such chains as the Hard Rock Cafe and McDonald's. Rather than depend on the spontaneous appearance of some boisterous and charismatic fan to lead the cheer, teams now hire professional mascots and, in case anyone might miss it, the instructions are displayed on a giant electronic scoreboard.

The travel and tourism industry has also followed the organizational model described by Ritzer. One of the more memorable marketing campaigns in recent years was a series of ads for the Holiday Inn hotel chain, which promised customers "no suprises." Similarly, American Express, in a long-running series of ads, made the claim that replacing lost or stolen traveler's checks in a foreign country is fast, easy and efficient with them (and, allegedly, a nightmare with those of their competitors). Mass-marketed tourist resorts such as Club Med offer a large selection of routinized activities in interchangeable exotic settings where a guest can stay without having to venture into the unknown and unpre-dictable environs of local life on a tropical island (ibid.: 23).

Yet, contrary to the principles which propel it, the fast food society often turns out to be neither efficient or inexpensive. Frequently a victim of their own success, theme parks and fast food restaurants generate long queues. "Big Macs" may be good value in America, but the case is different in Geneva, Berlin or Moscow where they are still considered a novelty. Why, then, has the

McDonald's model been so successful? Ritzer contends that what is really on offer is the possibility of fun. Fast food restaurants with their explosion of color and garish signs and symbols are entertaining in the same way that, traditionally, amusement parks have been seen to be. Unlike traditional restaurant menus which are presented as individual documents to be handheld, the fast food menu is displayed on a marquee which is reminiscent of the movie options at a local cineplex (p. 127). Some McDonald's outlets even have playgrounds and children's rides. Malls are designed to be fantasy worlds. Not only is the mall itself "a huge stage setting loaded with lots of props" but there are such entertaining extras as restaurants, bars, movie theaters, exercise centers and, on weekends, clowns, balloons, magicians and bands (p. 128). When Ritzer was completing the first edition of his book, the Mall of America near Minneapolis was not yet open, but he cites it as evidence of a future trend toward shopping malls as entertainment palaces.

What can explain the seemingly unstoppable spread of McDonalidzation? Ritzer points to three significant factors: economics (lower corporate costs as a result of rationalization equals higher profits), familiarity on the part of consumers (growing up with the Golden Arches), and an attunement to broader societal lifestyle changes (dual-career families who are pressed for time; greater mobility, including greater car use; increased affluence and available discretionary income). The first, lower corporate costs, refers to factors internal to the business world, whereas the other two touch the lives of the ordinary consumer. Inexplicably, Ritzer doesn't include on his shortlist something which he notes earlier on in his book: "our national obsession with amusement" (p. 128), although this would seem to be one key to understanding its desirability. We may be, as Neal Postman (1985) has termed it, "amusing ourselves to death," but nevertheless, this is an important trend in the final years of the millennium.

Ritzer's book has been much praised, but it has also been criticized for underplaying the cultural and symbolic aspects of the fast food society. Featherstone (1995: 8), for example, insists that McDonaldization not only entails economic efficiency gains but also represents a globalized cultural message which equates the "good life" with American commercial culture. Gottdiener (1997: 132) acknowledges that Ritzer's argument is persuasive but claims that he has missed an important point about the human interactive side of the fast food experience. Outlets such as McDonalds are successful, he maintains, not just because they follow rational techniques of production but because they offer easy-to-decipher signs and standardized behaviors, no matter where you go in the world. So too do theme parks, hotels, hospitals, casinos, airports, office buildings and other built spaces in which past experience proves to be a reliable guide.

While writing this section of the book, I encountered several good examples which highlight Gottdiener's point. As a regular patron of a downtown Burger King, I have come to appreciate the concise, almost robotic four-question interrogation by the counter server: "What would you like? To drink? For here? Salt or ketchup?" One day, feeling like a change, I went to a submarine sandwich bar. The specials were numbered, but the choices were more numerous, the direction of the queue was less clear, and you needed to tell the clerk behind the counter a lot of information: type of bread, length of sandwich, choice of toppings, size of beverage cup. This was too much for one patron several places ahead of me, who fled out of the store. An equally confusing incident happened to guests staying with me who, unacquainted with the routines of a popular local hamburger outlet, were left standing in limbo between the order desk and the preparation area where the burgers are dressed and delivered to the customer.

Nevertheless, Ritzer's thesis is useful in helping us to understand the organizational context in which fantasy cities develop. As we will see in Chapter 6, one of the leading principles of UED development is the minimization of risk. To optimize this, leisure merchants must be able to "roll out" new entertainment concepts across the country and the world in a standardized, predictable form very similar to that described by Ritzer for the fast food society. Furthermore, many of the elements of predictability and control which are central to the discussion in his book can be seen in the design and operation of Fantasy City.

The Theming of America

A second noteworthy trend is the proliferation of themed environments as part of the everyday social fabric. In his book, *The Theming of America*, urban sociologist Mark Gottdiener (1997) argues that since the 1960s new modes of thematic representation have come to organize our lives. In contrast to the past, the postmodern 1990s is awash in symbolic motifs created by commercial interests in order to promote mass consumption.

At the turn of the century, city structures tended to be monochromatic with relatively little symbolic embellishment. Space was functional and material culture was relatively straightforward. Gottdiener devotes several pages in his book to contrasting the early modernist city to the ancient cities of Athens and Beijing (formerly Peking), both of which possessed an overarching sacred symbolic structure which imbued the physical layout with meaning. With the arrival of the Industrial Revolution this rich iconography went into decline within secular society, whose leaders were practical men of business. Their consumption patterns were meant to proclaim their financial success and power, emphasizing luxury, ostentation and "conspicuous consumption" (Veblen 1925). Unlike their counterparts in ancient and medieval societies, ordinary people led lives stripped bare of signification, unless they were active in certain forms of religion, notably Roman-Catholicism.

In marked contrast, Gottdiener characterizes the history of the twentieth century as an escalating development of commodity fantasy themes by capitalist entrepreneurs eager to exploit the rising purchasing power of the swelling middle class. In particular, he points to the emergence of advertising as a crucial activity. Whereas sales people such as the once ubiquitous door-to-door "Fuller Brush man" had sold products on the basis of their utility and performance, marketing people now devised sophisticated psychological techniques with which they identified the insecurities and aspirations of particular socio-demographic population segments and then produced images of desire tailored to appeal to these perceived needs.

Such image clusters were not just restricted to advertisements in magazines and catalogues but also pervaded the built environment. Standardized suburban housing, for example, was differentiated and promoted through endowing subdivisions, streets and house models with names suggesting mountains, nature or tropical scenery. Despite the fact that minimal downpayments and low mortgage rates had made suburbia virtually open to all whites, developers continued to sell an image of an exclusive enclave of upwardly mobile Americans nestled close to the land (Palen 1995: 95–6). Shopping centers were architecturally themed to suggest a fusion of modernity and Old World familiarity, the latter represented by open courts, fountains, terraces and skylights (Rowe 1991: 126–7).

While Gottdiener's account is generally convincing, there are a few significant gaps and inconsistencies in his argument. Although he cites the world's fairs and commercial arcades as partial exceptions, Gottdiener labels the large industrial city of the nineteenth and early twentieth centuries as "hyposignificant," meaning that their symbolic content was limited to signifying functionality. Consequently, they "could hardly be called a themed environment" (1997: 42). This dichotomy between the functional modernism of the industrial period and the later era of thematization breaks down, however, insomuch as functionalism and modernization can in themeselves be considered broad themes (Purcell 1997). Curiously, he makes no reference to the "golden age" of public amusements (see Chapter 1). While they tended to look back into history for their imagery, fantasy entertainments such as those presented at Coney Island, Luna Park and the New York Hippodrome were elaborately themed, even by today's standards. So too were the movie palaces of the 1920s and 1930s. It's fair to say that it is no coincidence that contemporary megaplexes have modeled themselves after these exotic picture palaces: with their Hispano-Persian lobbies, Mexican-baroque auditoria and Italian-Renaissance ceilings, most of which "bore no ressemblence whatsoever to models closer at hand in the city or in the memories of those who resided there" (Nasaw 1993: 230). It is hard to understand, therefore, why Gottdiener would conclude that urban spaces prior to the 1960s were not particularly based around a theme and were not very entertaining.

At the same time, Gottdiener overemphasizes the extent to which the 1960s and 1970s landscapes were dominated by themed devlopments. While the advertising for suburban homes was theme led, the product itself was usually more mundane, unleashing a torrent of architectural and literary criticism of suburban vistas as homogeneous, bland and incoherent. Recall, for example, the first generation of multiplex theaters which were little more than "concrete screening rooms" with thin walls, sticky floors and overpowering sound systems (see Chapter 2).

Finally, Gottdiener's historical and semiotic approach isn't very helpful in telling us much about the political economy of Fantasy City. While he does a good job demonstrating how advertising paved the way to widespread popular acceptance of commercial images as a feature of everyday life, his account falters at the approach the 1990s, frequently reverting back to general bromides about those evil twin processes: commodification and mass media influence. Such broad forces do not explain the reason why projects which couldn't get off the ground in the 1980s have moved ahead in the 1990s. That is, the fact that the air may be pregnant with "motif milieus," as Gottdiener terms them, does not explain how or why these themes actually find their way to become finished UED projects.

Building synergies

The third major factor which has sparked the growth of Fantasy City is the increasing emphasis placed by corporate decision-makers on "synergistic" opportunities, otherwise known as "tie-ins." Along with "downsizing" and "globalization," exploiting synergies has become one of the dominant business strategies of the 1990s.

Consider, for example, the road to success traveled by three of the most successful individual entrepreneurs operating in the entertainment industry in the 1990s. Relationships guru John Gray supplements his best-selling advice books on gender relations with an "infomercial," audiotapes, weekend seminars, a CD-ROM, themed vacations, a string of "Mars and Venus" counseling centers and even a solo performance show which had its debut at the Gershwin Theater in New York, and at the time of writing is scheduled to continue at arenas across the US (Gleick 1997). Entertaining and home interiors doyenne, Martha Stewart, is no less devoted to building an empire of spin-offs. Her interrelated enterprises, all of which bear her name, include a syndicated television show, a radio spot, a magazine, a mail-order business and a line of designer bedlinen at K-Mart stores.

Perhaps the most accomplished Merlin of brand synergies is the British entrepreneur Richard Branson who has successfully embossed the Virgin brand name on a mind-boggling array of products and services, among them, Virgin Megastores (music, books, videos, computer games), Virgin Cinemas (the largest movie exhibitor in Britain), Virgin Atlantic Airways (the "no frills" successor to Laker Airways), Virgin Communications (publishing, educational computer software, film production), and Virgin Direct (consumer financial services). Like Stewart, Branson is an iconic figure, popping up as the principal in a series of "events," which range from attempting to span the globe in a hot-air balloon trip to modeling a wedding dress from Virgin Bride (another of his companies, founded on a suggestion from an enterprising employee). When BBC Radio asked 1,200 people who they thought would be most qualified to rewrite the Ten Commandments, Branson rated fourth behind Mother Teresa, the Pope and the Archbishop of Canterbury (Fabrikant 1997).

More or less the same strategy is pursued by the entertainment giants who are prime movers in the growth of Fantasy City. Observe, for example, recent events at Sony Corporation, the Japanese consumer electronics conglomerate which counts recordings, films and computers among its other entertainment related interests. Compared to some of its competitors, notably Disney, Warner Bros. and Universal, Sony has been slow off the mark to explore the synergistic potential of its varied holdings. But, early in 1996, Sony hired Matt Mazer, former chief of Disney's promotions department, to head up a new unit, the Gateway Group, which was given the task of exploiting the value of the Sony brand wherever it occurred in the consumer market place (Gelsi 1997: 20). Mazer began by assembling a web of tie-ins around his firm's existing contract to outfit cruise ships owned by the London-based Celebrity Cruise Lines Inc.,[1] with audio and video equipment. With Celebrity's approval, he arranged for the gala opening on board one of their ships to screen Hollywood movie *Jerry Maguire*, released by Sony-owned TriStar Pictures. As a lead up to the event, movies released by TriStar and Sony Pictures were placed in the ship's video-on-demand center, the gift shop was equipped with a Sony concept area, Sony PlayStations were installed in children's play areas and computer classes were arranged for passengers who tired of swimming and shuffleboard. The project became a floating demonstration platform for Sony products, witnessed by roughly 200,000 passengers a year and constituting a new outlet for its movie software (Gelsi 1997).

According to American media and entertainment consultant Michael Wolf, there are three significant ways through which commercial value is created or enhanced by implementing strategies such as that undertaken by Sony (Koselka 1995). First, incremental revenue streams from repackaging and/or reworking existing properties and distributing them in new formats. As far back as the 1950s, Walt Disney pioneered this stategy by putting together *Davy Crockett* episodes first shown on television into a feature film and instaling a "Crockett" attraction in the Adventureland sector of Disneyland. Today, the Disney Company continues the same practice, only on a larger scale. Animated movies such as *Beauty and the Beast* are turned into theatrical stage productions. Another Disney feature, *Hercules*, was launched at the newly renovated New Amsterdam Theater supported by a stage show and publicized through an "Electrical Parade" down Fifth Avenue in New York (see Chapter 4). Other entertainment companies have converted popular video games into movies (*Mortal Kombat*, *Street Fighter*) and films have become the basis for popular theme park rides (*Back to the Future*).

A second way of creating value is to forge cross-business opportunities. Much to the consternation of traditionalist hockey fans, Disney named its Anaheim professional hockey team the "Mighty Ducks" in order to take advantage of the recognition which flowed from the two movies (a third is planned) of the same name.

A third set of synergistic opportunities occurs through the creation of new businesses. One high-profile example is Dreamworks SKG, a company formed by three well-known Hollywood figures: record mogul David Geffen, former Disney executive Jeffrey Katzenberg and film director/producer Steven Spielberg. Dreamworks SKG constitutes a multifaceted entertainment factory whose projects include television production, movies, recordings and "Gameworks," a chain of super-arcades stocked with virtual reality games and other high-tech attractions.

Most of that which I have discussed so far has been a matter of "brand extension," transferring the cachet of one well-known brand to a line of further products. Synergies in urban entertainment districts also have a "value-added" component. As used by economists value-added suggests that the sum of the whole is worth more than the individual parts. A new car, for example, is something more than just tires, bumpers and seat covers. In its more popular usage, value-added means annexing new components in order to enhance the appeal of a venue or facility. It is possible to find examples of both in Fantasy City.

In spring 1997, the entertainment conglomerate Viacom Inc., opened its first Viacom Entertainment Store on the "Magnificent Mile" along Michigan Avenue in Chicago. At the grand opening benefit party, Viacom boss, Summer Redstone, acknowledged that "Viacom is not a household name," but suggested that by combining six of the company's high-profile brands – MTV, VH1, Nickelodeon, Nick at Nite, Paramount Pictures and *Star Trek* – a valuable synergy would be achieved which would raise the profile of the company as a whole. "It will be a powerful licensing tool," Redstone declared, "to help drive sales [of Viacom merchandise] in other retail outlets. This store represents a major step in a companywide initiative to drive merchandising revenues" (M. McCormick 1997).

Illustrative of the second meaning of value-added is the proposed building of a $20 million, 295,000-square foot factory outlet center in Jackson Township, New Jersey. Located less than a mile from the Six Flags Great Adventure Theme Park, the fifty-store center with well-known fashion brands such as Gap, Calvin Klein, Donna Karan and London Fog will be called the Six Flags Outlet Center. Further synergies will be cultivated through joint advertising and promotional efforts and by providing a free shuttle-bus between the factory outlet mall and the theme park. Juxtaposing the two facilities, announced Arnold Laubich, president of New Plan Realty Trust, the project developer, "provides enough alternatives to make it well worth the trip and a longer stay " ("Outlet center opens" 1997).

A longer stay, in fact, is the goal of most UED developments. Previously, suburban shopping malls served as social centers for a cross-section of groups in the community. On his two-year journey across America in the early 1980s, William Kowinski (1985) talked to teenagers who spent all of their leisure time at the mall, young mothers who browsed, shopped and schmoozed there, and even "mall rats," people who do nothing but hang out at malls. A decade later, this situation had changed. Many of the baby-boomer mothers had re-entered the work force and had less leisure time. Hit by the corporate downsizing of the early 1990s, consumers embraced the concept of "value retail" – brand-name goods at prices lower than those offered by department and specialty stores (Siegel 1996: 29). Tired of the hassle of fighting traffic on the freeways or muggers in the parking lot, millions of consumers looked to other alternatives – at-home catalogue shopping, on-line computer services, cable television shopping channels. Between 1982 and 1992, the average time spent on a mall visit dropped from ninety minutes to seventy-two minutes (Morgenson 1993: 107). With the growing popularity of stand-alone big box stores such as Home Depot and Price Club, a new in-and-out style of shopping was adopted. This had the effect of jolting retailers and developers into coming up with new strategies aimed at drawing consumers back to downtown and suburban malls and, once inside, keeping them there for longer. Entertainment has been widely touted as one way of achieving this aim, inspiring consumers to remain in the mall or store as long as possible.

Furthermore, value-added entertainment features are seen as necessary in order to attract a new breed of consumer who is hooked on fun. New York retail designer Simon Graj has observed that these customers shop as if they were sightseeing: "They're looking for and having the same kind of experiences that they would if they were on vacation or on a tour. . . . So if a retailer wants to sell product, they have to entertain you" (Kaplan 1997: 74). With this requirement to provide entertaining experiences, retailers as well as restauranteurs, arena and stadium managers and, increasingly, educators and cultural institutions turn to leisure providers such as the producers of simulation and giant-screen attractions. Notes veteran amusement park designer and producer Jack Rouse (no relation to James): "Theming is about adding value" (Zoltak 1997c: 18).

Converging consumer activity systems

This aggressively themed, value-added component of Fantasy City manifests itself in particular in the pace and degree of mutual convergence and overlap of four consumer activity systems: shopping, dining, entertainment and education and culture. This has give rise to three new hybrids which in the lexicon of the retail industry are known as shopertainment, eatertainment and edutainment.

Shopertainment

As far back as the 1890s, the great metropolitan department stores set out to attract downtown customers by providing free entertainment. For example, Siegel-Cooper, which opened at Sixth Avenue and 18th Street in New York in 1896, earned its reputation as "the big store" by offering an orchestra, art shows, tearooms and "spectacular extravaganzas" in its auditorium. One summer, the store mounted a six-week long, "Carnival of Nations," which climaxed in the August with an exotic show, *Phantasma, The Enchanted Bower*, utilizing light and color effects to highlight a cast which included a Turkish harem, a parade of Turkish dancing girls, a "genie of the lamp" and, in an early example of time–space compression, "Cleopatra of the Nile" (Leach 1993: 138). Not to be outdone, Marshall Fields opened its twelve-storey department store in Chicago in 1902 complete with six-string orchestras on various floors (Magyar 1997). In a similar fashion, McWhirters, a turn-of-the-century dry goods store in Brisbane, Australia, offered a fourth-floor tea room where tired shoppers could enjoy a cool sea breeze and a charming view of the river and suburbs. The opening of McWhirters' new premises in August 1931, was promoted with a series of three-hour entertainments which included a dancing demonstration by Phyl and Ray, Australia's leading adagio dancers, and a live revue advertising a leading brand of corset (Reekie 1992: 173–4).

Another way in which retail and entertainment activities converged during this era was through the spectacular electrical signage advertising both local and national businesses. Some of these displays were almost shows in themselves. In the summer of 1924, the highlight of Times Square was a three-storey bottle of Cliquot Club Ginger Ale which pictured a giant sleigh driven by a smiling Eskimo boy wrapped in white furs. With successive snaps of a six-foot whip, the boy prodded three companions to pull the sleigh and to retrieve the ginger ale which then set the name of the product flashing in the sky (Leach 1993: 341). Twelve years later, the City Bank Farmer's Trust Building, which contained a theater and a vast nightclub, the International Casino, was crowned by a huge electronic sign featuring a fish blowing bubbles advertising Wrigley's Spearmint gum (Gray 1997).

After the Second World War, suburban malls displaced downtown shopping districts as popular consumer destinations. At first, these shopping centers marketed themselves on the basis of easy automobile access and free parking. By the mid-1950s, however, mall developers rediscovered the appeal of turn-of-the-century department stores, transforming indoor spaces into theatrical "sets" in which a form of retail drama could occur (Crawford 1992: 22). The template for this new generation of enclosed malls was Southdale in Edina, Minnesota, a suburb of Minneapolis. Built by Victor Gruen, an Austrian urban architect who admired the covered pedestrian arcades in Europe, Southdale had as its focal point the "Garden Court of Perpetual Spring," an atrium filled with orchids, azaleas, magnolias and palms which bloomed even in the midst of the deep freeze of Minnesota winters. Enclosed malls like these increasingly took on a leisure role, playing host to movie theaters, restaurants, fashion shows, symphony concerts and high-school proms and other such public activities. Over time, however, these entertainment elements became routine; "the formula," complained Cesar Pelli, a renowned architect who was once a Gruen design partner, "is trite and everyone has learned how to reduce it to a minimum" (Kowinski 1985: 123).

In contrast, the West Edmonton Mall (WEM) in Alberta, Canada, could never be accused of minimalism, the largest shopping center in the world to date. Its developers, the Ghermezian brothers, explicitly and ostentatiously set out to bring the world of the theme park to the environment of the shopping center. Among other things, WEM contains a 15-acre amusement park, a 10-acre water park, a full-size ice-skating rink, the Fantasyland Hotel, a faux version of Bourbon Street in New Orleans, and a 2.5 acre artificial lagoon complete with a replica of Christopher Columbus' ship the *Santa Maria*, several mini submarines and electronically operated rubber sharks. Built in the early 1980s, the West Edmonton Mall is a bizarre almagamation of shopping, entertainment and social space. As Shields (1989: 158) has observed, WEM "is a world where Spanish galleons sail up Main Street past Marks and Spencer to put in at 'New Orleans'." West Edmonton Mall also radically changed the shopping center formula, boosting the footage dedicated to entertainment up to 40 percent, the largest proportion up to that time in a suburban mall. Seven years later, the Ghermezians succeeded in cloning WEM with their first American project, the Mall of America in Bloomington. The centerpiece of the Mall of America is "Camp Snoopy," an amusement park.

Retail and entertainment further dovetailed in the festival market places of the 1970s and 1980s (see Chapter 3). In contrast to mega-malls such as those in Edmonton and Bloomington, the two activity systems here were not just juxtapositioned but merged. The shopping and dining experiences constituted the entertainment in a visual environment which projected an aura of historic preservation. In case consumer interest flagged, stand-alone cultural and entertainment attractions such as science museums and aquariums were positioned in close proximity, frequently along the urban waterfront.

In the theme park cities of the 1990s, shopping, fantasy and fun have further bonded in a number of ways. As Margaret Crawford has observed, the two activities have become part of the same loop: shopping has become intensely entertaining and this in turn encourages more shopping. Furthermore, theme parks themselves have begun to function as "disguised market places" (1992: 16). This convergence is described as "shopertainment," a term also used to describe the cable television shopping channels which feature Ivana Trump, among others, selling an array of mail-order merchandise.

One form of shopertainment is the themed retail experience known as "experiential retailing." This is represented by NikeTown,[2] a retail theater showcase in New York. Opened in November 1996, on the site of the former

Les Galeries Lafayette, Nike's flagship store is "a fantasy environment, one part nostalgia to two parts high-tech, and it exists to bedazzle the customer, to give its merchandise sex appeal and establish Nike as the essence not just of athletic wear but also of our culture and way of life" (Goldberger 1997: 45). According to its creative director, John Hoke III, the store is designed like a ship in a bottle. The bottle in question is a simulated, old-style gymnasium made to look as if it was built in the 1930s or 1940s. This sense of age is created on the exterior through an arched limestone and sandstone façade with the numbers PS 6453 added, a reference to a time when boxers trained in the gym of the local public school. Inside, the old gym theme is continued with aged brick detail, wooden sports flooring, wireglass windows, gym clocks, wrestling mats and "authentic" bleachers reclaimed from a gym on Long Island.

The ship which is dropped into this old gym bottle is a high-tech cross between a store, a museum and a media experience. The latter is represented by a multi-media show which combines video projection, theatrical lighting and sound design, retractable screens and a sophisticated motion and show control system with which to show Nike mini-films celebrating the spirit of sports. In addition, the lobby is decorated with a giant elliptical media wall on to which the multi-media show is projected at regular intervals. Scattered throughout the four levels are screen bays where one can view a rotating series of short films about sports and sporting events, and banks of video monitors placed directly beneath which give the latest scores and other information in ticker-tape style. The museum aspect is represented by scattered exhibitions, showcases displaying sports trophies and memorabilia and a Nike shoe museum with 400 pairs of shoes which have been gathered over the years. The retail element of the store is more muted: one can buy Nike products at NikeTown but the store exists primarily to promote brand recognition.

There are other NikeTown stores in Portland, Seattle, Chicago, Atlanta and Los Angeles but the New York location best epitomizes the retail theater of the future. The production lighting and sound systems are highly sophisticated. The principal lighting designer counts among her credits Disney's Broadway production of *Beauty and the Beast* and EFx in Las Vegas. The show control system is similar to that employed at the T23D attraction at Universal Studios Florida. The chief sound designer worked on the show *Quidam*, staged by Cirque du Soleil, the Quebec circus troupe who have permanent shows running at the Treasure Island hotel in Las Vegas and at Disney World in Florida. Clearly then the best of Fantasy City entertainment technologies and design are incorporated in the service of retail programming.

Combining the same themes of nostalgia and interactivity is the 300,000 square foot, two-level Viacom Entertainment store in Chicago. Scattered throughout the store are thirty interactive stations or "experiential hooks" at which customers can morph the Nickelodeon Welcome Totem into the cable network's logo, send the logo spinning, respond via computer to an MTV poll or be "transported" from the Starship Enterprise using green-screen technology.

Juxtaposing these stations are a number of props and activities which celebrate the golden past of television and motion pictures: the entrance way to the Nick at Nite area is designed as a 1950s living room, and the "Paramount Flip Book" recreates brief physical performances by visitors in a style reminiscent of the early movies (Muret 1997a).

Less technologically elaborate but more brazenly commercial are the ubiquitous yet successful Disney and Warner Bros. stores. Of these, Disney is the largest with 530 retail outlets spread over eleven countries, but Warner Bros. is said to have a greater appeal to adults who regard Bugs Bunny and other Warner Bros. cartoon characters as having a funkier image than their Disney equivalents. The Disney and Warner Bros. outlets are closer to traditional retail stores than NikeTown and the Viacom Entertainment Store with television monitors dotted throughout the clothing and souvenir displays continually showing cartoons, film clips and promotional material. In addition, these stores explicitly target on-the-spot sales to tourists who are looking to bring home a branded memory.

In the late 1990s, Disney has opened a new chapter in shopertainment with the debut of its 50,000-square foot World of Disney megastore in the Disney Village Market place in Orlando. In contrast to the smaller downtown and shopping mall stores, World of Disney is organized into a series of themed rooms (the Villain's Room, the Enchanted Dining Room) radiating from a central display area. It offers an astounding array of products from flavored "Polynesian" salad dressing to a set of silk Mickey Mouse pajamas. If successful, it's envisaged that the World of Disney will be rolled out to strategic markets across the globe (Tippit 1996).

Eatertainment

A second synapse of consumer activity systems in the city is "eatertainment" [3] in which the former boundaries between eating and play are collapsed and recast into something new. The act of eating, notes David Altheide (1997: 21), becomes "eventful in many senses of the word," even to the extent that the food itself may become secondary to the amusement experience. Dining and entertainment, of course, have always been closely linked from the time of medieval banquets with jugglers and bards to modern-day supper clubs with big-name Hollywood entertainment. One of the most popular and participatory forms has been the neighborhood diner with a jukebox in every booth. Indeed, the presentation and consumption of food is itself often a setting for entertaining displays: these can range from the pyrotechnics of the server flambéing a boozy dessert at the diners' table to the Benihana of Tokyo (a Japanese restaurant chain) chef who presents a dazzling display of swordmanship in dicing chicken and beef on the counter in front of restaurant patrons. This synergy between the two activities has reached its zenith, however, in the fashion for themed restaurants.

Themed restaurants

A combination of amusement park, diner, souvenir stand and museum, themed restaurants are projected to be a $5 billion business by the year 2000 (Angelo 1996). Most of the first generation of themed restaurants gross upwards of $10 million per year in revenue with several, notably the Planet Hollywood units at Disney World and the Forum Shops, grossing a record $45 million and $35 million respectively.

Themed restaurants, however, are not a recent phenomenon. *Amusement Business* publisher Karen Oertley (1996), remembers going as a child to a restaurant called the Hamburger Express where your meal was delivered to you from the kitchen on the flat car of a tooting, puffing, model train. When I was in graduate school in the mid-1970s, the place for celebrating a special event in Columbus, Ohio was the Kahiki, a Polynesian-themed eatery with exotic fish, a waterfall and various generic artifacts that suggested the South Seas via Hollywood.

The Hard Rock Cafe

The present generation of themed restaurants can trace their origins back to 1971 when Peter Morton and Isaac Tigrett, two footloose 22-year-olds from wealthy American families, created the Hard Rock concept in London. By most accounts, the Hard Rock's success was as much serendipity as it was strategic planning. When rock legend Eric Clapton's guitar was mounted on a hook on the café's wall, fellow pop star Pete Townshend of The Who insisted that his guitar join Clapton's, penning a note which read "Mine's as good as his." This initiated one of the Hard Rock's most distinctive features, its rock memorabilia collection, now centrally supplied from a warehouse in Orlando and rotated between venues at regular intervals. During the first few years, Tigrett and Morton moved into merchandising offering shirts, hats, watches and coffee mugs displaying the Hard Rock logo, items which contributed significantly to the company's revenue (Covell 1996: 228). These items were popular with tourists because it allowed them to return home with the evidence that, not only had they gone to Europe, but that they had gone somewhere fashionable. Indeed, in its twelve years, the Hard Rock Cafe was primarily an outpost for American rock and roll culture abroad, complete with hamburgers, ribs and apple pie. It was also a magnet for celebrities from the entertainment world: Steven Spielberg, for example, reputedly ate lunch there every day during the filming of *Raiders of the Lost Ark*.

In 1982, the Hard Rock brought its concept to the US, opening an outlet in Los Angeles. Among its financial backers were a handful of celebrities including Spielberg. This was the genesis of the concept of celebrity investors which has since been perfected by rival restaurants Planet Hollywood and the Official All Star Cafe. A year later, however, the co-founders who had been feuding for several years finally fell out and went their separate ways. As part of the corporate divorce, the world was divided with Morton's territory including the US from Chicago westwards, Israel, Australia and Brazil, and Tigrett's receiving the rest. Tigrett, a noted eccentric and follower of the Indian guru Sai Baba, subsequently sold his stake to restauranteur Robert Earl in 1988 for $100 million. After a stormy five years, Earl, who had gone on to open Planet Hollywood, sold his shares to minority partner, British entertainment conglomerate Rank Organisation, leaving Rank with fifteen fully owned Hard Rock Cafes and twenty-six franchised units while Morton's company owned thirteen restaurants and oversaw four franchised outlets. In 1996, the Hard Rock Cafe empire was united again when Rank acquired Morton's share for $410 million. As part of the deal, Morton retained the right to license the Hard Rock Cafe name for the casino business in his former territory, having successfully marketed the concept in Las Vegas with the first Hard Rock Hotel and Casino (Orwall 1996a).

Planet Hollywood

Inspired by an idea originally put forward in 1989 by film producer Keith Barrish for a restaurant called the Hollywood Cafe, Robert Earl opened the first Planet Hollywood in New York in 1991, one block away from the New York Hard Rock Cafe. Instead of rock and roll, Earl and Barrish, working with Anton Furst, the set designer on the first *Batman* movie, decorated their restaurants with costumes and props from Hollywood movies. Although celebrities such as Henry Winkler, Willie Nelson and John Denver had invested in Morton's Hard Rock Cafe in Los Angeles, their involvement had been largely passive and their appearances at the restaurant informal. Earl deliberately courted celebrities such as Bruce Willis, Demi Moore, Arnold Schwarzenegger and Sylvester Stallone, convincing them to become investors and make scheduled live appearances. By November 1995, Planet Hollywood had expanded into a chain of twenty-eight restaurants: twenty-one in the US and seven overseas. Collectively, the chain grossed $270.6 million in 1995 (Levine 1995: 184). Today their sites include New York, the Mall of America, the Forum Shops and Walt Disney World. In July 1997, Planet Hollywood announced a joint venture with AMC Entertainment Inc., a major operator of megaplex theaters. Together, the two companies plan to develop eight to ten "Planet Movies by AMC" complexes by the end of the millennium, and a further five to ten a year after that. Within the complexes, customers will be able to watch movies, eat at restaurants with movie themes and shop in stores selling movie-related merchandise ("Planet Hollywood and AMC in venture" 1997).

More than any other commercial player in Fantasy City, with the exception maybe of Disney, Planet Hollywood has managed to ingratiate itself into the celebrity-soaked, media-purveyed public life of America. When American gymnast Kerri Strug achieved her fifteen minutes of fame in Atlanta by maintaining her landing despite a ripped left ankle ligament, it wasn't long before her Olympic leotard ended up on display in Planet Hollywood, San Diego (Friend 1996).

Rainforest Cafe

The final member of the triumvirate of themed restaurant chains is the Rainforest Cafe.[4] The brainchild of former nightclub owner, Steven Schussler, the Rainforest Cafe recreated the tropics in the Mall of America in Bloomington, Minnesota, complete with live parrots, mechanized birds and monkeys, a 20-foot high fiberglass giraffe and fake thunder and lightning which can be heard every seventeen minutes. If the biology of the rainforest was not entirely accurate, Schussler's business sense was. The company's stock climbed from $6 a share at its initial public offering (IPO) in April 1995 to $22 in October, and by 1 July 1996 it had risen 700 percent before splitting three for two (Angelo 1996). Its market capitalization now stands at roughly $450 million, with each café costing around $7 million to open (Damsell 1997). Flush with the proceeds of its IPO, the company moved forward to open further restaurants at the Woodfield Mall, south of Chicago, Disney World in Orlando, the Gunnie Mill Mall (Illinois), Tyson's Corner mega-mall in McLean, Virginia and in the Stratosphere Tower in Las Vegas,[5] following a marketing strategy of locating in the first or second highest ranked tourist attraction in each state (O'Brien 1996a). In April 1997, Rainforest Cafe, Inc. announced a newly forged partnership with the Elephant & Castle Group, a Canadian company which operates British-style pub restaurants. A further six Rainforest Cafes are slated to open across Canada by the end of 1998 (Damsell 1997).

Other themed restaurants

With the success of Planet Hollywood, the Hardrock Cafe and the Rainforest Cafe, the floodgates are opening to a tidal wave of new themed eateries. With a host of superstar athletes as partners (Shaquille O'Neal, Andre Agassi, Wayne Gretsky, Joe Montana, Ken Griffey Jr., Monica Seles), Robert Earl has gone on to open a 650-seat sports-themed restaurant, the Official All Star Cafe in Times Square and is initiating the concept elsewhere. He has further plans to launch a Marvel Mania chain themed around the popular comic superheroes and villains, in partnership with financier Ronald Perelman,[6] formerly Marvel's controlling shareholder. Under the guidance of veteran developer and restau-rant designer Larry Levy, Steven Spielberg, Jeffrey Katzenberg and Mirage Resorts chairman Steve Wynn have created The Dive, a nautically-themed restaurant which gives the impression of being underwater in a submarine. At present, The Dive has venues in Los Angeles, Barcelona and adjacent to the Fashion Mall in Las Vegas. Disney has joined forces with illusionist David Copperfield to build a chain of magic-themed restaurants called Copperfield's Magic Underground; the first two sites are due to open at the Walt Disney

World Resort in Orlando and at the corner of Broadway and 49th Street in New York. The five-level Manhattan venue is to include a 430-seat restaurant with levitating tables and disappearing diners, a 2,000 square foot magic retail shop, and even a well-marked "secret entry" ("Presto!" 1997). Other putative chains are themed around racecars (NASCAR Cafe, Race Rock) and motorcycles (Harley Davidson Cafe); soul music (Motown Cafe), 1950s music (Dick Clark's American Bandstand Grill) and country and western music (Country Star, Wildhorse Saloon); fashion (Fashion Cafe) and entertainment (Billboard Live).

Perhaps the most unusual establishment is the Jekyll and Hyde Club in Manhattan. As it name suggests, the theme is horror – four floors of it. Acting on a suggestion by staff from Walt Disney Imagineering who were dining at his pub, The Slaughtered Lamb, D.R. Finley, together with project designer Dan Hoffman, spent several years building what they intended to be the first fully-fledged theme park restaurant. The Jekyll and Hyde Club has in residence a talking gargoyle and sphinx, animatronic musicians Femur and Patella and a Frankenstein act with a monster who descends from the roof of the club to the first-floor grand salon on a slab amid billowing clouds of dry ice (Cashill 1996a).

In contrast to UEDs in general, themed eateries aim at a slightly younger clientele – 16–35-year-olds. These restaurants, notes Art Carlson, an executive with the Dick Clark's chain, reflect the MTV generation where restaurant patrons not only eat out to enjoy the food but also expect to be bombarded with free entertainment (O'Brien 1996b). This expectation is further enhanced when the themed restaurant is an integrated component of the food service in a theme park or urban entertainment destination, for example, the new 13,000 square foot ESPN World at Disney's Boardwalk which includes a restaurant, broadcast center, sports bar and interactive sports arcade.

Themed eateries also differ from some other UED components in that they are seen by their owners as being compatible with casino gaming. Peter Morton is explicitly aiming to use his Hard Rock Hotel and Casino operations to attract a younger segment of the gambling market (Orwall 1996c). Two Planet Hollywood casino hotels bankrolled by ITT, the parent of Caesar's Palace, are on the drawing board. The Rainforest Cafe has not yet announced plans to open a casino but its largest shareholder is Lyle Berman, chairman of Grand Casinos, Inc.

Meanwhile, there is considerable concern in the hospitality industry that the themed restaurant market will eventually become saturated. "By the year 2000," warns Steve Routhier, vice-president of marketing for the Hard Rock Cafe, "the highway will be littered with themed restaurants gone awry" (O'Brien 1996a: 3). Already we are seeing some evidence of this with many of the second generation restaurants finding it difficult to recreate the sense of excitement and the iconic status of the Hard Rock and Planet Hollywood. The Fashion Cafe is said to be dying; The Dive has been slow to catch on and even The Jekyll and Hyde Club has not attracted the crowds at its Village location in Manhattan that it has in midtown (Zoltak 1997c: 26).

Edutainment

A third location for converging consumer activity systems is in "edutainment" – the joining together of educational and cultural activities with the commerce and technology of the entertainment world. The notion that "learning is fun" has achieved almost canon-like status, and can be seen in evidence from the animated performing letters and numbers on *Sesame Street* to the laser-rock star shows in urban planetariums. Nowhere has this edutainment trend been more prolific than in the area of museums.

In the first decades of the twentieth century, the great museums in American cities were transformed from institutions which were seen as inaccessible to ordinary people, to become part and parcel of urban industrial life. Spearheading this alliance between museums and business was a new cohort of curators – Morris D'Camp Crawford (American Museum of Natural History), Stewart Culin (Brooklyn Museum), John Cotton Dana (Newark Museum) – all of whom imitated Fifth Avenue display strategies in their exhibits and offered their museum facilities to industrial designers from all walks of business (Leach 1993: 164–73).

At the same time, museums also began to make effort to become more entertaining as well as educational. Displays became more sophisticated as collections were interpreted around distinct historical and cultural themes. Among the devices used to enliven exhibitions were period rooms, natural habitats, dioramas and live demonstrations (Glaser and Zenetou 1996: 18). Museums in Fantasy City have taken this a stage further. They employ "new media, new techniques of interactivity and new styles which have more in common with the funfair or theatre than with a traditional museum" (Macdonald 1996: 2). This is not accidental. The overwhelming commercial success of Disney theme parks in the 1970s and 1980s was recognized by museum directors and curators, many of whom have chosen to look to a winning formula in order to enhance their own marketability. As the commercial coordinator of a British history museum has been quoted as saying, "we're a family fun day out, not a stuffy museum – you can't afford not to be these days" (Wolfram 1997).

What can museums learn from theme parks? On one level this can be seen as simply a case of museums needing to catch-up by adopting whiz-bang theme park technologies such as advanced audio-animatronics. EPCOT, Neil Postman (1991) notes, is "so to speak, the world's largest animated diorama," which suggests that the Disney imagineers have simply scooped their museum colleagues by updating and expanding a technology which was originally the province of the latter.

There may, however, be another sociocultural dimension to consider. Margaret King, a cultural analyst who once served as Development Director of the Please Touch Museum in Philadelphia, views the relationship between theme parks and museums as essentially "a question about the dynamics of and between education, entertainment and acculturation" (1991: 7). Theme parks, King suggests, attract customers because they offer a form of stability in a world where change has accelerated at a rapid pace (ibid.: 8). By contrast, museums have tended to actively embrace change, mounting shows that attempt to reach out to diverse sections of the community. Or, to put it more bluntly, theme parks present a nostalgic vision of Main Street USA for affluent WASP visitors while museums try to promote cultural understanding of minority populations whose stories have heretofore been given short shrift.

In such situations, public museums often find themselves in a bind. Tourists, by and large, prefer romanticized and fictional representations of history and geography, even if these are distortions which are rife with postmodern currents of time–space compression. Museum programmers, on the other hand, take their educational role seriously, striving to accurately reflect local communities in time and space. Julia Harrison (1997) highlights this dilemma in her case study of the Bishop Museum of Ethnology in Hawaii. Faced with market competition from the Polynesian Culture Center theme park, the largest single attraction in the Islands, the Bishop Museum has attempted to broaden its appeal to a wider audience while at the same challenging "trivialized glosses" held by many tourists of what constitutes the local community and experience (1996: 36). Harrison argues that tourists are more open to the presentation of a distinctive "localness" than is generally assumed especially if this is packaged using a wide range of high-tech media. So far, however, the Hawaii of the Polynesian Cultural Center and the Aloha Center festival market place (see Chapter 3) seems to be winning.

With many other museums, however, the line between education and entertainment has blurred to the extent that it is difficult to know which is paramount. As a tie-in to the release of the blockbuster film *Jurrasic Park* in 1993, the Museum of Natural History in New York mounted an exhibition called "The Science of Jurassic Park" featuring movie robots and models. The sequel, *The Lost World*, was matched by another exhibit at the Museum – "The Lost World: The Life and Death of Dinosaurs" – which included dinosaur replicas contributed by Steven Spielberg's production company and a videotaped tour featuring actor Jeff Goldblum, who played a scientist in the movie as one of the narrators. At times, it seemed "more like a movie set than a museum hall" (Gill 1997: C-2), although the Museum, somewhat disingenuously defended the mix as helping visitors "distinguish fiction from reality" (Newborne 1997: 94).

Science museums and space centers as well have been embracing edutainment for some time. Blazing the trail was the Exploratorium, housed in the Palace of Fine Arts building in the Marina district of San Francisco. Founded in 1969, the Exploratorium, followed soon after by the Ontario Science Centre in Toronto, was one of the first museums to adopt an interactive, "hands-on" approach to science education. Another leader has been NASA's Johnson Space Center in Houston, Texas, which offers the audience both a simulated space flight experience and a chance to go behind the scenes and discover how things work. On the East Coast of Florida, the Kennedy Space Center Visitor Center attracted 2.5 million visitors in 1996. The newest attraction at the Kennedy Center is the Apollo/Saturn V Center which covers an area the size of the National Air and Space Museum in Washington DC. Designed by Bob Rogers' company, BRC Imagination Arts, the presentation uses a historical storyline and theatrical effects to instruct visitors about the Apollo program. As the simulated flight begins in the Firing Room Theater, "the lights change, a rumble can be heard, and the room shakes just as it did during the real launch" (O'Brien 1997a). Also of note is the Pacific Space Centre in Vancouver which is opening a new theater using a seventy-seat simulator and software package developed by SimEx Inc., a Toronto company which developed the Tour of the Universe Attraction at the CN Tower in Toronto in 1984. The Centre plans to show SimEx's "Virtual Voyages, " a series of science speculation films.

If any one thing can be said to represent an obstacle for the advancement of public museums toward becoming full-scale entertainment destinations it is the economics of edutainment. To deliver a level of technological sophistication equal to that of the theme parks, museums would have to charge theme park admission prices. There are several problems with this, not least of which is their present dependence on school tours which cannot afford to bear the higher tariff. One well-known big city museum recently commissioned plans from a theme park designer for a stunning, futuristic, high-tech makeover but has had to put the project on hold because of this dilemma.

One possibility is for museums and science centers to become privately oper-ated institutions. In a sense this has already happened with the success of facilities such as EPCOT and the Rock and Roll Hall of Fame. In what is perhaps the Rolls Royce of simulated experiences, a private company, Casey Aerospace Corporation is poised to build a $50 million space station center in Orlando. For a fee of $10,000, would-be astronauts receive space flight educa-tion, experience weightlessness in a specially equipped aircraft, watch an IMAX film which shows the visual impact of space flight, and, to remember the experi-ence, take home a videotape of their adventure together with a personal astronaut-style flight suit ("Next step: the space station" 1997). At this price, only a very special niche market is targeted, but it does suggest that in Fantasy City there will be increasing competition between the private and public sectors for the attention and dollars of tourists and other visitors.

Part III

ENTERTAINING DEVELOPMENTS

Hailed in some circles as the salvation of crumbling downtown districts and suburban malls, urban sports and entertainment complexes are clearly a hot growth area in the contemporary urban real estate market. Are they assembled in the same way as the "Corporate City" of the 1950s and 1960s, with their high-rise office buildings, cookie-cutter shopping centers and apartment towers? Or is it necessary to devise a new development model for these projects? As we will see, there is a huge cast of public and private players. Most of the giant real estate development firms from the immediate past are involved. So are today's huge entertainment firms: Disney, Universal, Sega, Sony, Warner Bros., Rank, Ogden. Then there are the casino czars – Steve Wynn, Kirk Kerkorian, Donald Trump – who are behind the aggressive theming of Las Vegas and Atlantic City. Added to this are a host of new players – native and riverboat casinos, Asian conglomerates, simulated attraction pioneers, themed restaurant entrepreneurs and even Michael Jackson – creating a varied and complex development medium. We begin with the private partners who are front and center in the financing, building and operation of Fantasy City.

Figure 6.1 "The development riddle": The Sphinx, Luxor casino-hotel, Las Vegas.
Source: Ruth Hannigan.

6

THE "WEENIE" AND
THE "GENIE"

The business of developing Fantasy City

In the not too distant past, the process by which a residential suburb, shopping plaza or commercial office tower was built was relatively straightforward. A developer would acquire a parcel of land; line up financing from a bank or insurance company; obtain approvals plus, more often than not, a package of subsidies, tax breaks and improvements from various levels of government; and, in the case of retail and commercial projects, organize a roster of tenants. Profits flowed from a combination of rents and leases, percentages of sales, land appreciation, tax writedowns and concessions. These last two profit boosters refer to measures which allowed developers to claim depreciation on their projects, even as they were rising in market value. The capital cost allowance (CCA) concession in Canada during the 1960s and 1970s, for example, allowed developers to show huge paper losses on their income properties on their corporate tax returns, even though their audited financial statements indicated considerable profits (see Lorimer 1978: 64–5).

By way of contrast, consider the components required to assemble and bring on stream the 42nd Street Redevelopment in mid-town Manhattan, an 11 acre, $1.8 billion retail-entertainment project first proposed a decade ago. The development was spearheaded by public agencies at both the state and municipal levels whose responsibility it was to condemn existing buildings, design an overall plan, round-up private and public financing, induce key tenants to commit to the project, supervise signage and the restoration of nine theaters and manage a public relations campaign. Private partners in the 42nd Street project include four major entertainment companies (Disney, Tussaud's, AMC, Livent), three developers (Park Tower Realty, Forest City Ratner, Tishman Urban Development) and an insurance company (Prudential). *En route* to its eventual completion by the end of the millennium, the 42nd Street project will have survived a crash in the real estate market, forty-eight legal challenges and the imprisonment of one of its original choices of developer (on unrelated charges).

Not every urban entertainment project is as complex or as long in the making as the 42nd Street project but increasingly UEDs are taking on a character of their own which is demonstrably different than the real estate deals and partnerships of the past. In particular, the role of the developer is undergoing a major facelift. At an Urban Land Institute seminar on urban entertainment development in 1996, a succession of speakers noted this transformation. Real estate projects today, observed Bob Rogers (1996), a noted themed entertainment consultant, must deliver more than just location, structure and leases; they must also provide meaning and feeling. In this changing scenario, developers have become impresarios, locations their venues, façades and interiors their sets and stages, and retail tenants the characters and chapters in their story.

Of particular importance is the entry of big name entertainment companies into the public–private partnerships that have fueled urban development for much of the last century. As outlined in Chapter 1, the merchants of leisure during the "golden age" at the beginning of the twentieth century, often doubled up as shrewd real estate investors. In the 1990s this is once again the case. All the major entertainment moguls – Disney, Universal, Warner Bros., Sony – have divisions whose task is to locate potential destinations, both domestically and abroad, for future urban entertainment centers. Entertainment companies are increasingly key development partners, supplying both a distribution channel and branded or signature products which are vital to the success of a project. They are also hands-on partners, contributing to every aspect of planning, marketing, design and operations. On the eve of receiving Academy Award nominations for his film *Schindler's List*, director Steven Spielberg airfreighted a package of buns to his partners at the Levy Restaurant Group in Chicago. It was, he assured them, the answer to their problem in finding the perfect bread for a submarine sandwich to be introduced at The Dive (the nautical theme restaurant conceived by Spielberg and his Dreamworks SKG partner Jeffrey Katzenberg.) This degree of attention to detail is perhaps the exception rather than the rule but it demonstrates the extent to which the relationship between culture and capital in Fantasy City goes beyond the purely impersonal "structural" linkages which are frequently ascribed to the development of the globalized city.

Table 6.1 Selected US leisure and entertainment companies: sales and profits for 1996

Company	Sales (US$m)	Profits (US$m)
Walt Disney	21,180.0	1,467.0
McDonald's	10,686.5	1,572.6
Nike	7,801.0	673.1
ITT*	6,600.0	249.0
Ogden*	2,018.1	64.5
Hilton Hotels	1,900.1	156.3
Harrah's Entertainment	1,588.1	98.9
Circus Circus Enterprises	1,353.3	121.2

Source: "Corporate Scoreboard," *Business Week*, 3 March 1997, p. 95
Note: *Figures include non-entertainment related subsidiaries

The cast of players

There are five[1] major categories of institutional players who are centrally involved in conceiving financing, building and operating Fantasy City: corporate lenders, real estate developers, gaming and entertainment companies, retail operators and public agencies. In addition, a brisk trade in consulting and management contracts has arisen for leisure and theme park designers.

Corporate lenders

With the possible exception of Disney, few companies involved in developing urban entertainment destinations in today's cities have deep enough pockets to internally generate equity for new projects, most of which are capital intensive and expensive by industry standards. As a result, entrepreneurs must necessarily turn to a familiar source: corporate investors.

Financiers have somewhat of a mixed view toward UED projects. On the one hand, they are cognizant of the boom in entertainment in the 1990s and are eager to tap into this new source of revenue. On the other hand, they are nervous of engaging with an industry about which they know relatively little and with which they have had limited experience. This is especially true for the managers of large institutional pension funds. Risk avoiders rather than risk-takers (Short 1996: 162), the pension funds have jumped back into the real estate industry in recent years but most of their domestic investment has been channeled into office buildings and suburban shopping plazas rather than toward new downtown projects.

Urban entertainment destination projects are the offspring of a union between the real estate development and entertainment industries. Like real estate projects UEDs are bricks and mortar (or perhaps lasers and silicon chips) but they also contain a number of creative and marketing components. Economic value is determined not primarily through subdividing, renovating and other easily understood strategies for restructuring space but by branding and theming – concepts which have been brought in by the entertainment partners. Such hybrids are usually not very well understood by corporate investors who tend to think in more conventional terms. "The rule in real estate is that you need a track record," observes ULI executive Michael Beyard, and "for these urban entertainment complexes, there's very little track record yet" (Milner 1997b). To cope with this uncertainty, UEDs are frequently cloaked in more familiar concepts and language so that they appear as extensions of existing lending patterns and portfolios. In some cases, a project may even be phased in with the first stage constituting a more orthodox shopping center while subsequent phases incorporate more risk-loaded leisure and entertainment components, for example, a 3-D theater or a virtual reality arcade.

Investors have also been skittish about diverting available funds into UEDs as a result of their negative encounters in the past with REITS (Real Estate

Investment Trusts). REITS are packaged like mutual funds, sold like stocks and avoid paying corporate income tax by distributing at least 95 percent of net income to shareholders in the form of dividends. REITS have been around for more than a decade and include some of the largest real estate companies in the US, notably Simon Property Group, Inc. and (soon) Mort Zuckerman's Boston Properties. However, in the early 1990s, they lost considerable value as a result of a sharp downturn in the real estate and retail markets. One of the most spectacular instances of this was the plight of a REIT which held a mortgage on New York's Rockefeller Center and went into bankruptcy in May, 1990. Too often, they were seen as exit strategies by troubled companies that had lost access to traditional sources of financing (Morris 1997). Once hailed as the panacea of the real estate capital market, REITS further lost their luster because they turned out to be both passive and shareholder-oriented, favoring dividend maintenance and growth at the expense of providing cash reserves for purposes of upgrading and enhancing existing properties (McCoy 1994: 21). In the late 1990s, now that commercial real estate prices have almost fully recovered from their 1991–2 low however, REITS have mounted a spectacular comeback. With more than $1 billion in initial public stock offerings and $8 billion in secondary offerings in the first half of 1997, REITS are said to have achieved a new degree of legitimacy, attracting strong support from institutional investors for the first time (Morris 1997).

Aside from friends, family and acquaintances, often key figures in financing the start-up of urban entertainment projects, there are six other major sources of private money: venture capital funds, hedge and leveraged buy-outs (LBOs), strategic investors, initial public offerings (IPOs), specified purpose acquisition companies (SPACs) and real estate investors (Hackett 1995a: 27). Most of these sources will not even consider a project under $10 million and prefer at least a $20 million proposal. In addition, they have a very specific selection criteria. Mostly, venture capitalists, LBO fund managers and other lenders look to creating synergy and adding value to their existing investments. Despite their public image as fast movers, in fact, they don't like surprises, professing to deal with established companies with a sound operating history, a sterling track record and a Triple A credit rating. Rather than simply buying into a good development idea which may produce gold at the end of the rainbow, they want low debt structures, no conflict of interest, a growing cash flow and a prudent, committed owner who has a viable vision. [2] In this spirit, it is easier to find financing for a project situated within or adjacent to existing high traffic theme parks, casino or sports stadium locations, than it is to convince lenders to fund a totally virgin site. Universal's CityWalk in Southern California, for example, is a 1,500-foot street which provides the connector spine between three attractions: the 6,000 seat Universal City Cinemas, the 6,200 seat Universal Amphitheatre and the Universal Studios Hollywood theme park and tour (Fader 1995: 19).

When financiers look at a prospective urban entertainment project, there are a number of crucial considerations (Erichetti 1995). As previously noted, there will preferably be a critical mass of customers already present at the target location. Furthermore, there must be a pre-existing level of brand recognition or a high potential for this to develop. Once established, brand recognition is a powerful aphrodisiac with Wall Street investors. Planet Hollywood, for example, has a stock market capitalization second only to the fast food giant McDonald's, while the Rainforest Cafe stock rose 700 percent in the fifteen months since its April 1995 IPO (Angelo 1996). Lenders also look to the "roll-out" potential of a project; that is, how well it can be replicated elsewhere in the world. Projects which are considered to be "site specific," and, therefore, difficult to duplicate nationally and internationally, make investors nervous. Thus, the Observation Deck at the World Trade Center in New York, generally considered to be a technically well conceived project, encountered some funding resistance because it was not clear how it could be duplicated elsewhere (Hackett 1995b). Lenders look carefully at the source of the potential consumer demand. The ideal profile is a project which draws from both a regional base and a tourist market. Tourists are highly valued both because they spend more and because they are inclined to purchase logo-embossed souvenir items such as caps, jackets, sweatshirts, sunglasses and so forth, which have a higher mark-up than food, drink or entertainment expenditures. A regional visitor is desirable as well because of the potential for repeat visits. Additional criteria include the degree of competition, the amount of community involvement (or opposition), the nature of local market conditions and the quality of management and operational personnel.

Corporate financiers normally play a passive role in developing UEDs, but there are some exceptions. One of these is the investment banking firm J.P. Morgan & Co. Inc. which, through its subsidiary J.P. Morgan Real Estate Investment Bank, has taken an unusually active partnership role in several 1990s urban entertainment projects. In New York, Morgan not only gave financial advice and raised capital for the New York developers, Millennium Partners, but it also took an equity position in the residential portion of the Lincoln Square project. Its involvement in Coco Walk, the pioneering urban entertainment project in Coconut Grove, Florida, was also extensive; Morgan acted as financial advisors to the French financial institution that owns the facility. This commitment and participation is especially worth noting since the parent company has been building a reputation in recent years throughout the financial community as the "guru of the risk management business."[3] Another active player has been WHCF Real Estate Ltd., Partnership, part of Goldman Sachs & Co. As well as owning 22 percent of former Canadian real estate giant Cadillac Fairview, it has functioned as a scout for Millennium Partners, directing them to various sites in Montreal and Toronto (Milner 1997a).

Entertainment companies

With deep pockets, global business linkages, characters that can be signatured and branded, and a host of new interactive and immersive technologies, entertainment companies have become key players in setting the direction for the next generation of downtown development projects and exurban shopping centers.

As financial analyst Harold Vogel (1986) has noted, the entertainment industry has several distinguishing characteristics. First of all, a high level of risk is an accepted part of the funding equation. With motion pictures, network television shows, toys, video games and recorded music, the profits from a few mega-hits are required to offset losses from a slew of less popular offerings. It isn't surprising then to learn that of any ten major theatrical films produced, on the average six or seven are unprofitable and only one will break even. Second, entertainment products often derive a very large proportion of their financial returns from ancillary or secondary markets. Increasingly, this means commercial spin-offs, from high technology rides to cartoon character lunch pails. Third, marketing expenditures for individual products are proportionately large, sometimes almost as much as the product itself. Feature films are the leading instance of this but it increasingly applies to other entertainment activities. This can be seen in the blanket media advertising for live theater shows such as *Ragtime, Beauty and the Beast* and *The Phantom of the Opera*. Fourth, capital costs are relatively high. Thus, motion pictures routinely cost $30–$50 million with some rising to twice that number, while theme parks can cost in the hundreds of millions of dollars. Finally, many entertainment products and services are not standardized, varying widely in their financing arrangements, working arrangements and creative output.

Hollywood firms routinely engage in a number of risk reduction strategies (see Prindle 1993: 18–25). Some strategies such as vertical integration (combining the production, distribution and exhibition functions into a corporate whole) and audience research are generally well understood. Others are specific to the entertainment business and are sometimes controversial. "Completion guarantees" are a form of insurance often used by independent producers. In the case of "negative pickup," a major studio agrees to pay part of the cost of making a film on delivery of the negative. For the studio this reduces risk since it only pays for a finished product. Independent producers, in turn, can take a promise of payment on completion to the bank and use it as collateral. With "deficit financing," the producer has to pay part of the cost and try to recoup it through syndication, sale of foreign rights etc. if these revert back to the creators. Some film-makers and their advisors have been quite shrewd about this. For example, Alfred Hitchcock's agent, Lew Wasserman, a former studio head, worked out a deal for *Alfred Hitchcock Presents*, a television show which ran on network television between 1955 and 1962, in which the rights to the show returned to Hitchcock after the first broadcast (James 1997). Others, however, initially turned over these syndication rights to the networks and lost money since network licensing fees rarely cover all of the producer's cost. Even murkier are the "creative accounting practices" by which box-office champions such as *Forrest Gump* are officially classified as money losers. In one celebrated case, actor James Garner challenged these questionable practices in connection with his popular television series *The Rockford Files* and, after a decade of litigation, won over $5 million.[4]

The position of the giant entertainment companies is thus somewhat contradictory. On the one hand, they possess a number of resources which are vital in order to make UED projects work successfully. On the other hand, their operating style and corporate culture are considerably more high risk than is the case for the various lenders and developers with whom they must partner in order to bring these new hybrids to market.

While there are dozens of entertainment companies active in UED development, the three key players are Disney, Universal and Sony.[5]

Disney

Disney is clearly the dominant player among the entertainment giants. Not only has the company become a major force in films, television, recordings, theme parks, live theater, professional sports and specialty retailing, but it has also extended its influence into a number of far-flung nooks and crannies of the leisure and hospitality business from cruise ships and vacation clubs to state fairs. There is even an annual "Disney Animation Festival" in Argentina.

Unlike most other entertainment companies, Disney has had a significant land development connection for many years and in many ways. When they were assembling a site for a second theme park in Florida in the 1960s, Disney executives insisted on a buffer zone of 28,000 acres of undeveloped land. Initially, this seems to have reflected a desire to limit potential competition nearby and to ensure that no inappropriate business or land uses would impinge on the theme park. Eventually, however, Disney moved more aggressively into the role of a developer.

When Michael Eisner and the late Frank Wells assumed management control of The Walt Disney Company in 1984, they set up a new subsidiary, the Disney Development Company (DDC) in order to maximize the value of their land assets in this buffer zone. Ten years later, 9,000 acres had been developed in the form of hotels, golf courses, a camp ground, restaurants and shopping areas. The Disney Development Company also engaged in a series of outside consulting assignments not explicitly connected to the existing theme parks: designing the Johnson Space Center in Houston and the Gene Autry Western Heritage Museum in Los Angeles, participating in the redesign plans for the civic center in Seattle and proposing a major urban redevelopment in the California cities of Anaheim and Long Beach (Warren 1994: 98). By 1994,

DDC had expanded its roster of architects, planners and affiliated staff from the original seven employees to more than 700 (Marcy 1994: 37).

Walt Disney himself had originally conceived of EPCOT (Experimental Prototype Community of Tomorrow), opened in 1982, as a model utopian community of 20,000 permanent residents complete with a 50-acre, glass domed downtown, suburbs, manufacturing areas and cultural districts, linked by state-of-the-art transportation systems. Sadly, Disney died before he could act on this ambitious vision, and in 1966 the company decided to abandon its founder's plans for a fully-fledged community on the grounds that it implied too great a legal responsibility. In the years thereafter, Disney built various settlements, but they were all more or less transient resort colonies. In the late 1980s, however, Eisner decided to return to Walt's dream of building a town and initiated planning for a residential community called Celebration to be built on 5,000 acres in Osceola County, Florida adjacent to the Walt Disney World Resort. Celebration, opened in 1996, is an unincorporated town with a mix of different housing types, a school and teaching academy, and, in the future, a health campus and an office park. Despite it being the most comprehensively planned new town in America since Columbia, Maryland and Reston, Virginia were built in the mid-1960s, Celebration, claims architect and author Witold Rybczynski (1996) "is actually the opposite of Walt Disney's urban vision – more accessible, unthemed and less technology driven." It is also more vulnerable to real-life conflicts than the theme parks, as evidenced by a recent bitter clash over the school curriculum (see Pollan 1997).

Disney's first large-scale venture into 1990s-style urban entertainment destinations was "Pleasure Island," a 6-acre island entertainment complex within Disney World containing nightclubs, restaurants, shops and a ten-screen multiplex theater. Pleasure Island was a response to the success of Church Street Station, a night-time entertainment facility for adults in downtown Orlando built by developer Bob Snow. It wasn't an instant success, perhaps because the facility was aimed at a different market than the Disney theme parks. At the time of my writing this book, however, Pleasure Island seems to have caught on and is said to be operating at near capacity (Macbride 1995).

Despite its leadership position in the theme park industry, Disney has chosen not to cannonball into the big city entertainment market. If anything, it has been live theater which has drawn it in, notably the stage version of *Beauty and the Beast* which has enjoyed a long run at the Palace Theater in Manhattan and which ran for two years at the Princess of Wales Theatre in Toronto.[6] Encouraged by this, Disney has expanded its plans for producing other live stage shows in custom built theaters of its own, notably, the renovated New Amsterdam Theater in New York's 42nd Street development.

Disney's other point of engagement with urban entertainment has been through sports. "Disney equates sports and entertainment as being one," Tony Tavares, the President of Disney Sports Enterprises has stated. "They think the terms are synonymous and it certainly works from a synergistic standpoint"

(Zoltak 1996a). As the majority shareholder in both ESPN, the largest all-sports cable network in the US, and more recently in the Classic Sports Network, Disney has clearly been implementing this synergistic strategy to a large degree.

As long ago as 1961, Disney recognized the entertainment value of athletic activities, opening the "Celebrity Sports Center" in Denver, Colorado. This was a facility which included bowling alleys, a swimming pool, a restaurant and specialty shops.[7] The previous year Disney had combined sports and entertainment in another way by producing the opening and closing ceremonies at the Winter Olympics in Squaw Valley, California. Today, the company is involved in a variety of sports-related projects. In addition to its ownership of California professional hockey (Anaheim Mighty Ducks) and baseball (Anaheim Angels) teams, the company has developed Disney Ice, a 90,000 square foot facility adjacent to the Anaheim Civic Center which performs multiple functions: a training center for the Mighty Ducks, a venue for local and regional hockey leagues and a setting for skating-based community outreach programs (Johnson 1995: 14–16).

Disney's most ambitious athletic facility is Wide World of Sports, a $100 million, 200-acre international sports complex in Florida which has become the spring training home of the Atlanta Braves baseball team, as well as host to basketball's Harlem Globetrotters and Indiana Pacers. To attract young people and their families, Disney has a thirty-year agreement with the Amateur Athletic Union (AAU) which gives the sports complex access to 450,000 amateur athletes engaged in 221 national championships in 32 sports. Brand synergies include a major commercial presence by Nike, which runs the AAU basketball showcase, and the All Star Cafe which is due to open a restaurant in 1998. Here, the unscripted events and sentiments of amateur sport are juxtaposed with the planned inauthenticity of the surrounding Disney World complex. As Reggie Williams, a former professional football star now a Disney vice-president, told *New York Times* columnist Robert Lipsyte (1997: 40), "I love the true emotions of this place. But, when the tears dry, we can all go to Space Mountain."

Clearly this is only the tip of the iceberg. In 1995, the Walt Disney Co. established a division to develop a wide range of new businesses from location-based entertainment centers to sports restaurants. Within the company, a key task has been research and development on ways of downsizing theme park experiences in order that they may be incorporated into urban entertainment centers. Once perfected and patented, Disney's roll-out could be nothing less than global. If, for example, as part of its recent ten-year cross promotional deal with McDonald's Corporation, worth an estimated value of $1 billion, Disney were to rebuild the now somewhat aging McDonald's "Playlands" with new state-of-the-art technology, the synergy might be considerable, although strong corporate rivalries would probably scuttle such an arrangement.

Indeed, the only major entertainment opportunity that Disney has so far shunned is casino gambling, reflecting a probably well-placed concern that this linkage would tarnish its family-centered image. Certainly, it is true that Disney's film and television units have been willing to take a number of chances; from the release of such controversial films as *Priest* (about a gay priest) and *Kids* (showing under-age sex) to instigating "Gay Days" at its theme parks. Still, the parks in Florida and California are widely touted as family entertainment and therefore the company would be taking a considerably greater risk by introducing slot machines and blackjack tables to the Magic Kingdom.

Universal

If Disney is the Hertz of the themed entertainment business, the Avis is Universal Studios Inc. (formerly MCA Inc.). Universal has closely followed Disney's strategy of establishing theme parks in both California and Florida. Its Universal Studios Hollywood was one of the first and most successful projects to recognize the entertainment value of taking tourists behind the scenes on movie lots, while its east coast version, Universal Studios Florida in Orlando, has become Disney's main competitor in that city.

In 1993, the company opened Universal CityWalk in Universal City, California as a way of linking its theme park and tour to Universal City Cinemas, an eighteen screen multiplex theater, and to the Universal Amphitheatre, a live entertainment venue. CityWalk brought together more than forty tenants mixing popular or unusual local retailers and restaurants with upmarket national chains. Its roster includes "Out-takes," a video studio that casts patrons in classic movies, a "Nature Company" outlet with its own 40-foot rain forest, the Museum of Neon Art, B.B. King's Blues Club, Cinemania, a simulated ride by Showscan, and Wizardz Magic Club and Dinner Theater. According to surveys carried out at the site by the company, over 70 percent of the target market has visited CityWalk at least once, with 80 percent returning at least once again. This translates into 25,000 daily visitors and strong retail sales[8] of over $500 per square foot in some units (Fader 1995).

In the near future, the company plans to open a version of CityWalk at its theme park in Orlando. Universal Studios CityWalk Florida is designed as a two-tiered promenade of entertainment and dining experiences including the world's largest Hard Rock Cafe; a television production center which offers guests a chance to watch live shows and celebrity interviews being taped; the NASCAR Cafe, a restaurant with a racing car theme; a sixteen-screen, 5,000-seat Cineplex Odeon Megaplex complete with its own eateries, cafes and shop; "Bob Marley: A Tribute to Freedom," modeled on Marley's Jamaican house and garden; and "CityJazz" which will include the Down Beat Jazz Hall of Fame.

Unlike Disney, which develops most of its projects internally, Universal has taken on several joint venture partners. Its partner in the expansion of Universal Studios, Florida, into a major destination resort is the British entertainment corporation, Rank, proprietors of the Hard Rock Cafe chain. The resort will include CityWalk, Florida, Universal's Islands of Adventure (a new theme park due to open in 1999), four themed island hotels with a total of 4,300 rooms, more than 300,000 square feet of conference and meeting space, a golf course and lodge and a tennis center. In building the Portofino Bay resort and the Royal Bali Hotel, which at a combined cost of $600 million represents the most expensive American hotel planned outside of Las Vegas in recent years, Universal has offered a 50 percent stake to Loew's Corporation, the hotel chain controlled by the Tisch family of New York (Pacelle and King 1996). And, together with Sega Enterprises and Dreamworks SKG, Universal will attempt to become a dominant force in the family entertainment center business by building 100 high-technology arcades by the year 2000.

Universal changed its ownership in 1995, with 80 percent of its stock being purchased from Matushita Electric Company of Japan by Seagram, the Canadian liquor and orange juice company. To finance the purchase, Seagram's chairman, Edgar Bronfman, sold off Seagram's controlling interest in Dupont, the Belgian-based chemicals company. Bronfman justified the change in emphasis from chemicals and plastics to movies and theme parks by citing the rising importance of the entertainment economy, although some market analysts and dissident shareholders suggested that a brief stint in Hollywood in the 1980s had hooked Bronfman on the idea of becoming a film mogul. Whatever the case, Universal still appears to be on course to consolidate its hold as the runner-up to Disney as the leader in theme parks and urban attractions. And, like Disney, it has hesitated in becoming involved in designing entertainment for families who go to gambling casinos, although its alliance with Loew's Hotels would seem to suggest a synergy which could be activated by purchasing or joining forces with one of the half dozen major public casino companies.

Sony Corporation

Starting its corporate life in a bomb damaged Tokyo department store in 1947, Sony Corporation has gone on to pioneer a number of technological innovations: the transistor radio, the videocassette recorder, the Walkman and the compact disk. In an attempt to diversify, the company spent more than $5 billion in the late 1980s to expand into entertainment, purchasing CBS Records and a pair of American movie companies, Columbia Pictures and TriStar Pictures (A. Pollack 1996: 10).

Sony's star-crossed journey from a world leader in electronic consumer goods to the victim of a fiscal mugging in its disastrous reign as owner of Columbia and TriStar has been widely documented, most recently in the book *Hit and Run* (Griffin and Masters 1996). Indeed, by November 1994, five years after acquiring Columbia Pictures Entertainment Inc. for $5 billion, Sony Corporation was forced to write-off slightly more than half its investment ($2.7

billion).[9] What has not been highlighted in the business and entertainment press, however, has been Sony's more adept and successful participation in the first generation of urban entertainment projects in America.

Over the last decade, Sony has engaged the location-based entertainment business in several notable ways. Together with Blockbuster and PACE Entertainment, Sony owns and operates the leading chain of amphitheaters in the eastern US. In 1989, Sony acquired Loew's, the theater chain originally built by Marcus Loew in the 1920s. It is the Sony–IMAX theaters, however, which have catapulted Sony into the front ranks of urban entertainment enterprises. IMAX brings to the relationship its expertise as a supplier of advanced technology 3-D theater systems. Sony, on the other hand, functions as a combination of developer, film-maker and capital-raiser. Their first project, the Sony–Imax Theater at Lincoln Square in New York has been highly successful – the single highest grossing screen in the US.[10] In spring 1995, Sony Corporation and IMAX Corporation signed a three-year agreement that calls for two new Sony–IMAX 3-D theaters to be built in San Francisco and Berlin as well as for a mutual exchange of technology.[11] The Sony–IMAX theater in San Francisco is part of the final phase of Metreon, a large-scale mixed-use, urban center which brings together components of recreation, entertainment, education and technology in a 40,000 square foot, four storey complex which is expected to draw over two million patrons per year. UEDs such as this, commented Sony Theaters executive vice-president, Joyce Storm (1995), are "a superb vehicle" to capitalize on her firm's diverse products and merchandising signatures which include musical artists, the theater exhibition circuit, film properties, electronics and a cable television network.

Real estate developers

The land development industry has an altogether different profile from their partners in the world of entertainment. In the 1960s, it was dominated by thousands of small-time entrepreneurs, some of whom built successful development corporations. By the late 1970s, however, the industry had consolidated squeezing out these "buccaneers" in favor of a new breed of professional owners and managers whose main concern was to ensure regular increases in assets and cash flow without the spectacular swings between success and failure which characterized the earlier entrepreneurial era (Lorimer 1978: 29). Their analogue in the financial community is the conservative institutional lender who regards real estate investment much like an annuity, paying out a fixed amount over a long period of time.

Real estate, like the agricultural industry, is, however, cyclical, responding both to wider economic conditions and to supply and demand factors within specific cities and regions. When, as was the case in the early 1990s, the property market collapses, higher-risk financial players move in to bottom-feed, scooping up mortgages cheaply and reselling them once recovery beckons. This introduces a certain measure of volatility into the industry, although it doesn't come near to matching the roller-coaster ride which is characteristic of everyday life in some sectors of the entertainment business.

Unlike entertainment companies, property companies have not traditionally branded either themselves or their holdings, the conventional wisdom being that they will stand on their own merit. One of the few possible exceptions to this is the Reichmann family whose name became synonymous with quality rental properties. In recent years, some property developers have attempted to brand themselves by establishing a reputation for standardized designs or superior service, but the degree of name recognition is still probably much less than is the case in other industries (Cohen 1998).

One carry over from the earlier era is the relatively high degree of decentralization. Unlike the entertainment sector which is concentrated in a handful of cities – New York, Los Angeles, Toronto – major development firms are spread out across the country in centers such as Chicago, Indianapolis, Cleveland, Pittsburgh and Dallas. To succeed, developers need to keep a close ear to the ground, since much of their task involves ensuring positive outcomes with regards to public sector decisions concerning subsidies, tax policy and the regulation of construction (Fainstein 1994: 219). This is also true for some parts of the entertainment industry, notably cable television, but in general land developers are required to keep a stronger local presence.

If not exactly the same old gang, the developers who are central in bringing urban entertainment destination projects to market are anything but neophytes. Most of them cut their teeth building office buildings and suburban and downtown shopping centers in the 1970s and 1980s, and have grown into developing UEDs through accumulated experience with mixed retail-entertainment projects.

One of the most renowned developers currently active in this area is Melvin (Mel) Simon of Indianapolis, who started in the business in the 1960s building small community plazas. Along with his one-time rival Edward De Bartolo, Simon became the emperor of shopping center builders in the 1960s and 1970s. His Simon Property Group Inc., which he operates together with his brother and son, recently acquired DeBartolo Realty Corporation making the combined company the largest privately held real estate company in the US with a market capitalization of $7.5 billion.[12] Although not the ones who conceived the project, the Simon Group were brought in as managers of the Mall of America and are part owners (22.5 percent). In partnership with Sheldon Gordon, Simon is the developer of the Forum Shops in Las Vegas. Another of his projects, the Circle Center Mall has brought the UED formula to downtown Indianapolis with the fourth floor of the shopping center given over to virtual reality games, themed restaurants, bars and movie theaters.

Formerly a movie producer, Mel Simon is a curious blend of pragmatist and visionary. At industry gatherings, he is the irascible voice of experience, refusing to be swept up into the high-tech entertainment dreams of his younger colleagues. At the same time, inspired by a "life enhancement" exhibit which he witnessed in Montreal several years ago (which included a blood pressure monitor, a surgery room and an interactive nutrition counselling display), he has given some thought to fashioning a commercial version of this which would be suitable for incorporation into UED projects. Thus in addition to entertainment and sports, "wellness centers" could become an important component of these projects. This has created widespread industry talk about "Mel's black box"[13] ("black box" refers to the entertainment retail formula of the future that will turn around the fortunes of hundreds of presently marginal shopping centers).

Simon Property Group Inc. is worth watching not only because of its size but also because it has expressed interest in doing something other developers have stayed away from in America: bringing the UED to the suburban mall. The concept of the theme park, of course, has been featured at the West Edmonton Mall and the Mall of America but Simon's aim is to achieve this within a smaller space. With its hefty portfolio of older plazas, Simon Property is in an ideal position to retro-fit larger and mid-size malls with the technology of the downtown UED, thus providing direct competition. Not coincidentally, the fundamental pieces of Cafe-at-Play (see Note 13) are said to be "scaleable" and capable of being downsized to fit any urban entertainment destination (Halliday 1996).

Simon's partner in the Forum Shops, Sheldon Gordon, is a California-based developer who is actively planning and building a number of high-profile projects both in the US and overseas. His 500,000 square foot "Sportsplex" in Scottsdale, Arizona promises to be a state-of-the-art amalgam of themed sports environments, television broadcasting facilities and participatory sports events, together with a continuous manufacturer's trade show and exhibition. The Gordon Group Holdings, Ltd. recently purchased Atlantic Pier in Atlantic City, New Jersey, and, with partners from Hong Kong, has plans to develop Battersea Power Station in London, England as a combination of Sportsplex and the Forum Shops. Together with the DeBartolo Entertainment Group, Gordon is acting as the master developer of the Grand Bay Hotels development at Monte Lago, a $300 million resort hotel casino project which is to be part of a $4 billion luxury residential golf resort community.

Himmel and Company, a Boston firm that built a number of high-profile projects in the 1970s and the 1980s – Copley Place (Boston), Water Tower Place (Chicago), Reston Town Center (Virginia) – is now working on entertainment enhanced shopping areas in Seattle and Chicago. Millennium Partners, initially a builder of middle-class homes, successfully developed the Lincoln Square project in Manhattan with its high-grossing Sony–IMAX theater, multi-level retail stores and the largest health club in New York, and is the lead firm in the Metreon center in San Francisco. Its potential future projects include a residential and entertainment complex in downtown Toronto (in partnership with Cadillac Fairview Corporation) as well as properties in Boston, Washington, Miami, Chicago and Montreal (Milner 1997a).

Forest City Enterprises Inc. is a major vertically integrated national real estate management and development firm with $2.5 billion in assets whose high-profile entertainment related ventures include Tower City Center (Cleveland), The Showcase (Las Vegas) and part of the 42nd Street Redevelopment project in New York. Although its headquarters are in Cleveland, Ohio, where it has been active in the real estate business since the 1930s, Forest City Enterprises has recently become a major figure in the future redevelopment of Brooklyn in New York. This is largely due to the financial backing it has provided for developer Bruce Ratner, a member of the company's founding family. New York's Commissioner of Consumer Affairs from 1978 to 1982, Ratner, through his Forest City Ratner Companies, has pursued several projects that other developers haven't wanted, including the Metrotech Center in downtown Brooklyn and a proposal to revive the Loew's Kings movie theater in Flatbush, once known as the "crown jewel of Brooklyn" (Rohde 1997).

And what of James Rouse and Ernest Hahn, the pioneers of downtown development in the 1970s who were lionized in the book *Downtown Inc* (Frieden and Sagalyn 1989)? Rouse, the Svengali of the festival market place, whose projects in Boston and Baltimore first inspired the retail-entertainment renaissance in downtown and waterfront areas of American cities, retired from the Rouse Company in the early 1980s to found a non-profit corporation, the Enterprise Development Company. Rouse and his long-time associate Marty Millspaugh went on to experiment with the establishment of scaled-down versions of Faneuil Hall and Harborplace in a number of medium-sized cities. Rouse died in April 1996.

The Rouse Company stopped building festival malls a decade ago[14] but has continued to pursue a number of other projects, some of which incorporate urban entertainment components. In Baltimore, it participated in the building of the Columbus Center, a state-of-the-art research and education marine biotechnology and archaeology center. In February 1996 the Rouse Company announced that it had purchased vast tracts of land and buildings in Las Vegas and Los Angeles from the Howard Hughes Corporation for more than $520 million, the last remnants of the business empire of the late, reclusive billionaire (Sterngold 1996a). It is not yet clear how it plans to develop these properties, although it is worth noting that several components – the Fashion Show Mall on the Las Vegas Strip and the huge Playa Vista development in Los Angeles, site of the new Dreamworks SKG movie studios – have the potential to form the nuclei of entertainment centers.

The Hahn Company, which built the Horton Plaza in San Diego and Plaza Pasadena in California, was eventually acquired by Trizec Corporation, the Toronto-based real estate giant who is North America's third largest developer with interests in seventy-two properties across Canada, in addition to the thirty-eight malls owned by Hahn. Then in a move that stunned the investment community, TrizecHahn was in turn purchased by and merged with Horsham Corporation which is controlled by the Canadian millionaire, Peter

Munk. This was significant because, despite its size, TrizecHahn had a shortage of cheap investment capital with which to finance growth. By merging the two concerns into a new real estate company, Munk combined the portfolio and expertise of Trizec with the bountiful cash of Horsham Corporation, which in turn had a major holding in Barrick Gold Corporation, the world's leading gold producer (McLaughlin 1996), thereby creating the second largest publicly held real estate company in North America with $6 billion in assets. In 1997, the newly constituted TrizecHahn went on a shopping spree, purchasing $2.1 billion in commercial real estate across North America including the Sears Tower in Chicago.

Among the holdings which TrizecHahn acquired as part of its purchase was one of the best known downtown malls in the US – the Horton Plaza in San Diego, California. Ernest W. Hahn Inc., the original developer, opened Horton Plaza on 9 August 1985. With its brightly colored buildings and extensive entertainment facilities it now occupies the position of San Diego's third largest tourist attraction behind Sea World and the zoo. Soon after the merger was announced, TrizecHahn Corporation dove head first back into the entertainment business, announcing a $200 million, 450,000 square foot retail and entertainment complex to be built at the Aladdin hotel and casino in Las Vegas. In a second venture, the Los Angeles Community Redevelopment Board asked the company to begin negotiations on redeveloping Hollywood Boulevard, including a legendary showbusiness icon, Mann's Chinese Theatre and the nearby Walk of Fame (Craig 1997). In a third major announcement, TrizecHahn has been named as one of two developers for a 44-acre tract of former railway land near Toronto's waterfront. As part of its $100 million capital investment, TrizecHahn will construct a retail and entertainment complex next to Skydome, the sports and entertainment stadium, and the Metro Convention Centre. In addition, the company will lease, develop and operate the CN Tower, the largest freestanding structure in the world and Toronto's top tourist attraction with 1.4 million visitors annually.

Munk is no stranger to the leisure and hospitality business, having at one point operated a chain of South Sea hotels and almost selling the Egyptian government a scheme to build a $400 million resort city behind the Pyramids. However, the force behind TrizecHahn's current expansion into the urban entertainment business is David Malamuth, the former vice-president of development at Walt Disney Imagineering. It was Malamuth who managed Disney's renovation of the New Amsterdam Theater and spearheaded its participation in the 42nd Street Redevelopment project.

Finally, it is worth noting the entry of Zev Buffman into the UED business. Buffman is unusual insofar as he comes from the entertainment industry rather than the real estate business. Starting off as a Broadway producer in 1960, Buffman later branched out to produce live television programs such as the Emmy awards. In 1988, he took a sabbatical from live theater to become a founding general partner of the Miami Heat basketball team, helping to put together a $32.5 million financing package. Rather than return to Broadway, Buffman has gone on to exercise his multiple talents in a wide range of endeavors, from producing entertainment at the Forum Shops in Las Vegas to building amphitheaters in conjunction with the PACE–Sony–Blockbuster group.

As chairman of TZBG Inc., Buffman's inaugural plunge into developing urban entertainment on a large scale was the proposed $127.5 million country and western themed "Old Town Entertainment Center" in Temecula, a small community in California's wine district. This was scheduled to open Christmas 1997. However, after facing a barrage of financing and legal problems, Buffman moved the planned venture to Murrieta, a neighboring community. The opposition in Temecula came from a small group of concerned citizens who were able to use California's strict environmental laws to stall the project in court. Along the way, Buffman announced that he was merging the Old Town Entertainment Center with "RogersDale USA," a retail and entertainment project which was initially slated to be built on a site next to retired movie stars Roy Rogers' and Dale Evans' existing museum in Victorville. At the time of writing, construction has yet to begin. The planned project combines a 2,200 seat opera house, a 1,400 seat cabaret theater and a 100,000 square foot Wild West arena, together with various other standard UED components: a motion simulation theater, a giant-screen theater, an interactive center, a food court and 10,000 square feet of specialty retail space. The theater facilities in Old Town are designed as an incubator for new shows which it is hoped will subsequently move on to venues in New York and Las Vegas as well as to venues managed by Ogden Entertainment who has signed on as the facility manager for Buffman's entertainment center.

Although he is not a novice at raising capital, Buffman speaks a somewhat different language than many of his real estate development colleagues. Rather than discuss sales/investment ratios and earnings multiples, Buffman, a skilled promoter, emphasizes the qualities of passion and vision as the moving force behind successful urban entertainment projects, an approach which leads some industry veterans to wonder whether he can actually bring a project of this size to market. At the same time, Buffman is known for his practical attitude in finding and creating new public revenue sources, notably hotel and theater ticket taxes. Thus "Old Town" represents an interesting test of the role of impresario as developer in Fantasy City.

Retail and entertainment operators

In some respects, the retail-entertainment line-up of urban entertainment centers in the 1990s is similar in format to that of the suburban malls of the past, since, generally speaking, it's the same cast of operators. Whereas suburban malls feature branches of downtown department stores and national clothing chains, UEDs court merchants whose products tap directly into the leisure experiences of their customers: the British-based music retailers, Virgin Records

Megastores and HMV; the bookstore chain, Barnes & Noble and Borders; and the decidedly middle-class Seattle coffee chain, Starbucks. Most urban entertainment projects, already built or on the planning board, host one of the top three themed restaurants – Planet Hollywood, the Rainforest Cafe and the Hard Rock Cafe – as well as a multiplex cinema and some form of large format, 3-D movie attraction.

Retail and entertainment operators are perhaps the most reluctant players in UED development. Rarely do they initiate the wider vision of what the project will look like; instead, they are asked to participate on faith by the developer or entertainment company. Exceptions to this are innovators such as Nike or Dave & Busters which build their own stand-alone attractions or else anchors such as Nordstrom's, the Seattle-based department store, which are lead players in more conventional mixed retail-entertainment projects.

Like corporate investors, retail and entertainment operators have a fixed objective, typically an operating profit of 25 percent of gross revenue. With the top-ranking UED projects this is not a problem. The Forum Shops in Las Vegas boast an annual retail volume of $1,220 per square foot. Clyde's Restaurant in the Reston Town Center turns over $10 million in business – over $1,000 per square foot (figures for 1994). Coco Walk in Florida draws retail sales of $600 per square foot (excluding the movie theaters), equal to Rouse's most successful market place project, Bayside in Miami. Yet despite the potential for profit, the risks are greater than for more conventional projects. Operating costs are higher; merchandising is more intensive compared to traditional retail outlets, requiring more capable and better trained staff; and there is less of a margin for error. As I have already noted in Chapter 5, the themed restaurant industry is facing a major shakedown with many operators finding it not as easy as they thought to follow in the steps of the Hard Rock Cafe.

Developing UEDs: Risk management strategies

Property development, according to British land economists Peter Byrne and David Cadman (1984: 1–7), is a dynamic process which is characterized by varying levels of uncertainty and risk in each of its three phases: acquisition, production and disposal. Some of these uncertainties can be contained but others are more difficult to control and must be accepted as part of the risk associated with bringing a project to market.

Byrne and Cadman note that the factor of time-scale is especially cruel to the property development industry because it restricts the degree of certainty which can be achieved. Compared to other industries, the time difference between the conception of a project and the finished product is fairly long, leaving the developer vulnerable to changes in consumer preference, the rise and fall of economic cycles and changes in interest rates (1984: 7). In the face of this challenge, principals in the development process must choose between short or long term estimates, judging the viability of a project on the basis of how the market is performing at the time or, alternatively, how it is likely to look in the future. Predicting the future is an uncertain art resulting in so-called "educated" guesses turning out to be wrong. During the 1980s, for example, financial institutions in Britain and the US, flush with excess capital, were persuaded by overly optimistic estimates as to the need for office space in New York and London, only to find that a number of unanticipated factors and events resulted in a frenzy of over building (Fainstein 1994: 221).

As noted earlier in this chapter, the development of UEDs involves an especially high level of uncertainty and risk because it represents new territory. Although the success of the Disney amusement parks, of themed restaurants such as the Hard Rock Cafe and Planet Hollywood, and of a few pioneering retail-entertainment destinations such as the Forum Shops and CocoWalk suggests a potentially bright future for this type of hybrid development, the difficulties encountered by some of the festival market places a hint at a less optimistic scenario.

In an attempt to contain and control the uncertainties associated with financing, building and operating urban entertainment projects, each of the four categories of players which I have just discussed here (investors, developers, entertainment companies, retail and entertainment operators) have worked out a number of "risk management strategies" (see below, Table 6.2).

Table 6.2 Risk management strategies in urban entertainment development projects

Player	Risk/weakness	Risk management strategy
Corporate investors	• low return on capital	• stricter lending criteria and guidelines
Real estate developers	• undercapitalization	• use of conventional leasing terms
	• low occupancy and rents	• pre-leasing
	• community resistance	• prepaid and minimum guaranteed rents
		• community involvement
Entertainment companies	• lack of real estate experience	• use of planning tools (charrette, computer modeling)
	• incomplete knowledge of project mix	• strategic partnerships
	• low attendance	• the "weenie" and the "genie"
Retail operators	• high infrastructure and operating costs	• landlord/tenant improvement allowances (TIs)
	• elevated customer expectations	• percentage rents
		• staff training programs

For *corporate investors* the number one concern is the return rate on their capital. Chastened by the excesses of the late 1980s and the subsequent real estate downturn and losses of the early 1990s, today even venture capitalists attempt to work within fixed parameters in order to minimize their risk potential. An urban entertainment destination project is generally expected to reap a return of 15 to 20 percent. In order to guarantee this level of return on their money, banks and other corporate lenders usually insist on a number of conditions before extending investment funds. Prospective developments should, for example, show a high level of pre-leasing, often as high as 70 percent. At least 50 percent equity is required. A shorter term (7–10 years) is offered compared to other kinds of retail financing. Developers must demonstrate a potential cash flow of at least 1.5 the debt service and ideally this figure should be closer to 2.1. These guidelines are not set in stone but they do provide a fixed set of expectations with which corporate investors can approach and assess UED projects without having to evaluate what they deem to be "creative risk" (Hackett 1995a: 28).

Faced with these constraints, *developers* have been forced, in some instances, to describe urban entertainment centers in more conventional leasing terms, notably as mixed-use retail projects with an entertainment component. Even so, further difficulties can arise from undercapitalization, low occupancy and rents, and community resistance.

As we saw in the case of Freedomland and the ill-fated indoor theme parks of the 1960s and 1970s (see Chapter 2), undercapitalization puts the developer in a precarious position from the start, usually ensuring that the project will sooner or later falter. One reason for this is that UED projects are especially sensitive to the need for reinvestment or, as it is now called, "changeable software"; since they depend on patrons making a number of return visits. Even industry giants such as Disney, Universal and the Las Vegas/Atlantic City casino operators are vulnerable on this point, and, as a result, are constantly adding new attractions, hotels and even additional theme parks, Consequently, developers must enter into a project with sufficient capital or else risk having it falter or close after a short period of time.

To ensure sufficient capital, developers rarely take the option of going it alone. Any developer who might contemplate this strategy needs only to look at the woes encountered by London's Canary Wharf developers, Olympia & York, whose decision to be self-financing contributed to its eventual cash-flow problems during the real estate downturn of the early 1990s (Fainstein 1994: 219). Instead, developers turn to a repertoire of risk reducing measures, some well established in the industry, others relatively new. In concert with corporate investors, pre-leasing of retail and entertainment space is encouraged, sometimes with prepaid rents as well. As much as possible, minimum guaranteed rents are favored over percentage arrangements. Not only does the latter involve a higher degree of uncertainty but a project which is loaded down with percentage arrangements also attracts a lower level of financing (Erichetti

1995). Developers may also act to reassure lenders by signing up blue chip tenants or by approaching capital sources in tandem with a heavyweight partner or sponsor.

After receiving the go ahead by their investors, developers must then deliver a full roster of retail and entertainment tenants at the projected rents. Sometimes, however, this involves a greater risk than might be expected. Ken Himmel (1995), the developer of the Reston Town Center, has described his consternation when, four months before opening, a doubting Thomas operator told him: "We do not intend to open our theaters. You can take whatever action you want." Himmel was forced to negotiate a riskier percentage rent deal with another theater operator with the provision for conversion to a minimum guaranteed rent after five years. Fortunately for him, theater revenues have steadily risen.

In addition, UED developers can encounter sharp and sometimes unexpected community resistance. By purchasing a buffer zone of land around the site of its Florida theme park complex, Disney has been able to minimize potential problems with disgruntled neighbors in the Orlando area; however, the widespread dissent toward its now canceled colonial heritage theme park in northern Virginia, "Disney's America," did not appear to have been fully anticipated by the "imagineers." Opposition to one aspect of Himmel's six-storey retail-entertainment project in downtown Seattle led to a referendum on the project. Fortunately for Himmel and Company, the referendum passed with just over 60 percent of the vote. The Ghermezian brothers were not so fortunate in their campaign to build "American Dream," a $585 million entertainment mall which they proposed for the Washington, DC edge city of Silver Springs, Maryland (see Chapter 7). In this instance, the developers were clumsy in their initial handling of community opposition in Montgomery County, although in the end it was uncertainty over project financing that killed the proposal. Such cautionary tales clearly indicate that citizen approval should never be taken as a foregone conclusion, even in communities where civic approval has been formally extended.

To overcome community resistance, developers need to employ a number of strategies. Above all, it is necessary to recognize that the most successful and trouble free project is one in which developers identify with and articulate the goals of both the private and public sectors. James Rouse's associate, Marty Millspaugh, cautions that developers have to take into account a crucial shortlist of considerations: public standards for bidding, affirmative action, historical and architectural preservation, environmental impact. In short, public–private partnerships have to be precisely that, rather than just a convenient moniker for tax, zoning and regulatory concessions on the part of the city. Furthermore, the developer must communicate effectively and often with those whose daily lives will be touched by UED projects. In what may constitute a record, Zev Buffman conducted 117 meetings with community groups in Temecula in order to steer his "Old Town Temecula" project through the sea of public doubt. It is vital, he urges prospective UED developers, to "get them [the community] to buy into your dream."

Entertainment companies can in various situations function both as developers and as operators. In their role as creative partners, however, they face various hurdles. Above all, entertainment companies do not generally have the requisite experience with the real estate market that their development colleagues possess. No matter how dazzling a particular new entertainment technology might seem, it may not be sufficient to attract new investment capital or to wean consumers away from other activities. The short theatrical career of "Cinerama," a pioneering widescreen motion picture technology of the 1950s and 1960s, is a good example of a promising idea which simply wasn't commercially viable. Similarly, Sid and Marty Krofft, although inspired puppeteers, failed in their attempt at an indoor Atlanta theme park (The World of Sid and Marty Krofft) due to underfunding, the wrong formula, and being blind to competition from the nearby Six Flags Theme Park. As one veteran theme park designer kept repeating when I ran the names of some of the better known UED entrepreneurs past him, "He's bright enough but has he actually ever built anything?"

In order to better anticipate such situations, entertainment companies employ a number of planning exercises before a project is formally initiated. Long a staple among architects and urban planners, the "charrette" has become a popular tool for a number of the larger firms such as Disney, Universal and RKO. Buzz Price (1995) claims to have carried out seventeen charrettes between 1987 and 1995 for the indoor entertainment industry, including such high-profile projects as CityWalk, Camp Snoopy and the Hollywood Entertainment Museum. In each case, the project size, content and cost have all been positively influenced by the charrette. In addition, consultants such as Price have been asked to model the mix of entertainment, retail and real estate so that both developer and entertainment entrepreneur can have a more precise concept of how UEC synergies affect such key measures as attendance, per capita revenues and retail-entertainment dollars per square foot. Clearly this is light years away from the stereotyped image of how Hollywood projects are developed at poolside or over cocktails at a trendy restaurant.

To attract patrons to UED projects and thereby justify high rents, entertainment companies use two strategies, commonly known as "the weenie" and "the genie." The former refers to a single magnet attraction that draws people to the project in the first place,[15] much like the notion of the shopping center anchor store, while the latter describes the strategy of providing three or more choices for prospective visitors.

To handle the increased degree of risk attendant upon UED projects, *retail operators* make several moves in order to protect their pocketbooks. High-profile tenants demand (and usually receive) large landlord–tenant improvement allowances (TIs). Some insist on a guarantee of signage, and arcade and casino licenses before committing to the project. In cases such as that recounted by

Himmel (see p. 123), operators ask for percentage rents rather than the riskier minimum guaranteed rents.

Bringing the players together

Finally, it is important to consider how this new hybrid of real estate development and entertainment has taken the initial steps in overcoming a host of conflicting corporate traditions, mind-sets and operating structures in order to emerge as a distinctive industry in its own right.

Perhaps the most important linking mechanism so far has been the flow of creative and management personnel across existing industry boundaries. In particular, the Disney companies acted as rich talent pools, throwing out an increasing number of animators, designers and executives to every corner of the burgeoning urban entertainment industry. Bob Rogers, whose firm BRC Imagination Arts has designed among other things theme parks, world's fairs and space museums, started at Disney. Ex-senior Disney imagineer, David Malmuth, a principal in the negotiations with redevelopment officials in New York to restore the New Amsterdam Theater, is now an executive with real estate developer TrizecHahn. Mickey Steinberg, Chairman of Sony Retail Entertainment since 1994, previously headed up Walt Disney Imagineering where he was involved in building the EuroDisney theme park. The new Universal Studios Japan, due to open in 2001, includes among its project team Paul Lefrance, vice-president and executive project director, and Dave Burkhart, creative director, both formerly at Disney. Former Walt Disney Imagineering vice-president, Jon Snoddy, has gone on to become the design vice-president at Sega Gameworks in charge of creating entertainment centers.

A second important medium for bringing together the diverse players in the urban entertainment field has been the conferences and professional development seminars sponsored by the Urban Land Institute (ULI). While few participants publicly solicit partners at these events (as was the case with Andy Halliday, co-president of Simon Brand Ventures, at a 1996 seminar), there has been a high level of networking resulting in a number of new partnerships. Several top officials at major entertainment companies – Peter Rummell (formerly at Disney), Frank Stanek (Universal) – and real estate development companies – Mel Simon, James Ratner – are ULI trustees as well as serving on the editorial advisory board of the *E-Zone* where they are joined by such luminaries as Steve Wynn of Mirage Resorts Inc. and Michael Rubin of MRA International.

A third avenue is the well-known inter-organizational networking device of serving on corporate boards of directors. For example, Iwerks Entertainment, a major producer of simulation rides and films, counts among its directors Gary Matus, the vice-president of the Bank of America in Los Angeles, and Terry Van Gorder, President and chief executive officer of Knott's Berry Farm, the established California theme park. And, Jeff McNair, President of Toronto theme park design firm Forrec Ltd, sits on the board of Rank, the British entertainment conglomerate which owns the Hard Rock Cafe.

Finally, there are the time honored strategies of vertical and horizontal integration. While Disney or Universal might be thought to be the best examples of this, in fact, the highest levels of integration have been achieved by a lesser known but no less formidable conglomerate, Ogden Corporation.

A global company which focuses on three fundamental businesses – entertainment, aviation and power generation – Ogden earned revenues in 1996 of just over $2 billion. Until recently, the company was best known for its presence in the waste management business. By the early 1990s, Ogden Martin had captured almost 20 percent of the energy from waste market (i.e. electricity from incineration) in the US (Crooks 1993: 210), operating twenty-one plants with a capacity to process 20 tons of waste a day (Bator 1992: 152). In the 1980s, however, the company re-created itself as a services company, providing, among other things, concession food services, janitorial services, security, parking, facility management and concert promotions. In the 1990s, Ogden Entertainment holds interests in themed attractions, live theater, concert promotion, gaming, large format theaters, performing artist management, broadcast production services, recorded music and video development and food and beverage operations at arenas, amphitheaters, convention centers and other recreational facilities around the world.

Recognized for many years for its dominance in food service and venue management, Ogden began a concerted move into live and interactive entertainment attractions in the mid-1990s. In March 1995 it won the rights to manage and develop location-based entertainment attractions at the World Trade Center's Observation Deck in New York. The following autumn, it purchased half ownership in Metropolitan Entertainment, a New York concert promoter. Ogden's first major theme park acquisition was Silver Springs/Wild Waters, Florida's oldest tourist attraction, which it acquired in March 1996. In mid-1997 the company announced that it would become the major equity partner and would manage and operate the proposed $76 million Jazzland Theme Park in New Orleans (O'Brien 1998). Recently, Ogden has spread its net even further, acquiring the Enchanted Castle, the largest indoor themed entertainment complex in Chicago, and the first in a series of planned FEC developments (Muret 1997b).

One of Ogden's premier projects has been the development of a chain titled American Wilderness Zoo & Aquarium (AWZA), a nature-based theme attraction scaled down to a department store size (Evans 1997). Earlier, in 1995, it had taken the first step in this direction by acquiring Firehole Entertainment, a New York Corporation which operates the Grizzly Discovery Center, an attraction located at the entrance to Yellowstone National Park, which combines high-tech large format films with wildlife habitats.

AWZA is a simulated wilderness experience located within a controlled, indoor environment, the first of which is a section of the 1.7 million square foot

Ontario Mills Mall located at a junction between two heavily used interstate highways forty miles east of Los Angeles. It presents simulated eco-systems of five different regions of California – the Redwood Forest, the Mojave Desert, the High Sierras, the Pacific Shore and the Yosemite Valley – each with its own separate climate control system. American Wilderness Zoo & Aquarium is said to be an example of "immersion exhibiting" in which zoos and aquariums try to connect the public with the natural habitat of animals (Evans 1997: 38). One way of achieving this is through the forty seat Wild Ride Theater, a simulator ride in which the visitor feels the motion experienced by the animals themselves. The AWZA complex also includes a retail store called Naturally Untamed and a 440 seat large-screen theater which employs Iwerks technology. This latter attraction has been developed in conjunction with the County of San Bernadino whose museum system is to receive part of the funds generated by the facility.

In addition to AWZA, Ogden has announced a battery of joint ventures with a number of other prominent entertainment providers. It is heavily involved in co-developing, building and operating fifteen IMAX theaters in North and South America and Asia as well as financing, developing and producing large format films such as *Mark Twain's America* with Sony Corporation. Among its other leisure based activities are the leasing and operation of a gambling casino in the Palm Beach area of Aruba in the Caribbean, and a thirteen year contract to design and manage the Olympic 2000 Stadium in Sydney, Australia, the site of the opening and closing ceremonies, all track and field events and possibly, the soccer final (Melvin 1996a). As noted on p. 119, Ogden has joined forces with producer/developer Zev Buffman to act as both manager of Buffman's Old Town Entertainment Center and, potentially, as the host of shows first initiated at Murrieta.

Although only about a tenth the size of Disney in terms of sales revenue, Ogden may point to the future of entertainment conglomerates. Already it is active in certain areas – food services, concert management, casino gambling— which are beyond Disney's scope. It is unique in that it has a commercial interest in both the real (through its waste management arm) and the virtual (through American Wilderness Zoo & Aquarium) environments, and in the interface between the two (Grizzly Discovery Center). Although Ogden doesn't yet own an airline, it is capable of fueling the plane that carries you to your theme park vacation, preparing the food you eat in the airport and on the plane and handling your baggage. Once at your destination, Ogden may own the park, produce the themed and live entertainment you sample and supply your meals and snacks. It has the capacity, therefore, of bringing the players in the fledgling urban entertainment industry together in a number of new, more tightly co-ordinated ways.

Figure 7.1 "New life around Times Square": The Disney Store on 42nd Street, New York.
Source: Courtesy of Blaise Haywood.

7

CALLING THE SHOTS

Public–private partnerships in Fantasy City

"If you build it, they will come," this invitation, made famous in the 1989 baseball fantasy movie *Field of Dreams*, has special resonance for the theme park city of tomorrow. Battered by factory closures, shrinking federal subsidies and a deteriorating infrastructure, cities and towns across America are desperate for something – anything – to kickstart their stagnant economies. For local politicians and planners whose communities are faced with such dismal prospects, the first step to recovery is to join forces with a corporate savior in order to build a landmark project which, it is perceived, will constitute an economic miracle.

Of all the alliances to be found in the process of building Fantasy City, these public–private partnerships are the most sensitive and complex. While both parties broadly support a growth-oriented strategy, specific goals may differ sharply. Elected officials and public agencies tend to see UEDs as the most recent brand of magic elixir, providing jobs, tax revenues and, perhaps more importantly, a dynamic new image for the community. "Cities today cannot afford to rest on their laurels," advises Carol Rubin (1996), general counsel to the Silver Springs (Maryland) Redevelopment Program. "Urban managers must find ways to make them safe and secure and to attract tourist dollars."

Private partners from the entertainment and real estate development industries share this affinity for safety, security and tourist dollars but their bottom line is somewhat different. With the notable exception of James Rouse, who honestly seemed to be driven by a self-proclaimed mission to help rescue the inner city, most of the principal players in UED projects are more concerned with questions of practicality and profitability. Neither Robin Hoods nor robber barons, they must delicately balance what the city wants with what their investors and tenants need in order to create a financially successful development.

Depending on the nature and size of the project, the prime initiative may come from either the public or the private partner. In the case of large, multi-component entertainment districts, it is usually a city or state appointed urban redevelopment agency which comes up with the original concept and issues an RFP (Request for Proposals). The Metreon entertainment complex in San Francisco was put into motion in this manner. Alternately, public sector leads can subdivide the project into different parts and negotiate privately with companies that they wish to invite in as anchors or as developers. The 42nd Street Redevelopment Agency in New York pursued this latter line of strategy in convincing Disney to join its "42nd Street Now" plan.

A more common scenario, however, is for the private partner to approach the city seeking approval, and frequently assistance, in building an arena, ballpark, casino, amphitheatre, convention center or theme park. If the municipality is desperate enough, it may roll out the red carpet for the proposed project. More likely, however, a kind of extended courtship will ensue in which each of the parties will try to get a feel for the extent of the other's contribution and commitment. This getting to know you period may even be legally structured into a series of stages, each with its own benchmarks and deadlines. And, as can occur in some romantic betrothals, city–developer engagements may be broken off at the last minute, as happened in the case of the proposed "American Dream" entertainment mall in Silver Spring, Maryland (see "When a public–private partnership fails" below).

When a public–private partnership fails: Silver Spring and the "American Dream"

On 12 November 1996, Douglas M. Duncan, the politically elected Executive of Montgomery County, Maryland, ended an eighteen-month relationship when he announced he was unwilling to commit public funds toward the construction of "American Dream," a $585 million entertainment mall proposed by the Triple Five Group of Edmonton, Alberta, Canada. In many ways, this is a textbook case of how public–private partnerships can break down due to conflicting expectations and poor communication. At the same time, it also illustrates the potential difficulties inherent in exporting large-scale urban entertainment projects beyond the tourist-friendly downtown urban core.

The proposed site of American Dream was Silver Spring, a mature suburb of Washington, DC, which for a long time had been seeking to revitalize its city center. At one stage, Silver Spring seemed poised to become a major employment and residential node, but in the 1960s and 1970s the County opted to encourage growth in the I-270 highway corridor to the west of the city, leaving a downtown of abandoned storefronts. In the late 1980s, the community began to consider ways of revitalizing its downtown, culminating in plans for a $275 million office and retail center called "Silver Triangle." However, the Silver Triangle shopping mall project was abandoned when the developers failed to find a second anchor tenant willing to join Macy's department store.

Then along came Triple Five, the high-profile developers of the West Edmonton Mall and the Mall of America. The Triple Five Group is the corporate development vehicle for the four Ghermezian brothers of Edmonton. Originally from Iran where they were part of the Armenian minority, the Ghermezians started out in business selling carpets, but they soon moved into buying and selling land, and, later, developing shopping centers, office buildings and residential communities. Aggressive and persistent in their business dealings, they developed a reputation as being both bombastic and visionary.

For the Silver Spring site, the Ghermezians proposed building a 2.1 million square foot entertainment mall which would include an ice rink with seats for 1,000 people, wave pools for 3,000 swimmers, an indoor roller coaster, an IMAX giant-screen movie theater, a 500 room hotel called Fantasyland, a conventional multiplex theater, nightclubs, restaurants and upmarket stores. In addition, Triple Five agreed to restore the rundown Silver Theater to its former art-deco glory, provide underground parking for 2,000 vehicles and create several park-like esplanades for public use.

In their selling of the American Dream project, the Ghermezians had to overcome two major problems – achieving public acceptance and securing private financing.

From the beginning, the brothers got off on the wrong foot with the community. During the seven years that the former Silver Triangle project had been discussed, a groundswell of voter opposition had arisen and this carried over to the American Dream project. At the first public hearing to do with the Silver Spring Mall in September 1995, 700 Montgomery County residents crowded into a meeting hall while 100 more were shut out due to lack of space.

Instead of sending a representative skilled in handling town meetings, the Ghermezians decided to attend themselves – with mixed results. Feisty, given to hyperbole and handicapped by their strong accents, the Ghermezians were unable to reassure the lively crowd; and instead, came across as confrontational (Aguilar 1995: DM-2). "I have never seen a crowd like this," Neder Ghermezian later told a *Washington Post* reporter. "I don't mind working with people that are very vocal and educated. But I am afraid that they [the citizens of Montgomery County] might be too radical" (Pressler 1995: 2).

Eventually Triple Five did manage to overcome most of the public opposition to the project by instituting a concerted public relations campaign. At a second, less conflictual forum, the Ghermezians handed over the task of public presentations to a company vice-president and their lawyers. An advisory group was created with the power of recommending for or against plans for the project to the County Executive. In the fall of 1995, Triple Five sponsored an all-expenses-paid trip for nineteen residents and county employees to Edmonton and Bloomington to inspect the West Edmonton Mall and the Mall of America. Meetings were held with over forty community groups. Consultants' reports were commissioned into potentially problematic issues such as traffic volume and the economic impact of the mall.

Ultimately, however, it was financing which proved to be Triple Five's Achilles heel. In May 1996, Duncan set a 100-day deadline for the company to submit evidence of adequate private funding. If this was not satisfactory, the County would opt not to proceed to the next phase, which was the final development contract. After five months of trying to pursue funds themselves, in October 1996 Triple Five turned to Morgan Stanley & Co. to canvas potential private investors on their behalf. At this point in the story accounts of events differ.

Triple Five gave a financing report to Duncan in early November 1996 which it claims indicated "a strong level of potential private investment." However, Duncan rejected the proposed financing plan on the grounds that it didn't include specific evidence of backing from private investors beyond the $10–$15 million from Triple Five itself, money which would have come back to the company through fees. A large proportion of the disagreement seemed to revolve around what constituted commitment. The County insisted that Triple Five provide concrete evidence of commitment by interested investors and retail tenants. The Ghermezians, however, seemed to believe that it was sufficient to demonstrate an initial expression of interest by several prospective investors.

Another point of conflict was the level of public investment required. From the beginning, the Ghermezians made it clear that they expected public help, specifically in the form of low interest notes, industrial revenue bonds to be paid off over many years with revenue generated by the project after it was completed. However, later on Triple Five asked for a public contribution of up to $235 million, mostly in the form of tax breaks and direct grants, a request which was considered too expensive by Montgomery County officials. Furthermore, in the package presented to the County in November 1996, the County was said to have been asked to make up any shortfalls in funds from other public sources and to grant

Triple Five a freeze on property, personal and real estate taxes for a decade following the project's completion (Perez-Rivas and Pressler 1996). Instead, the County suggested a limit of $150 million to the public contribution, a cap which Triple Five officials claimed was set at the very last moment in the meetings leading up to the termination of the deal (Perez-Rivas 1996).

In summary, several lessons can be learnt from the rocky road traveled by Triple Five and their American Dream project. First, there is still a sizeable gap between the zealous enthusiasm for urban entertainment projects, as seen at industry forums, and the conservative mandate of private investors, especially away from the tourist zones of Orlando, Las Vegas and New York. American Dream was considered too ambitious, too expensive and too controversial. "People that have money in real estate, and especially retail, only want A+ projects," Steven Clayton, a Chicago-based investment consultant, told the *Washington Post*; while at the same time they remain wary of "unusual" retail projects (Pressler 1996). While it's true that Triple Five did build mega-projects in both Edmonton and Minnesota, there were several crucial differences. In these two previous projects, entertainment was a significant extra to the retail shopping mall, but it was not the sole anchor as would have been the case with American Dream. Perhaps the only instance where this style of project seems to have been a success is the Irvine Entertainment Center in California, and this probably has to do with its ideal location. Additionally, the Mall of America project, the Ghermezians' initial plunge into the US retail market, was co-developed with Simon Properties, the veteran American mall developer who took over management responsibility thereby reassuring investors of a strong measure of experience and stability.

Second, it is questionable whether full-scale UED projects can survive outside a city center. Although Silver Spring was located in the general orbit of Washington, it possessed no other independent tourist attractions and was part of a suburban fabric studded with regional malls and big-box stores. With a population of 85,000 within a two mile radius, it could have worked only by drawing from a wider regional market and from the Washington, DC tourist trade – not an impossible task, but not a certainty. As Anthony Dearing, chief executive of the Rouse Company observed, "you can't build a big regional shopping center on a speculative basis . . . without leasing agreements from large retailers, such projects are nearly impossible" (Haggerty 1995). American Dream not only lacked large retail anchors such as Nordstroms, Macy's or Bloomingdale's, but it also lacked convention facilities. In this development context, public–private partnerships run the risk of becoming unacceptably skewed, with the public partner having to assume too much of the financial risk. Ironically, traditional theme parks, such as the Six Flags chain, are generally a better bet, unless, like the ill-fated "Disney's America," they impinge on sacred historical sites.

Public contributions to UED development

While UED creation has increasingly necessitated new roles and relationships for its private partners, the contribution of the public sector has mostly followed a familiar repertoire of subsidies, concessions and guarantees. These fall into four broad categories: land acquisition/condemnation, infrastructure upgrades and additions, financing and tax benefits, and regulatory relief.

Land acquisition/Condemnation

In the downtown redevelopment projects of the 1970s, cities routinely expected to have to assemble the site on which a future shopping center would sit. This is still the case in those cities which are especially eager to renew a declining downtown. Thus Indianapolis assumed responsibility for land acquisition in its partnership with the Simon Property Group as part of its contribution to the construction of the Circle Center Mall.

It is more common, however, for public authorities to arrange development deals so that the land is not just a free gift. As an example, consider the agreement between the city of Anaheim and Disney regarding the Disney Ice Center. This deal has been structured in such a way that Anaheim deeds a thirty-two-acre site to the Disney Development Company via "Disney GOALS," a public charity which subsequently leases the land back to Disney in return for $50,000 per year and 500 hours of free time for community skaters (Johnson 1995).

In addition to land purchase, for a long time public partners have assisted private builders in site assembly by using one of their most powerful tools – condemnation. This is facilitated by the legal right of "taking by eminent domain" which allows for the immediate possession of private property for public use. Exercising its eminent domain powers has allowed cities to assemble parcels of land at reduced time and cost and this can be a highly sought-after concession.

Sometimes cities have concluded that condemnation is an overwhelming prerequisite for attracting public interest. In 1984, Philadelphia authorized the condemnation of inner-city buildings in order to build a new convention center, even though financing was not yet available. Similarly, redevelopment planners in New York convinced themselves that intended changes to Times Square could not happen without moving out the pornographic book stores and other undesirable activities: something which it then proceeded to do, cleaning out 500 businesses over a 10-acre area. At Camden Yards, Baltimore, the public authority used its condemnation powers to complete the assembly of 25 acres of land on which the new baseball stadium was to be built. On occasion, the municipality may even agree to underwrite the cost of tearing down existing buildings. In St Louis, for example, the public partners took on the responsibility for demolishing the existing Kiel Auditorium, the historic Children's Building (to provide additional parking) and the city jail (considered geographically too near to the new facility) as part of its contribution to the building of the Kiel Center, the region's primary indoor arena for sports and leisure events including the home games of the St Louis Blues hockey team (Rosentraub 1997: 297–8).

Infrastructure improvements

Even in cases where wholesale condemnation is not required, public partners are often asked to help make a UED project possible by effecting a number of infrastructure improvements, some of them potentially quite expensive. The most common variety of these are road and transit additions and reconfigurations which are deemed necessary in order to make an entertainment complex accessible from the freeways which encircle and bisect many American cities. In Philadelphia, federal and state transportation agencies spent $58.9 million to build three major on/off ramps from the I-95 expressway to the newly emergent entertainment area along the Central Waterfront and Penn's Landing. Across the river, Camden County, New Jersey put up $15 million for road and transit improvements, as well as paying for site clearances and the land itself, in order to secure the Blockbuster–Sony Music Entertainment Center ("E Center") for Camden, one of the most economically depressed cities in America. Elsewhere in the state, public authorities agreed to relocate Route 120 to the eastern perimeter of the Meadowlands in order to open up 55 acres of land for a proposed UED development.[1] In this case, highway reconfiguration was also to be accompanied by the extension of the New Jersey Transit rail lines from a new transfer station at Seacaucus allowing 20,000 passengers per hour at peak times to pour into the sports and entertainment pavilion. Transportation improvements similarly played a role in another stillborn project, the "Disney's America" theme park which was to be built in a rural part of Prince William County, thirty-five miles west of Washington, DC. Governor George Allen had committed the state to providing $163 million in public improvements, including widening a long portion of the I-66 ahead of schedule (Langdon 1994).

Municipal authorities may also be approached to relocate existing natural gas lines and other utilities or to build new ones in previously unserviced areas. Thus, in Philadelphia the PIDC (Philadelphia Industrial Development

Corporation) negotiated with the Philadelphia Gas Works to install a gas line along the central waterfront in anticipation of future leisure and entertainment-oriented development, while, in Indianapolis the city assumed complete responsibility for utility relocation related to the Circle Center Mall.

Finally, cities are often asked to build parking facilities to serve new downtown entertainment facilities. St Louis, for example, took on the responsibility for building a $24.5 million parking garage to serve patrons of the Kiel Center. Since this often requires construction of multi-leveled structures which are costly to operate and maintain, municipalities may opt to use such facilities for other purposes, for instance to serve the needs of nearby employees in public office buildings.

Financing

Gone are the days when cities could afford to finance private projects directly out of the public coffers. Brushes with bankruptcy, taxpayer revolts and declining transfer payments from senior levels of government have made politicians and public officials considerably more cautious in distributing direct investment money. Only in communities that seem hopelessly mired in poverty, crime and unemployment is this still seen as a politically viable, if not always economically sensible, option.[2] In Camden, the state-supervised Casino Reinvestment and Development Authority and the Urban Development Authority jointly put up $11.5 million to erect the "E Center" in the hope of extending the beehive of UED activity along the waterfront in Philadelphia to its cross-river poor cousin in New Jersey.

Elsewhere, public partners turn to a rather complex repertoire of more indirect and thus more politically palatable financing strategies: tax increment financing bonds, loan guarantees, sales, entertainment and "sin" taxes (duty on alcohol and tobacco), naming rights and personal seat licenses to name a few. Of these the first, tax increment financing (TIF) is the most popular form to have been carried over from the previous era of downtown shopping malls and festival market places.

TIF is a mechanism which allows redevelopment agencies to capture increases in property taxes in specially designated districts and then recycle them in order to pay back the debt incurred in order to build facilities such as sports arenas and convention centers. The appeal of TIF is twofold. First, the increased revenue which is generated by redevelopment projects is protected against being cast back into the vat of general tax revenues. Second, once approved by the city council, tax increment bonds do not require subsequent voter approval, making them secure against the changing winds of local politics. Tax increment financing has been used as part of the financing package for the Circle Center Mall in Indianapolis, in the relocation and expansion of Elitch Gardens amusement park to downtown Denver and is to be one of several means of financing a new football stadium in Nashville, Tennessee. While they appear to be failsafe, TIF bonds are opposed by some in the local community who would prefer that any revenue should go wholly or partly into paying for schools, social service programs and other major sources of municipal expenditures. In addition, they are open to criticism on the grounds that, once in place, they insulate expensive mega-projects from being scaled down or even canceled.

Of the more recent revenue streams, two seemingly bright stars are naming rights and personal seat licenses. In the past, the right to name an arena or stadium has traditionally been a perk of ownership or in the hands of the community. While some buildings were named after the team itself (Tiger Stadium, AstroDome, Maple Leaf Gardens) or after its geographic location (Fulton County Stadium, Three Rivers Stadium), some owners' names (Busch Stadium, Wrigley Field) also became enshrined. Today, the name of the facility is shamelessly deeded to corporations who are willing to pay an average of $1–$2 million per year (Muret 1996a). Among some of the pricier name sales in recent times have been for Pacific Bell Park in San Francisco ($50 million), the TWA Dome in St Louis ($1.3 million annually for twenty years) and Bank One Ballpark in Phoenix ($1.3 million annually for thirty years). In some cases, an existing facility will even be renamed as a money-raiser. The Brendan Byrne Arena in New Jersey's Meadowlands sports complex, for example, was rechristened the Continental Airlines Arena in return for a payment of $29 million.

At first glance this appears to be a "win-win" situation, at least for new facilities. While some people may be offended by the colonization of place names by major corporations (General Motors Place, Ford Centre for the Performing

Table 7.1 Naming rights: selected Canadian and American major league sports venues 1990–97

Venue	Cost (US$m)	Length of terms (in years)
America West Arena, Phoenix	26	over 30
Bank One Ballpark, Phoenix	66	over 30
Canadian Airlines Saddledome, Calgary	15	over 20
Continental Airlines Arena, East Ruttherford, New Jersey	29	over 12
Corel Centre, Ottawa, Ontario	25 (C$)	over 20
Ericsson Stadium, Charlotte, North Carolina	20	over 10
General Motors Place, Vancouver, British Columbia	20	over 20
Key Arena, Seattle	15	over 15
Miller Park, Milwaukee, Wisconsin	41.2	over 20
Pacific Bell Park, San Francisco	50	over 24
RCA Dome, Indianapolis, Indiana	23	over 20
TWA Dome, St Louis,	26	over 20
Tropicana Field, St Petersburg, Florida	46	over 30
USAir Arena, Landover, Maryland	10	over 10

Source: Amusement Business, 24 June 1996; 5 January 1998, pp. 13–14

Arts), this is not a new phenomenon. The "robber barons" of the late nineteenth century – the Carnegies, Morgans and Vanderbilts – helped to establish their philanthropic reputations by endowing and naming public libraries, museums, art galleries and theaters. Some of these took on a wider symbolic meaning: to perform in Carnegie Hall, for example has long been synonymous with reaching the pinnacle of excellence and fame in music performance. While it may seem improbable that sports venues named after airlines (USAir Arena, Delta Center) could take on the same mystique, it is worth recalling that a generation of North American children grew up delighting in the direction, "Take a Ride on the Reading," which the inventors of the board game Monopoly named after the Reading Railroad.

The issue of naming becomes more complicated when venues which spark a deep cultural resonance are tampered with. To change the name of Yankee Stadium for purely monetary reasons would no doubt raise an outcry among both fans and players. College football wouldn't be the same if the event and the venue were changed from the Rose Bowl to the name of a computer software company. None the less, names sometimes do change, especially in the case of an old facility being rehoused to a new one. For example, the Montreal Forum was an established sporting icon, but its name was changed when it moved into new premises, becoming the "Molson Centre" after the brewery which owns the team.

Personal seat licenses (PSLs) are one-time payments which are mandatory in order to secure the right to be a season ticketholder at a sports stadium or arena. The PSL concept was pioneered by the Carolina Panthers professional football team which has sold nearly 60,000 so far, thereby raising about $100 million (after taxes) of the $187 million needed to build the privately funded Ericsson Stadium in Charlotte. Also gaining from this scheme is St Louis which raised $74 million through the sale of 52,000 PSLs in order to finance the cost of moving the Rams football team away from Los Angeles.[3]

It is not uncommon for the larger urban entertainment projects to combine a variety of different public financing vehicles. Gateway Center in Cleveland is financed by loans, state capital grants, naming rights for the ballpark and arena, and a group of bonds totaling nearly $275 million, of which $117 million is backed by county "sin" taxes in liquor and tobacco; and by parking revenues and the sale of premium seats in the two sports facilities which together are expected to produce $158 million. Even this wasn't enough to cover construction overruns and extras such as office space and luxury restaurants; when the sin taxes fell short the County had to guarantee more than $120 million in construction bonds through property taxes (Rosentraub 1997: 201). In addition to TIFs, the relocation and rebuilding of Elitch Gardens in Denver is being paid for by $14 million in general obligation bonds, a $7 million city of Denver loan and an $18 million mortgage from the Colorado Housing and Finance Authority and from the Denver Employees Retirement Plan.

Regulatory relief

Finally, governments are often asked to utilize or waive their regulatory powers in order to facilitate the building of entertainment related projects. In the 42nd Street redevelopment, for example, Forest City Ratner negotiated a set of "as is" rights as a condition of their entering into the project. This automatically entitled them to a cabaret license, an arcade license and unlimited signage – normally valuable and difficult to obtain privileges in a competitive economic environment. On occasion, the requests for regulatory relief touch on matters which exceed local government powers. In Denver, relocating and expanding Elitch Gardens Amusement Park necessitated a joint agreement of the federal Environmental Protection Agency (EPA) and the Colorado Department of Health which allowed Elitch to cap the new park site with clean fill rather than having to remove the contaminated soil. This reduced the cost from an estimated $10–$12 million to $1.2 million (Stern 1995:13). Before the conversion of the central waterfront in Philadelphia into an entertainment district could proceed, the PIDC approached Congress with the request that it declare the central waterfront "non-navigable." This was necessitated by an obscure federal law which gave the US Army the authority to stop development projects in river areas in cases of national security, thus acting as a deterrent to developers seeking to secure financing since no project could obtain a clear title (Selhat 1995).

Privatizing partnerships:
The rise of business improvement districts

Unlike the standard public–private partnership in which the urban redevelopment authority or other coordinating body is state funded, in some more recent versions the agencies are privately financed. The most common model is the Business Improvement District (BID). The International City/County Management Association has put the number of BIDs in the US at 1,200, with the BID phenomenon beginning to spread in the late 1990s to Europe, the Caribbean, Australia and South Africa.[4] In spirit, BIDs are an updated version of the neighborhood businessmen's associations of the past which promoted commercial activity along main streets by putting up Christmas decorations, sponsoring prizes for the best decorated shop window and by holding "Midnight Madness" sales on warm summer nights. BIDs play a similar role but in addition they have legal status which allows merchants and property owners in commercial districts to tax themselves in order to provide an expanded repertoire of services. Some of these services – street cleaning, garbage pick-ups, security patrols – mimic and even replace city services which have steadily fallen victim to government budget cuts. In other cases, however, BIDs have mounted a much more ambitious program. The Grand Central Partnership, a BID in midtown Manhattan which was established in 1988 and covers over a fifty-three block area, not only employs uniformed street cleaners and security guards and supervises the illumination of Grand Central Station, but it also runs a tourist information booth, sends political lobbyists to the state capitol in Albany and issues its own bonds which are backed by annual levies on building owners within its district. With financial resources approaching $5 million annually, the Grand Central Partnership has been able to assume the role of a non-profit developer; creating outdoor restaurant areas, a pedestrian mall and redesigned streetscapes (Zukin 1995: 33–5).

In their new role as developers, BIDs have begun to embrace urban entertainment in various ways. Zukin charges that they are increasingly prone to follow Disney's lead in identifying theme and style with public order. This means both securing consumption space by limiting public access and controlling visual design, key elements in the success of the Disney theme parks. On 34th Street in Manhattan, for example, the local BID acting on a report commissioned from retail consultants, undertook a campaign in the early 1990s to strictly enforce municipal regulation of signs and setbacks in order to combat the existing jumble of stalls, news-stands, murals and oversized signs which was thought to violate Disney World-style values of cleanliness, security and visual coherence. In Times Square, the BID has transformed its private sanitation force into Disneyesque "cast members" with bright red jumpsuits and caps designed by a theatrical costume designer to match the trash cans (Zukin 1995: 66–7).

In a fourth Manhattan BID, the Alliance for Downtown New York, strategies to make public space more attractive for both tourists and investors have reached a new level. Supported by a self-imposed levy on area business owners and by grants from business and philanthropic foundations, the Alliance has been considering ways of transforming Lower Manhattan from a daytime-only financial district to a round-the-clock residential and tourist location. One plan is to create a high-tech state-of-the-art "heritage trail" which would link-up and create a coherent "tourist cloverleaf" marked out by digital sidewalk guideposts. In addition, the Alliance plans to use part of its war chest as an incubator to stimulate public and private investment in the area. One indicator of the potential financial clout possessed by this $8.6 million BID is its credit rating which amazingly is higher than that of New York itself (Weisbrod 1995).

Creating political acceptance:
Community sensitive UED developments

While municipalities are often asked to bend over backwards to facilitate the construction of entertainment-based projects, private partners too must make certain concessions in order to make their developments more acceptable to community residents. Unlike politicians and planners, the future neighbors of these theme parks, stadiums and arenas, and mixed retail-entertainment complexes do not always enthusiastically embrace these facilities on the basis that they will provide jobs, tax revenues and a new image for the area. More typical is the experience of North Stonington, Connecticut, the potential site of a new theme park in the Six Flags chain,[5] whose citizens have expressed concerns about traffic, noise and air pollution and the protection of the aquifer which supplies water to the town of 5,000 residents (Melvin 1996c).

One response by entertainment companies to such difficulties is to treat locals to a day at other existing venues in their chains. When Six Flags chairman and chief executive officer Larry Bouts sent a letter to each of the 5,000 residents of North Stonington offering them free admission and lunch at Six Flags Great Adventure in Jackson, New Jersey, a three-and-a-half hour drive away, 1,500 residents took up the offer, almost a third of the town (O'Brien 1996e). In a similar fashion, the Triple Five Group sponsored an all-expenses paid trip to the West Edmonton Mall and the Mall of America for nineteen residents and public employees in Montgomery County, Maryland, as part of a public relations program to win over public opinion in favor of their proposed entertainment super-mall "American Dream" (see p. 132). In some cases, however, a more substantive contribution is required.

In communities with sizeable minority populations, project proponents increasingly find it necessary to make provisions for training and hiring quotas of blacks, Hispanics and native people. In order to help create political acceptance and demonstrate a linkage between the project and the surrounding neighborhoods, the convention center authority in Philadelphia created a $10 million fund ($1 million per year) earmarked for a minority jobs training program for the convention center and the adjoining Marriott hotel. In the case of the E Center, the State of New Jersey insisted as a condition of its financial contribution that Pavilion Partners hire most of the workers from the economically depressed city of Camden. In addition, Pavilion Partners agreed to turn over the building eighty nights a year to the non-profit Southern New Jersey Performing Arts Center, which had previously won a $12 million state grant to build its own home in the neighborhood (Takiff 1995)

With the Metreon entertainment center in San Francisco the developers, Millennium Partners, knew from day one that they would have to reach out to the community in order to secure approval. In an earlier phase of the Yerba Buena development, so star-crossed that the journal *Progressive Architecture* proclaimed its opening "nothing less than miraculous" (Woodbridge 1994), the San Francisco Redevelopment Agency (SFRA) and its allied interest groups had initially attempted to displace the existing population of poor residents who were living on welfare in residential hotels in order to build a convention center complex. Refusing to be evicted without a fight, some of the residents established an organization called Tenants and Owners in Opposition to Redevelopment (TOOR). Linking in a common cause with Bay area environmentalists and an angry taxpayers group, TOOR sued the pro-Yerba Buena coalition in federal court for illegal displacement of the residents, only agreeing to drop the litigation in exchange for receiving guarantees of funding for new low-rent housing units, relocation benefits and improved social services (Hartman 1973). Given this legacy of controversy, it was vital that the SFRA rather than the private developer be viewed by the public as managing the construction operation and maintenance of the entertainment center project (Sagalyn 1997: 1961) and that the developer appear sensitive to the concerns of the local community.

To ensure the political survival of the second phase with its fifteen movie screens, IMAX 3-D theater, live performance spaces, restaurants and family attractions, Millenium took on a partner, WDG Companies – a San Francisco-based, minority-controlled firm with twelve years of development experience. Furthermore, the land deal between the developers and the SFRA required that at least half the tenants and construction companies building the center represent women and minority-owned firms. From a short list of architects nominated by the SFRA, the developers selected Cathy Simon of Simon Martin-Vegue Winklestein Moris of San Francisco, one of the largest female-owned US design firms (Wetmore and Sause 1995). Described by SFRA president Jon Henry Kouba as "a real San Francisco-style project" (Levy 1996), the Yerba Buena entertainment complex went farther than most towards the goal of becoming a community sensitive retail-entertainment project.

Public–private partnerships and Urban Economic Growth

In the relentlessly upbeat official discourse promoting the growth of Fantasy City, the benefits of public–private partnerships and the projects they support are rarely called into question. The traditional wisdom, "a rising tide lifts all ships, " seems to be the governing principle and such partnerships are assumed to be in the best interest of the community. Yet, in reality, the downtown landscape is still littered with the remnants of failed experiments – discarded pedestrian malls, struggling festival market places – which have not only neglected to consider the character, history and unique potential of the particular neighborhood and community but also have not delivered the jobs or commercial spin-offs as predicted. Because most UED development is still so recent, it is hard to reliably determine its economic effect. One activity, however, for which there are plenty of statistics is professional sports venues.

Professional sport as entertainment

Sports has become a defining part of our life and culture, infusing a wide range of events, activities and institutions from the social life of high schools and colleges to holiday celebrations. Not everyone is a sports fan, but enough people are so that professional sports have taken the role of a common cultural currency – around the office water cooler, in taxi cabs and on the street. In her study of cultural knowledge in the private security industry, sociologist Bonnie Erickson (1996) found that, beyond work itself, the primary source of cultural capital (see Chapter 4) among those in her sample was a knowledge of popular sports personalities. Unlike fast-food restaurants which are much utilized but little discussed, sports provides something to talk about, regardless of class position. Winning a championship is one of the few occasions when people from all walks of life spill out into the streets in a spontaneous urban celebration, followed by an official parade.

Considering the extraordinary value that our society places on sports personalities, facilities and consumer products, it is not suprising that these should be an integral part of the developing Fantasy City. "Comeback cities" such as Baltimore, Cleveland and Denver have all recently constructed open-air baseball stadiums with natural grass surfaces designed to evoke the ambience of the intimate ballparks of yesteryear, situating them in downtown entertainment areas. Miami's soon to be built new arena which will house the Miami Heat professional basketball team will be part of a 70-acre development near the expanded port area which is to include ships, restaurants and parks. Skydome, Toronto's domed baseball stadium with a retractable roof is right in the middle of the city's entertainment district with its sports bars and cafes, collectibles stores (selling sports cards and other memorabilia) and even the Hockey Hall of Fame. Plans are currently underway to build both a major UED development next to the stadium as well as a combined hockey–basketball arena at the eastern flank of this district. Even Yankee Stadium, a long-time baseball shrine in the blue-collar environs of the Bronx, is rumored to be heading for a new location either in the New Jersey sports-entertainment complex or in midtown Manhattan where, as the New York Times notes, "its value as a mecca for tourists and visitors from around the country and from the suburbs who are looking for entertainment in the context of an urban experience would be enhanced" ("West Side Yankees" 1996).

Furthermore, sports culture spills over into a number of other aspects of life in Fantasy City. The Official All Star Sports Cafe, the newest member of entrepreneur Robert Earle's roster of themed restaurants, is decorated with sports memorabilia and counts many well-known atheletes among its group of celebrity investors. The ESPN theme restaurant, which draws its inspiration from the US cable television channel specializing in sports coverage, is now one of the top draws at the World of Disney resort in Orlando. Wayne Gretsky, the Canadian hockey player who almost single-handedly sold hockey to star-besotted Los Angeles and who now reigns triumphant in New York, is active in a multiplicity of urban projects from Wayne Gretsky's restaurant in Toronto's theater district to "Wayne Gretsky's Iceland," a chain of sports facilities which include ice rinks, virtual reality games, fitness facilities, training clinics, a children's lounge and a sports bar offering instant video replays of in-house events (Macdonald 1995). Las Vegas, the world's biggest theme park, has for a long time featured championship boxing matches at its casinos, although a recent attempt to bring a Canadian Football League franchise to Las Vegas was not successful. Indeed, along with motion pictures, sport has become one of the leading sources of theming and branding in Fantasy City. As I mentioned in Chapter 5, Niketown in Manhattan is a trendsetter in the world of "shopertainment," with its clever mix of nostalgia and high-technology. Sports Realm in Baltimore is a key component in the second generation of waterfront retail-entertainment development in that city. Sportsplex, Sheldon Gordon's reworking of the Galleria in Scottsdale, Arizona, promises to be a creative amalgam of sports theme retailing, entertainment and showmanship.

Equally, the sporting events themselves have incorporated large amounts of entertainment components. Jumbo scoreboards in stadiums and arenas have become entertainment centers with a selection of video games, fan contests and other events which sometimes overshadow the action. Between periods or at half-time sports teams put on increasingly lavish shows complete with laser light effects and special sound systems. Even the singing of the national anthem becomes an opportunity for established and would-be celebrities to take a star turn. Each year, the union of sports and entertainment peaks at the Superbowl where the on-field extravaganza (in 1996 it was a Cajun-themed spectacular with country singer Mary Chapin Carpenter and a supporting cast of singers and dancers) is matched by the advertising on television which features such stars as Michael Jackson.

Chasing franchises

Among urban politicians and business people, it is widely perceived that a city without a professional sports team and a first-rate facility quickly falls outside the mainstream (Rosentraub 1996). As a result, cities court and are courted by sports franchise owners. Since the number of applications normally outstrips the number of available franchises, owners have frequently been able to play one city off against another, sometimes even engaging in bidding wars. Teams frequently change names and locations. In 1984 the Baltimore Colts, a football franchise once quarterbacked by the legendary Johnny Unitas, became the Indianapolis Colts. A decade later, the Cleveland Browns left town for Baltimore, as had the St Louis Browns baseball team forty-one years earlier. With their Browns now morphed into the Baltimore Ravens, Cleveland has been promised a new team sometime before 1999, the name as yet undetermined. Similarly, Nashville voters approved new tax initiatives worth $80 million to fund a football stadium to house the team currently playing as the Houston Oilers. The Oakland Raiders left for Los Angeles and then returned to Oakland; while Los Angeles' other football team, the Rams, are on the move to St Louis.

Typical of the 1990s version of this "sports franchise game" (Shropshire 1995) are the maneuvers associated with another professional football team, the Seattle Seahawks. The Seahawks joined the National Football League in 1976 and have been playing since that time in the King Dome, a domed facility which is generally regarded as dreary and earthquake unsafe. During the winter

Table 7.2 New major league sports venues opened 1996–98

Facility/location	Cost (US$m)	Major tenants
Core States Center (Philadelphia)	200	NBA 76ers, NHL Flyers
Bank One Ballpark (Phoenix)	187	MLB Phoenix Diamondbacks
Carolinas Stadium	184	NFL Carolina Panthers
Broward County Civic Arena (Sunrise, Florida)	172	NHL Florida Panthers
Cookes Stadium (Landover, Maryland)	150	NFL Redskins
MCI Center (Washington, DC)	150	NBA Wizards/NHL Capitols
Pepsi Center (Denver, Colarado)	150	NBA Nuggets/NHL Colorado Avalanche
Ice Palace (Tampa, Florida)	125	NHL Lightning
Marine Midland Arena (Buffalo, New York)	123	NHL Sabres
Nashville Arena (Nashville, Tennesse)	120	TBA

Source: Amusement Business, 24 June 1996, p. 18; 16 June 1997, pp. 14, 16
Key: MLB (Major League Baseball); NBA (National Basketball Association); NFL (National Football League).

1996, Seahawk owner Ken Behring, a California developer who bought the team in 1988, was reported by the local press as going on a shopping expedition for a new city for his franchise. Fueling his tour of Los Angeles and Orange County was the decision by King County to build a new baseball-only stadium for the Seattle Mariners who previously had been sharing the King Dome with the Seahawks. One plan on offer was Anaheim's idea to create "Sportstown," a $1 billion sports and entertainment complex just two miles away from the gates of Disneyland. At the center of Sportstown would be a 70,000 seat football stadium which would house the former Seattle Seahawks. According to a city spokesperson, "What we want to do is basically redefine how people are entertained . . . and convince people to spend all their entertainment dollars in Anaheim" (Serrano 1996).

Enter Paul Allen. The co-founder of the Microsoft Corporation and the eighth richest man in the world, Allen, who lives in a compound on Mercer Island, already owns a professional sports team – the Portland Trail Blazers of the National Basketball Association. With the Seahawks' fate up in the air, Allen acceded to requests from local politicians and business leaders and agreed to buy the team but only if the financing for a new $425 million stadium was approved in a statewide referendum. So as to ensure the vote was held, Allen agreed to foot the $4.2 million cost of the election. And to ensure that the voters approved the proposal, stadium backers through a pro-stadium group called "Our Team Works" poured $3 million into an intensive TV advertising campaign. The financing package on which Washington state residents voted specified that money for the stadium would come from special lottery games, taxes on stadium admissions and parking, various sales tax credits and deferrals and an eight-year extension of the 2 percent hotel room tax in King County (Goldberg 1997). On election day, 17 July 1997, the plan barely scraped through with the yes votes outnumbering the no votes by a margin of 50 percent to 49 percent.

Why is it so important for cities such as Seattle to keep its sports franchises? Euchner (1993) argues that it's not a case of economics, but rather the symbolic significance they come to represent. In communities which are otherwise fragmented by class, race and ethnicity, sport constitutes a common denominator, the last remaining point of identification. Granted, this may be a "contrived community" (Smith 1979) which conveniently papers over important social conflicts and inequalities but nevertheless it has a strong political hold. Forty years after owner Walter O'Malley moved the Brooklyn Dodgers baseball team to the West Coast,[6] their demise is still lamented among New Yorkers and no mayor with any political sense would ever permit the Yankees or the Mets to relocate outside the city.

Be that as it may, academics, policymakers and politicians still continue to ask whether it is economically viable for cities and towns to spend billions of dollars for the financing and construction of stadiums and arenas to be used by professional sports teams.

Justifying economic subsidies to professional sports

With a few exceptions, it is fair to say that professional sports teams have generally had a less positive economic effect on the urban economy than one might expect. One of the most outspoken advocates of this conclusion has been Mark Rosentraub, an urban policy professor at Indiana University. In his definitive book on the subject, *Major League Losers*, Rosentraub (1997: 3) makes the charge that "a welfare system exists in this country that transfers hundreds of millions of dollars from taxpayers to wealthy investors and their extraordinarily well-paid employees." Rosentraub, of course, is referring to the hefty subsidies demanded by professional sports team owners in order to keep their franchise in town. This subsidy system is regressive in two ways. First, only one of the partners in the relationship – the team – shares in any revenues or profits earned from the operation of the stadium or arena. Second, while team owners pass on the cost of investment to fans who attend games, the public sector partner must ask the tax-paying public-at-large to support the facility through higher taxes.

In a steady stream of studies which he has conducted since the late 1980s, economist Robert Baade (1988; 1990; 1994; 1996a; 1996b) has consistently reported that there are few instances of a correlation between a city's adoption of a team or construction of a stadium and increases in real per capita income – a finding remarkably similar to that of Levine on the effects of waterfront development in Baltimore (see Chapter 3). Furthermore, both Baade (1990) and another sports economist Roger Noll (1974) have suggested that rather than creating new sources of leisure dollars, what in fact happens is a realignment of consumer spending. This means that individuals and families simply shift around a fixed amount of time and money for leisure activities. Does it matter, Baade (1996b: 36) asks, whether a city derives its tax revenues from sports entertainment or from recreation provided by the local theater?

More justification for granting economic subsidies to sports teams may be evident if one factors in activities which economists term "intangibles." In a 1996 report on the impact of major league baseball teams on the local economy of Chicago, it is estimated that a Chicago baseball franchise produces about $3 million worth of intangible benefits in an average year and up to $11 million in a peak year, that is, a championship season. Intangibles here are described as indirect publicity and media exposure such as name recognition and television footage of the city skyline and other local attractions (City of Chicago 1986). In 1995, documents designed to support the case for building the new Washington Redskins football stadium in Prince Georges County in suburban Maryland, the late Jack Kent Cooke claimed, perhaps with some degree of hyperbole, that each US citizen would, on average, read about the facility thirty-five times a year (Leonhardt 1997).

Less quantifiable but also important are other intangibles such as creating a sense of excitement and civic pride. Referring to the new Gateway entertainment complex in Cleveland which includes Jacobs Field (baseball), and the Gund Arena (basketball), Rosentraub (1996: 26) concedes that even if the 4.6 million visitors each year to sporting and other events do not generate any new jobs or downtown development, they do make the downtown area a livelier place. Furthermore, Gateway has helped to establish the city's reputation and image, neither of which were very positive in the days when Cleveland was better known as the site of the Cuyahoga River which became so polluted with industrial waste that it once caught fire.

In addition to its image benefits, it is also possible that the excitement generated by civic campaigns to keep sports teams in town may create the illusion of economic success, thus holding together and energizing a civic coalition which then goes on to undertake other, potentially more useful, redevelopment efforts. In Indianapolis, for example, there is some evidence that public–private partnerships created to retain the Colts (football) and Ravens (basketball) teams helped to maintain the coalition and attract new members, thus generating a sense of vitality that contributed to and maintained a two-decade long focus on downtown development (Rosentraub 1997: 239).

Despite their symbolic value, however, professional sports teams and facilities rarely constitute a good financial deal for the city. Contrary to the hype, professional sports franchises are essentially small-scale businesses, which account for no more than half of 1 percent of jobs or salaries in any urban county with 300,000 or more residents, this compares against other leisure facilities such as restaurants and bars which provide nearly 7 percent of jobs and manufacturing which continue to account for about 17 percent of employment (Rosentraub 1997: 143). With only about 100 full-time, year-round employees, a sports team produces approximately the level of employment equivalent to that of a large department store (Perez-Pena 1997: 31). By contrast, casinos are far greater sources of revenue. While the most successful teams in professional sports, the New York Yankees and the Dallas Cowboys normally bring in around $100 million in annual revenue, visitor inputs into Clark County, the site of the Las Vegas casinos and hotels, topped $20 billion in 1995. As the experiences of Atlantic City, and of the various cities which have hosted riverboat casinos have shown, Las Vegas may be unique in this regard but even here the numbers are often larger than is the case for major league sports teams.

In short, there are plenty of reasons to be cautious in rushing to embrace the economic benefits of sports and other entertainment venues in Fantasy City, especially where the public partners in these projects may end up liable for a hefty percentage of the development costs. Still, as Fainstein (1994: 141) has pointed out, rather than totally dismiss public–private partnerships on moral grounds, it makes more sense to ensure that the public component has a greater degree of control and shares more in the proceeds. What this means is that cities are well within their bounds to firmly say 'no thanks' to major league team owners and other leisure merchants who attempt to strongarm communities into taking on bad deals just to get or keep sports franchises, casinos and the like. At the same time, entrepreneurial public–private partnerships can some-times function positively, especially where there are controls in place to ensure that the public sector will gain from its involvement (Fainstein 1994: 136).

Figure 8.1 "Theming Las Vegas style": New York New York hotel-casino, Las Vegas.
Source: Ruth Hannigan.

8

GAMBLING ON FANTASY

Las Vegas, casinos and urban entertainment

Of the thirty-two films to star Elvis Presley[1] one of the most successful was *Viva Las Vegas* (1964). Playing an aspiring auto-racing champion who is forced by circumstance to work as a bellhop, Elvis, together with romantic foil Ann-Margret, take Vegas by storm framed by a succession of glitzy backdrops – neon-lit casinos, poolside patios and even the Hoover Dam. It soon became a case of art imitating life: from 1969 until his death in 1977, Elvis was the king of Las Vegas, playing the Hilton (formerly the International Hotel) in month-long gigs, three to four times a year. Twice a night, clad in his trademark white-studded jumpsuit, The King would reprise his movie persona singing "Viva Las Vegas" to standing-room-only crowds. Likewise, Ann-Margret was known as the "Queen of the Strip," headlining at the Riviera Hotel in a show which began with a production number featuring twelve motorcycles. Both Elvis and Ann-Margret had hotel suites named after them – Elvis at the Las Vegas Hilton and Ann-Margret at Caesar's Palace – a privilege reserved exclusively for the two stars of *Viva Las Vegas* (Graham 1989: 128–9; 178).

Over the years Elvis' Las Vegas has taken on American icon status – with its neon cowboys, topless showgirl revues, quickie marriages in the Chapel of Love and nightclub acts starring headliners such as Wayne Newton and Tom Jones. It became the favorite stomping ground for the boisterous antics of the Hollywood "Rat Pack" – Frank Sinatra, Dean Martin, Peter Lawford, Shirley Maclaine and Sammy Davis, Jnr. Championship boxing matches were often staged there with an impressive turnout of sports and show business celebrities. America during the 1960s, wrote cultural historian William Weathersby (1994), " was on a spending spree and Vegas was its luxurious playground."

By the mid-1970s, however, Las Vegas had begun to lose some of its appeal. The younger generation was more likely to head to stadiums and arenas[2] to see rock bands like the Grateful Dead and Santana than to the casino nightclubs to see Sinatra and his fellow crooners. Risqué floor shows were not only becoming more expensive to stage but they had joined beauty contests on the hit-list of the burgeoning women's movement. In 1976, Las Vegas' virtual monopoly over casino gambling was broken when the State of New Jersey licensed Atlantic City as a gaming center.

Twenty years later, Las Vegas is once again booming. There are so many new projects underway that, as urban critic Mike Davis (1995) has noted, it resembles "a vast highway construction site." Recently, Las Vegas celebrated the opening of its one-hundred-thousandth hotel room, a milestone unmatched anywhere else in the world. Among the projects being built at the time of writing this book, are: Bellagio, a $1.4 billion version of a northern Italian resort complete with its own $30 million 12-acre artificial lake set on the grounds of the former Dunes Hotel; Paris, a 2,500 room hotel and casino which will stand out thanks to a 50-storey replica of the Eiffel Tower and other Parisian landmarks such as the Arc de Triomphe and the Champs Elysees; and Paradise, a $1 billion tropically-themed casino, hotel, retail and entertainment complex opposite Circus Circus to be operated by seven different gaming companies.

Inspired by the example of Las Vegas, cash-strapped cities and towns around the world are turning to legalized gambling as a revenue source. With its seventy-three licensed casinos, Moscow has become not only the political capital but also the gaming capital of the new Russia. With a dash of historical irony, it was announced that American actor Chuck Norris, the star of *Walker, Texas Ranger* and, during the Cold War, a string of anti-Communist action films such as *Invasion USA*, would be opening Chuck Norris' Supper Club and Casino – a six storey, $20 million complex in Red Square (Cashill 1996b). Post-apartheid South Africa has just enacted a National Gambling Act which will legalize casinos throughout the unified country (previously they were legal only in the black "homelands"). Already most of the big gaming companies – MGM Grand, Hilton Hotels, ITT Corporation – have been exploring casino-resort opportunities in South Africa in conjunction with heavily capitalized local partners.

In the US, dozens of riverboat casinos have dropped anchor in Illinois, Indiana, Iowa, Louisiana, Mississippi and Missouri, and tribal-run casinos are thriving in Connecticut, Michigan, Minnesota, South Dakota and in several Canadian provinces. Colorado has become a center for limited-stake gambling. A host of other gambling activities are spreading rapidly, although not without some fierce opposition: video lotteries, electronic gambling machines in bars and convenience stores, off-track telewagering theaters (one is being built several blocks from where I live in Toronto as part of a future residential development package). This "new landscape of luck," as Robert Goodman (1995: 1) describes it, is backed by sophisticated state-of-the-art marketing, shaped by "theming" consultants who create mythical dream worlds and plotted by demographic experts who target the socioeconomic profiles of potential players.

While Las Vegas constitutes a fantasyland in itself, it has recently begun to merge and morph with Disney-style theme park entertainment as well as incorporating the leading themed restaurant concepts. Some observers have declared Las Vegas unique, insisting that it can't and won't be imitated. But others see it as a template for urban entertainment in the next millennium. Doug Trumball, the designer of the "Back to the Future" ride, ventures that "in Las Vegas you

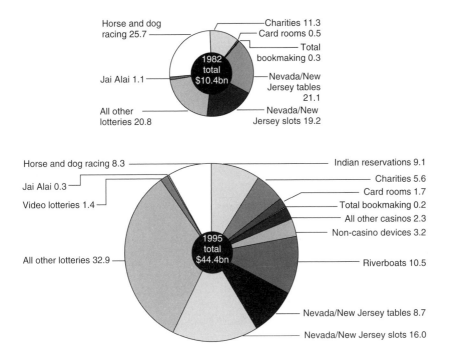

Figure 8.2 Gambling growth in the United States, 1982–95: gross revenues by industry, % of total.

Source: 'A busted flush' (1997). © The Economist Newspaper Group, Inc. Reprinted with permission. Further reproduction prohibited.

will see things happening that are far in advance of anything in Orlando or Hollywood. What's going on there . . . gives us a glimpse of what we will see everywhere" (Provost 1994: 253).

One major aspect of what's going on in Las Vegas is the rise of themed attractions both within and outside of the casinos. In Buccaneer's Bay, a $30 million artificial lagoon outside the Treasure Island casino-hotel, a full scale naval battle is staged four times a day between a Spanish galleon and a British frigate. Next door at the Mirage, a volcano blows its top with perfect regularity in an outdoor setting of waterfalls and lagoons. One of my favorites is the "Show in the Sky" in Masquerade Village, a food, entertainment and gaming center at the Rio Suites Hotel and Casino just off Las Vegas Boulevard. On a 950 foot-long track suspended 13 feet above the casino floor, a parade progresses complete with floats and bands celebrating carnivals in New Orleans, Venice and Rio. Perhaps the most patrician themed space in the city is the Forum Shops, a Roman-themed shopping street crowned by a vaulted ceiling painted to look like a natural sky whose appearance is changed by computerized lighting

Do as the Romans do

Imagine it's the year 2010. You have impetuously decided to escape the never-ending crush of deadlines at your home office for a weekend of fun in Las Vegas. It's been years since you were last there, but the place everyone recommends is the venerable casino-hotel Caesar's Palace, once again in the limelight for its amazing Forum Shops. Fifteen years ago, in 1995, the Forum Shops had essentially been an upmarket shopping center leading into Caesar's Palace, albeit unlike any other mall in America. With its Roman-themed shopping street, animatronic statues found in The Festival Fountain, and, the most spectacular of all, a hand-painted sky ceiling featuring computerized lighting to emulate the different periods of the day, the Forum Shops had always been an unique experience. Now, with the completion of the second and third phases, it is the talk of the Las Vegas Strip.

On your approach to the entrance to Caesar's Palace, you discover on one side a cul-de-sac which is approximately two blocks long and is lined with stores and restaurants. At the far end is a Roman-style court where an eight-minute show is about to take place. Just like in Disney films, inanimate objects are magically transformed and are able to speak. The Festival Fountain announces that Caesar will shortly ascend to the throne of the Emperor. Within minutes, Caesar himself arrives at the court with his Roman guard and invites onlookers to his coronation in the Great Hall.

The Great Hall is enormous – measuring 100 feet in diameter, 90 feet high and with a capacity for 3,000 guests. Here, too, inanimate objects speak, notably the oracle figures located in the four columns, which can also turn and, together with a large obelisk, recede into the fountain. All of a sudden, a huge throne arises out of the center of the 20 foot high aquarium. Animatronic figures also emerge: Atlas and his two children and Poseidon. When Caesar announces that neither of Atlas' offspring is fit to rule Rome, the room appears to explode. Flames shoot up; water seems to cascade from the ceiling creating a sensation that the room is sinking.

Beyond the Great Hall is a building which resembles a Roman forum. On entering, you look up and see a Roman hill town complete with a three-dimensional sky projected from above and below. Like the Great Hall, the forum is also immense: the size of two football fields and 100 feet high. Not only are there shops and restaurants in the town, but on the floor of the forum is a Roman "pleasure faire" with jugglers, magicians, musicians and stalls. Its easy to "do as the Romans do" in this fantasy space as togas and masks are on sale which you can wear to the Roman-style Mardi Gras that takes place every night until two in the morning. And, of course, if this isn't enough there's always the action in the casino.

Source: Gordon (1995)

devices to emulate the passage of the sun from midday to dusk (see "Do as the Romans do" p. 154).

Casino capital: Ownership Consolidation and change in the gaming industry

As in the case of real estate development and the entertainment industries, in recent years there has been a notable shift in the gaming industry away from ownership by a clutch of colorful individual entrepreneurs towards a more muted corporate-style control. This is not to say that there aren't a number of flamboyant, controversial types in the casino world – Donald Trump, Steve Wynn and Kirk Kerkorian are just three who stand out – but increasingly they are the exception rather than the rule.

The early history of casino gambling in the state of Nevada reveals a collection of visionary, if often erratic figures. Prior to the Second World War, one of the leading purveyors of gaming action in Reno, which overshadowed the smaller Las Vegas scene until the 1950s, was Raymond I. Smith. Smith, a former carnival showman who founded and managed Harold's Club, the first Nevada casino to attempt to lure customers through creating entertainment experiences, is remembered today for his ethically dubious, but initially successful, marketing ploy of putting a mouse instead of a silver ball on the casino's roulette wheel. Another colorful promoter was former Texas bootlegger Benny Binion, proprietor of Binion's Horseshoe casino, who among other things initiated the practice of giving away cocktails to customers. As a publicity stunt, Binion once put a million dollars in $10,000 bills on display in the lobby of the Horseshoe. Las Vegas lore also includes the gangster, Benjamin "Bugsy" Siegel, memorialized by Warren Beatty in the movie *Bugsy*. Together with "Billy" Wilkenson, Siegel founded the Flamingo, the first casino to feature big-name nightclub entertainment. He is also credited with moving the casino scene away from downtown Las Vegas to the Strip. Unfortunately, Bugsy Siegel met an untimely end, murdered allegedly on the order of organized crime bosses who were not happy with his considerable overspending on construction costs at the Flamingo. Finally there was Howard Hughes, the eccentric and reclusive billionaire who bought a full house of casinos (Frontier, Landmark, Silver

Slipper, Sands, Desert Inn) in the 1970s, thereby enhancing Las Vegas' reputation as a hot spot of money and celebrity.

Casino ownership was radically altered in 1969 by a decision taken by the State of Nevada which made corporate ownership permissible.[3] While this initially opened the door to Hughes' Summa Corporation to become the largest corporate owner of gaming operations in the state, a more significant result was the entry of several large hotel chains – the Hilton, the Sheraton (through its parent company ITT Corporation) and the Pratt Hotel Corporation. These experienced hospitality providers had the advantage of operating worldwide reservation services through which they could snag potential customers for their casino-hotels. Furthermore, they brought a strong measure of legitimacy to an industry which had suffered for years from an association with criminal activity. So as to emphasize this recently acquired respectability, a new corporate name was given to gambling – "gaming." [4]

Further corporate respectability was achieved through the decision of a number of Las Vegas casinos to turn to the stock market in order to obtain new investment capital. In 1971, Bill Harrah, a major casino-resort owner in northern Nevada, went public with 13 percent of his holdings, raising $4 million. He was eventually followed by Circus Circus Enterprises, Caesar's World Inc. and others. Ironically, much of the growth in casino securities in the 1980s was kick-started by the future junk bond king Michael Milken who as an up-and-coming salesman at Drexel-Burnham in the 1970s had put together a $100 million issue of high-yield debentures for Ramada Inns Inc., owners of the Tropicana hotels in Las Vegas and Atlantic City (Provost 1994: 214–15). Later, in 1980, Steve Wynn built the Atlantic City version of the Golden Nugget on a raft of junk bonds floated by Milken, using the Golden Nugget in Las Vegas as collateral (Christenson 1997: 9).

In the 1990s, the corporatization of casino gambling has taken a new direction. In the same way as a series of mergers, acquisitions and takeovers in the communications industry has culled the field while creating a small number of major corporate players – Time-Warner, Viacom, Disney – the gaming industry has consolidated, even as the boom in the construction of new resorts and attractions has continued. According to one insider, Glen Schaeffer, president and chief executive of Circus Circus Enterprises, "there are too many public casino companies for the set of opportunities available over the next few years . . . five or six companies in gaming are going to determine the future of the industry" (Orwall 1996b: A-1).

Initially these "opportunities" were expected to expand geographically like wildfire, but voter opposition has been consistently more widespread than expected. Pro-casino initiatives have been defeated at the ballot box in more than thirty states since 1994 including Florida, Connecticut, Massachusetts, Rhode Island, Wyoming and New York. As community disenchantment with gambling magnifies, the casino owners have strategically retreated to Las Vegas and Atlantic City, their two long-time home bases. Growth, it has been decreed, will occur both through the building of new mega-sized destination resorts like Bellagio and Paradise, and through the acquisition of mid-size casino companies with key locations along the Strip and on the Boardwalk. Already, Hilton has acquired Bally Entertainment Corporation, owners of Bally's Las Vegas. Bally's, weakened by over financing and by competition from Excalibur, a 4,000 room medieval-themed hotel which opened in June 1990, had committed itself to building a new project, "Paris," on 25 acres adjoining its existing casino. However, as its CEO Arthur Goldberg told the *Wall Street Journal*, "after the takeover, we build it with 6% money rather than 12% money" (Orwall 1996b: A-10), a testament to the lower cost casino capital available to the Big Five gambling companies: Circus Circus Enterprises Inc., Hilton Hotels Corporation, Mirage Resorts Inc., MGM Grand Inc. and Harrah's Entertainment Inc.

One casualty of the spread in borrowing rates has been the $550 million Stratosphere Tower hotel and casino. Badly situated at the downtown end of the Strip,[5] the Stratosphere has the dubious honor of being the first large-scale flop in the "New Las Vegas." Grand Casinos Inc., the Minnesota-based company who own the Stratosphere, financed its completion by selling $203 million in notes at an effective interest rate exceeding 19 percent, making it a nearly fatal millstone around the company's neck when attendance failed to meet expected levels (Orwall 1996b).

Rolling on the river: The turbulent career of riverboat gambling

One of the most colorful historical images associated with the American South is the sight of a paddleboat steamer chugging down the Mississippi, while below deck a party of high-stakes gamblers in string ties and cowboy boots bluff and bet their way to Nachez and New Orleans. The film *Maverick*, based on the popular 1960s television series of the same name, celebrated this period with Mel Gibson, James Garner and Jodie Foster as a trio of wheeler-dealers immersed in a make-or-break poker game on a riverboat.

Contemporary riverboat gambling had it beginnings in the state of Iowa[6] which licensed two riverboats – one in Dubuque and one in Davenport. The initial success of these floating casinos generated a rolling wave of competition up and down the Mississippi River. Riverboat gambling was the final piece in an economic revitalization strategy which, in the 1980s, had seen the legalization of lotteries and of horse and dog tracks in a state which had been battered by recession, manufacturing losses and plummeting farm income.

So as to assuage any fears of Iowa becoming the new setting for Las Vegas- or Atlantic City-style gambling, The Excursion Gambling Boat Act of March 1989 spelt out a set of conditions for licensing. Bets were limited to $5 each; players could not exceed a maximum loss of $200 per excursion; poker was not allowed; and only 30 percent of floor space on a boat could be given over to gambling. It was, at least initially, more of an attempt to sell Mark Twain nostalgia to what local promoters thought would be a tourist rush than it was an appeal to the serious gambler. In a remarkably appropriate match, the *Diamond Queen* was launched as America's first modern-day riverboat casino on April 1 1991 by Howard Keel who had played a gambler in the film version of the Broadway musical *Showboat* in 1951 and Vanna White from the television game show *Wheel of Fortune*, once the subject of a music parody by Weird Al Yankovic.

However, Iowa's naïveté soon became apparent. Unlike Las Vegas where the majority of visitors to casino-hotels are out-of-state tourists, Iowa's riverboat patrons were locals who specifically went to gamble. Recognizing this, the neighboring state of Illinois passed the Illinois Riverboat Gambling Act in 1990 allowing poker as well as just about every other type of betting activity, a reflection of a local political culture that had always been both pragmatic and opportunistic (Haley and Truitt 1995).

To the south, the State of Mississippi brought in riverboat gambling with a set of liberal conditions which set no limit on the type of game, the size of individual bets, total player losses or number of casinos. By spring 1995, Mississippi had attracted thirty-one riverboats, nine of them in Tunica located in one of the thirty poorest counties in the US. Three other states – Lousiana, Indiana and Missouri – also jumped aboard, creating the potential for a riverboat jam.

Iowa was the first to feel the heat of competition when the *Diamond Lady* and its sister ship the *Emerald Lady* left for Biloxi, Mississippi in 1992 after a forced settlement with the city of Fort Madison only a year after first being floated. Within two years, the Mississippi riverboat gambling market was saturated. Bell Casinos Inc. filed for Chapter 11 bankruptcy in August; Palace Casinos Inc. sought protection from its creditors in bankruptcy court in December and a third, Treasure Bay, defaulted by the year's end. Another riverboat owner, President Riverboat Casinos Inc., announced plans in July 1994 to relocate to the Iowa–Nebraska border (Labalme 1995). This decision was no doubt influenced by the lifting of restrictions by the State of Iowa which removed betting and loss limits on its riverboats, allowed them to operate around the clock, legalized new games, relaxed the limit on how much space was allowed for gambling and reduced the required cruising hours.

Whereas the riverboats along the Mississippi were stripped-down operations catering primarily to local markets, a plan proposed by Chicago mayor, Richard M. Daley, in June 1993 was far more ambitious. Chicago had initially been shut out of the riverboat gambling rush by 1990 legislation which encouraged riverboat gambling in smaller communities such as Joliet, Illinois, but kept it out of the big cities. Chicago now tried to jump into the fray: Daley proposed to create a $800 million entertainment district on 150 acres along the Chicago River. The planned complex included up to five riverboats with a total of 6,000 gaming positions together with an entertainment center boasting high-tech, movie-based, virtual reality attractions, "similar to Epcot Center or Universal

Studios in Florida."[7] It would, claimed Mayor Daley's assistant Diane Aigotti, bring an additional $3 billion a year in tourist revenue and 14–18,000 new jobs to Chicago.[8] Chicago's entertainment center would also contribute generously to city and state coffers: the proposal called for a 25 percent state gaming tax (shared 75 percent to the State of Illinois and 25 percent to the city of Chicago), a city "franchise" fee of 8 percent, a "special service entertainment district fee" (to compensate the city for providing public services), a $2 admission fee to be split between the city and the state, a $6 admission surcharge to be allocated to the Chicago Board of Education, and an additional $1 admission surcharge, half of which would be used to compensate existing municipalities with riverboat casinos for lost business and half to do the same for the horse racing industry.[9] With such an array of taxes and surcharges, Chicago's erstwhile gaming entertainment district effectively priced itself out of the market; gaming venues in Colorado, for example, are taxed at a rate of 15 percent while Nevada levies a 6.25 percent tax on gambling with no state, individual or corporate income tax.

Riverboat casinos have generally encountered rapids rather than plain sailing. Promoted as a fertile source of employment, riverboat casinos have been a big disappointment. In Tunica, Mississippi, a community so poor that it has been called "America's Ethiopia," most of the casino-related jobs went to residents of nearby Memphis while the local crime rates skyrocketed (Shapiro *et al.* 1996: 56). A study by Earl L. Grinols, an economist at the University of Illinois at Champaign, concluded that they had little discernible impact on reducing unemployment levels (Grinols 1994). Similarly, the riverboat casinos have not acted as effective catalysts for the revival of local economies. Owners of businesses near Harrah's casino in Joliet, Illinois quickly discovered that riverboat customers rarely venture further than the casino parking lot. Even pawn shops suffer since gamblers prefer to use automatic teller machines (Shapiro 1996: 56). The only new downtown business to open in Joliet, reported the *Boston Globe*, was a small, take-out coffee shop (Goodman 1995 29). On their travels throughout the state of Mississippi in 1993–94, Peter Tarlow and Mitchell Muesham (1996) reported some new growth of restaurants and hotels in riverboat communities but they also were told by various attraction managers that senior citizen tour buses were being diverted from local sites to the casinos.

By 1995, the riverboat gambling business had reached saturation point and casinos were beginning to relocate or go bankrupt. One report by investment brokers Salomon Brothers Inc. estimated a 54 percent drop in operating profits at riverboat casinos in Mississippi between 1993 and 1996. As a number of the small operations founder, the Las Vegas casino companies have begun to move in looking for bargains. For example, the medium-sized Boyd Gaming Corporation of Las Vegas entered the Illinois market through its acquiring the East Peoria riverboat operator Par-a-Dice Gaming Corporation, while Mirage, despite its vow to stick to its casinos in Nevada and New Jersey, is building the

Beau Rivage, a $500 million riverboat project in Biloxi, Mississippi which is scheduled to open in December 1998 and seems likely to squeeze out the remaining small operators.

Golden reservations: Casino gambling on tribal lands

An altogether more successful venture than the riverboats in non-traditional gambling areas has been the casinos operated by Canadian and American Indian tribes. In the US, this dates back to 1986 when the Supreme Court ruled that the State of California had no legal authority to close a native-run bingo operation since the Native American band was deemed a "sovereign nation." Two years later, the Federal Government adopted the Federal Indian Gaming Regulatory Act which permitted gaming on tribal lands in states which allowed it, although the legal power of individual states to regulate Native American casinos on tribal land remains cloudy.

Since 1989, 184 tribes in twenty-six states have opted to offer some form of Vegas-style gambling, but only about two dozen of these are larger, high-traffic facilities. In New Mexico, for example, six traditional Indian pueblos located within an hour's drive of Santa Fe, a tourist magnet which in 1992 was voted the number one destination by readers of *Condé Nast Traveler*, operate full-scale casinos, helping to generate $200 million a year in gaming revenues (Johnson 1996). Other hotbeds of tribal casinos are Wisconsin and Minnesota. The latter is unusual in that it is the site of an urban gaming operator, the Fond-du-Luth Casino, jointly operated by a Chippewa Native American tribe and the city of Duluth on downtown land occupied by a Sears outlet. After a shaky start in 1988, the casino brought in over $32 million in profits by 1991 (Pagano and Bowman 1995: 120). According to figures from the General Accounting Office, Native American gaming in the US generated gross revenues of nearly $4.5 billion in 1996, earning it the sobriquet among some tribes as the "new buffalo" (K. Pollack 1996). It is important to note, however, that eight of the larger facilities accounted for 40 percent of the $4.5 billion (Alvarez 1997), the rest being much smaller operations which typically employ no more than forty to a hundred people.

The most profitable of these is the Foxwoods Resort Casino, opened by the Mashantucket Pequot Indians on their 2,000-acre reservation near Ledyard, Connecticut. The largest casino in the US, it draws over 50,000 visitors daily to its 200,000 square feet of gambling space. Foxwoods is at the center of a market area population of just over 27 million, 50 percent larger than the market area for Atlantic City.[10] Equally significant is the fact that the adjoining state of New York does not allow casino gambling, making Foxwoods the only location[11] at present within easy commuting distance.[12] Foxwoods is also unique in that it is the only casino outside Nevada and New Jersey to have enthusiastically embraced themed entertainment. As opposed to the symphonic-scale extravaganzas of Las Vegas, Foxwoods has brought in smaller-scale location-based entertainment products supplied by Iwerks Entertainment of Burbank, California. Iwerks' package has four components, each using a different technology: a giant screen auditorium which can feature film or live action; a simulation theater in which three different films can be shown; "virtual adventures" such as riding with "Robo-Cop" or battling aliens; and a 360-degree dance club with a changing collage of music videos and customized electronic displays. Unlike the larger Vegas shows, these location-based entertainment attractions span from fifteen minutes to a maximum of an hour and a half and are frequently updated and changed so as to retain the interest of a clientele who visit often but for short periods of time. Some in the industry, however, have suggested that the day-trippers who patronize Foxwoods are mature patrons who are bused in primarily for the gambling and are unlikely to seek out activities such as high-tech dancing or virtual adventures.

The Mashantucket Pequots have flaunted one of the cardinal rules of Las Vegas by installing windows in the Foxwoods casino. Many years ago, Vegas gambling czars decreed that casinos should be isolated worlds, containing no windows or clocks. This was not only to sustain the fantasy by shutting out the real world, but to confuse the circadian rhythms of their patrons, who might otherwise depart the gaming tables when the sun comes up (or goes down). The Pequots, however, ignored this accepted wisdom, evidently out of a sense of pride in the natural beauty of the cedar forest which surrounds Foxwoods.

Tribal-run casinos have a mixed relationship with government and with mainstream gaming operators. On the one hand, the money-making potential of American and Canadian Indian gaming is both recognized and coveted. Foxwoods, for example, contributes $137 million annually to the state coffers in Connecticut, making it a major revenue source in a region which has seen more than its share of factory closures and lay-offs.[13] Furthermore, tribes in the gaming business have proven to be generous political donors. The Mashantucket Pequots were the top gambling givers in the US in 1995 with donations of $465,000 almost evenly shared between the Republican and the Democratic parties (Shapiro 1996: 55). New Mexico tribes contributed $250,000 to the political campaign of Republican governor Gary Johnson, who has continued to strongly support the signing of a new gambling pact which would impose a minimum of state regulation in return for a share of the casino proceeds (Johnson 1996). Corporate casino operators, even while they lobby to undercut the monopoly of native-run casinos, have sought out joint projects. Harrah's Entertainment Inc., for example, reached an agreement in June 1996 with the Prairie Band of Potawatomi Indians for a $37 million casino-hotel project near Topeka, Kansas.

At the same time, there have been concerted efforts against tribal casinos. In 1993, a number of congressmen from Nevada and New Jersey introduced bills to curb Native American gaming by making them subject to state approval and by requiring that the tribes make income records available for government review. This was interpreted by Native American gaming officials as an attempt to protect the Atlantic City casinos of Donald Trump, who shortly thereafter sued the Federal Government and the tribes on the grounds that they violated his rights to equal treatment under the US Constitution (Goodman 1995: 117). Since then, Texas politician Bill Archer, chairman of the influential House Ways and Means Committee, has twice (once in 1995 and again in 1997) introduced a bill to tax tribal business revenue including casinos, bingo halls and betting parlors, only to see the measure die after furious lobbying from the Indian Gaming Association and other aboriginal organizations. In the most recent proposal, a 34 percent tax would have been levied, raising $1.9 billion in new tax revenue, an attractive sum for Republican politicians who had promised $85 million in tax cuts and credits in their 1997 budget package (Alvarez 1997).

In the early 1990s, Steve Wynn, proprietor of the Mirage and Treasure Island casinos in Las Vegas, waged an aggressive, expensive but ultimately unsuccessful campaign in Connecticut to convince state legislators to license non-native casinos. In particular, Wynne and the Pequots clashed over the rights to develop a seaside property in Bridgeport. Initially, Governor John Rowland opted for the Mashantucket plan for a $875 million casino project, but in November 1995, the legislature decided to maintain the status quo and rejected the possibility of any new casinos. By the end of his Connecticut campaign Wynne had spent $10 million with nothing to show for it.

Does gambling represent the "new buffalo" as some of its proponents claim? Certainly the Mashantucket Pequots could be forgiven for thinking so. A small band of only 350 members, the Pequots receive 75 percent of the revenues from the Foxwoods casino. This tax-free money is divided between just fifty families. Members receive a guarantee of casino or reservation employment, free health care and educational expenses through graduate school and yearly bonuses. The tribe has even chosen to rescue a nearby prep school which was down on its financial luck but still possessed of a pedigree. In return, Pequot students attend the school and parents have a say in its running. In a similar fashion, Casino Rama, a gambling casino on a Chippewa reserve near Orillia, two hours drive north of Toronto, is predicted to gross $C200 million in 1998 (Walker 1997), at least half of which will go to Ontario's 131 Canadian Indian reserves to pay for roads, schools, community centers and other infrastructure projects (Welsh 1996).

Yet, casino gambling is not without its drawbacks. Some native people fear that the inflow of visitors and cash will result in an increase in broken families, domestic violence, child abuse and economic crime. Others fear that the economic dependencies created by tribal-run casinos will discourage any efforts to maintain traditional lifestyles and values. It is worth noting that much of the theming of native-run casinos is a curious mix of indigenous and exogenous cultural elements. Casino Rama, for example, operates a Canadian Indian gift shop and a laser light show with a "Circle of Nature" theme side by side with The Willows, a Chinese restaurant which caters to its major client base.[14] As

162

one elder on the Rama Reserve mused on the eve of the casino opening, "remember, nothing will be the same again" (Welsh 1996: WS-1).

Casino gambling: Economic savior or junk food development?

Like the other components of the rapidly emerging Fantasy City, casino gambling has been touted as an economic savior which will transform struggling downtown economies, converting them into clones of Las Vegas with its double-digit growth rate and booming economic base. As an example, proponents point to Inglenook, a low to moderate income community of 115,000 located in Southern California. Inglenook saw the addition of a casino to the fabled Hollywood Park Racetrack contribute 800 new jobs and a tenth of its annual municipal operating budget, thus elevating property values and helping to improve local schools and public services. Boosted by its casino experience, the city even felt empowered to compete for a National Football League team (Myers 1995). Also cited as a success story is East St Louis, a municipality in south-western Illinois whose economic situation was so desperate that it required a special piece of legislation, the Illinois Financially Distressed Cities Act of 1990, to save it from bankruptcy. Reardon (1997: 246) claims that the decision by the State of Illinois to award a riverboat casino license to East St Louis in 1991, "has been the single most important factor in the city's economic recovery," creating more than 300 new jobs for local residents, generating millions of dollars in new tax revenues,[15] and dramatically expanding the city's retail sector.

Usually, casinos come to town amid a flurry of optimistic economic projections. The temporary casino in Niagara Falls, Ontario, for example, is expected to employ 3,000 people, while creating spin-off employment for an equal number in Niagara and across the province (Rice 1996). "It's lifted the spirits of the whole city," a construction supervisor on the project told a visiting out-of-town reporter. "Old, little, depressed Niagara Falls is no longer depressed . . . everyone in the world is coming here and investing" (Vander Doelen 1996: A–5).

However, the more typical experience is that of Atlantic City which has not reaped great benefits from its casinos,[16] despite their contributing nearly 70 percent of the tax levy. At the same time as celebrities such as Donald Trump and Merv Griffin were building their "castles" along the Boardwalk, the city was losing people, businesses and jobs. Since 1978, the year casinos were first introduced to the city, 100 of the city's 250 restaurants have closed. Its population now stands at 38,000, a tenth less than when gaming was first established. Property values have declined. There has been little demand for new housing, manufacturing and warehouse space. Although the Atlantic City casinos collectively employ more than 40,000 people, wages are relatively low; one 1981 study found that a third of the hotel jobs in the city paid less than $10,000 per annum (cited in Gregory 1992). Rather than returning to its turn-of-the-century glory as a resort city, America's second gambling capital is still pretty much like it was as depicted in Louis Malle's 1981 film, *Atlantic City*: seedy, crime-ridden, and going nowhere. Except for the casinos, John Jerde (1995), the designer of a long string of projects including the Freemont Street Experience in Las Vegas, freely admits that Atlantic City is "a kind of a burnout." Nor is this likely to change in the near future. As Robert Goodman (1995: 11–12), a well-known critic of the gambling industry, has noted, plans to spend $100 million to expand Atlantic City's airport, rebuild its convention center, and beautify the approach roads to the casinos and their surrounding boardwalk areas have more to do with concealing depressed areas from visitors traveling to the casinos than it does with reversing the massive deterioration of non-casino sections of the city.

In the early 1990s, as part of a campaign to bring non-tribal casino gaming to the state of Connecticut, Steve Wynn proposed the investment of $350 million in an entertainment-convention-casino complex in Hartford, a community hard-hit by a recession which was suffocating the entire US economy. In their report, titled "The Other Side of the Coin: A Casino's Impact on Hartford,"[17] a local grass-roots coalition, CREN (Citizens' Research Education Network), identified six major problems which they predicted would develop if a casino were allowed to operate within the city: (i) job losses; (ii) public costs to exceed public revenue; (iii) higher crime rates; (iv) a negative impact on non-casino businesses; (v) failure to develop tourist and convention businesses aside from casinos; (vi) the creation of an unhealthy urban environment, especially for Hartford's youth.

Wynn's proposal, argued CREN, was the latest in a series of "quick fix" projects which had ultimately done nothing to improve the life and economy of the city. As noted previously in this chapter, Mirage was shut out of the state, largely for political reasons, but CREN's hit-list of potential problems associated with a Hartford casino-entertainment complex is a reasonably good summary of the darker side of gaming development outside of Las Vegas.

Perhaps the most exhaustive examination of the impact of casinos on the local community is Patricia Stokowski's (1996) before–after study of casino tourism in Gilpin County, Colorado (see "Fool's gold" p. 165). Stokowski paints a gloomy picture of gaming development as an effective solution for enhancing the sustainability of economically stalled rural communities. While some positive economic benefits do ensue, Stowkowski's study reveals that this is at the cost of the very soul of the community. Like the depressed town in Friedrich Durrenmatt's 1962 play, *The Visit*, whose residents murder one of their own in return for promised riches, the Colorado mountain towns of Central City and Black Hawk are depicted as sacrificing their unique qualities of place and community in order to attract gambling dollars. The dynamics which underlie such a decision are embedded in pre-existing conflicts and paradoxes in community life, notably the spirit of boomtown-style individualism that creates and legitimizes a sense of passivity among its citizens. In the political vacuum so created, a "growth machine" composed of local business people and politicians (who are often one and the same) embrace and often personally profit from gaming. When the construction dust settles and the dice begin to roll, local citizens suddenly find that life isn't the same as before; there are traffic and parking problems; City Hall is too busy dealing with casino expansion plans to take your call; and even the night sky isn't dark any more. Even more ominously, gaming tourism hijacks the history and culture of the community, repackaging it in ways that make it palatable with the frontier fantasies of casino visitors. As one resident confided to Stokowski, "it's not a better place to live now; it's a better place to do business" (1996: 185).

Fool's gold: gambling comes to Gilpin County

Once described as the "Switzerland of America," Gilpin County, Colorado is a former gold mining area which fell on hard times at the turn of the century when the cost of deep-rock mining began to soar. Over the course of the twentieth century, the population size steadily declined, falling to around 3,000 in the late 1980s. Furthermore, the urban infrastructure had begun to crumble, most noticeably the water system in Central City which had fallen into a state of severe disrepair. County residents were by and large a collection of die-hard individualists who chose to endure the problems of rural mountain living as the price for being left alone.

The introduction of gambling as a solution to Central City's woes closely followed the growth machine politics as outlined by Logan and Molotch (1987). Local politicians and businessmen met informally for several years to discuss ways of promoting "economic development." In 1989, they formally organized themselves into a non-profit body, "CCPI" (Central City Preservation Inc.), kicking off their pro-gambling movement with a letter from the Mayor to the local newspaper suggesting that legalized gambling, if kept at a manageable level, could provide jobs and boost the slumping economy. With the support of a second town, Black Hawk, CCPI members undertook a concerted campaign to place an initiative on the statewide ballot which would legalize limited stakes gambling (i.e. slot machines, poker and blackjack with bets not to exceed five dollars) in the two towns as well as in a third, Cripple Creek. To promote the legalization of gambling, CCPI members played on two particular concerns. They tapped into community anxiety over the weak economy; proponents of "Amendment 4," the pro-gambling measure, utilized a "rhetoric of despair" claiming that without gambling Gilpin County was destined to become a ghost town. At the same time, recognizing the widespread support for keeping the County's rich historical legacy alive, it was insinuated that gambling was consistent with the history and culture of Gilpin County and that it would assure local and state historic preservation by increasing tourism. It was also intimated that gambling operations would be decentralized and low-key rather than Las Vegas-style casinos, thus supplementing tourism rather than constituting its core.

Once successful in securing the required legislation, however, a different picture emerged. Instead of non-casino gambling, with a few slot machines placed in local businesses as believed, the local growth machine chose to allow free market, virtually unrestrained casino development. "Gaming" venues proliferated. Whereas on opening day, 1 October 1991, there were seven casinos in Central City and Blackhawk, by the end of the following summer this number had ballooned to forty-one casinos. And, contrary to the prior claims of proponents that gambling would not change either the look of the County or the lifestyle of its residents, the community costs of gaming development soon became evident.

In economic terms, the casinos had a mixed impact. In all three jurisdictions – Central City, Black Hawk and Gilpin County – substantial new revenue flowed into the government coffers, but the casinos also required huge increases in expenditure: for traffic control, police protection, improvements in the water and sewage systems, and even for public relations. By 1993, for example, the Marshall's Office in Central City had grown from just a few officers in pre-gambling days, to fourteen uniformed officers and five information and administrative personnel. This is all very well as long as gaming revenues keep flowing. But if demand for gambling declines, as is frequently the case, municipalities are left in the lurch, having to pay for extensive expenditure commitments with declining revenues. Thus "addictive economies" (Freudenberg 1992) such as gambling create a dangerous dependency on a single industry.

In the private sector of the County, the economic impact of gaming development has so far brought mixed results. Initially there was a land rush which made some local property owners instant millionaires. Entrepreneurial types opened parking lots, bed and breakfasts and various cottage industries related to gaming. Prospective small-time casino operators, however, have had a more difficult time, especially once the large gaming corporations began to move in. Consistent with the experience of other communities in a similar situation, there has been little economic spill-over from the casinos to the immediate surrounding neighborhood.

Almost all the existing cafés, restaurants and saloons closed when the buildings in which they were situated converted to casinos. Since property in the commercial zone of each town is assessed at the casino rate, few if any replacements have appeared.

In terms of employment opportunities the situation is again a mixed one. On one hand, local residents who wish to work in the casino industry can usually find a job, most of which are year-round. Wages are higher than in pre-gaming days and health-care benefits often go with the position. On the other hand, most local residents do not have, or cannot obtain the licensing and training to work in the higher income jobs in the casinos, thus limiting their employment choices and incomes. Furthermore, the advent of gaming tourism has led to an increase in the cost of living, notably in housing, which neutralizes the advantage of higher wages.

Socially and culturally, the impact of gaming and tourism development on the community has been even more powerful. Two of the most serious concerns expressed by residents have been to do with parking issues and traffic volumes. Although residents were guaranteed residential parking by permit, both Central City and Black Hawk adopted a pay-for-parking system on the main street which costs locals and casino visitors the same amount. Parking violations are strictly enforced. Parking spots downtown are difficult to find. Formerly quiet highways and streets are deluged with heavy traffic.

Parking and traffic issues are just part of a larger wave of change which is seen by many residents as eroding the former, more relaxed, mountain lifestyle. Strolling and socializing along local sidewalks is now difficult, as gamblers hurry from casino to casino, directed by traffic control guards. New residential subdivisions have been started to house casino employees who have migrated from outside the County. Local community festivals and celebrations which had traditionally marked the social calendar of Gilpin County, notably the annual "Jazz Fest," suffered a drop in attendance as gaming development produced a new year-round economy. When they were revived, they became professionally produced events sponsored by casino interests. Even the night sky has been transformed, no longer appearing completely dark as a result of the light from the new hill-top parking lots.

And what of historic preservation, one of the primary reasons given by proponents for the necessity of gaming development? While local preservation boards, particularly in Central City, were reasonably successful in keeping downtown exterior façades relatively intact while controlling a frenzy of neon signage, interiors were gutted and transformed so as to fit casino owners' pre-conceptions of the Old West. Undertaking a kind of risqué Disneyfication, both casino operators and local officials attempted to create a contrived version of community history and culture which was intended to tantalize visitors with the notion of gambling as a slightly immoral activity carried out in a "Wild West" setting. Thus, the entrance gate to the Miner's Mesa parking lot above Black Hawk was designed to look like a composite, generic mining structure, thereby dwarfing an original, weathered, old mine-shaft house; female casino greeters were costumed to look like "ladies of the evening," an image reiterated in the "Shady Ladies of the Motherlode," a troupe of civic ambassadors in Central City; and Harvey's casino in Central City featured a fake exploding gold mine.

Finally, the structure of local community leadership and power was affected by the triumph of gaming development. Starting in the construction period in 1990, casino owners and industry representatives emerged as powerful and influential figures in the towns of Gilpin County. Outside consultants were hired in Black Hawk and Central City to advise local government on a wide range of town development issues. One such advisor, David Stahl, a project coordinator with a Boulder land consulting firm, went on to become the interim City Manager of Central City, although not without considerable local opposition. Not surprisingly, these new decision-makers had a vision of community development which unabashedly favored gaming expansion. To be fair, so did the leadership contingent which brought in the casinos in the first place; on opening day, for example, both the mayors of Black Hawk and Central City resigned from their posts, having converted a portion of their commercial businesses into casino areas. Nevertheless, community business and local government leaders quickly lost the power to advance their own interests and were drawn into the issues and agendas as defined by the casino owners.

Gaming development, Patricia Stokowski observes, has "become the great social experiment of the late twentieth century" (1996: 284). Her in-depth study of the Gilpin County experience clearly indicates that realistically the experiment is more a Faustian bargain in which the community has lost its ability to act independently. Many residents, she discovered, now question whether the economic gains which accrue from gaming development can ever compensate for their lost lifestyle and sense of local control. One solution is for communities to become proactive in their dealings with gaming development, insisting that the values of the host be respected. In rural places such as Gilpin County where most residents just want the freedom to do their own thing, and local government is dominated by business owners who stand to gain from casino development, this isn't very likely however. Ironically, it was only after Pandora's box was opened and local residents discovered that life was no longer the same, that they began to collaborate, forming the Gilpin Residents Protective Association and other citizens' groups and initiating a series of recall motions against local politicians. Sadly, by the time this happened, it was too late to effectively halt the juggernaut of gaming and tourism development.

Source: Stokowski (1996)

Future developments

If the theme park has come to the casino, the question we must ask is, will gambling become an integral part of the developing Fantasy City? One segment of the urban entertainment industry – themed restaurants – has already enthusiastically embraced the synergy between Hollywood and Las Vegas. In June 1996, ITT Corporation, the parent company of Caesar's Palace, announced that its gaming unit had agreed to develop several large casinos with the Planet Hollywood chain. This builds on an existing relationship in which a Planet Hollywood restaurant is already a major tenant in the Forum Shops. As an initial move, ITT plans to spend $1.3 billion to build a 3,200 room hotel and casino in Las Vegas and a 1,000 room hotel and casino on the Boardwalk in Atlantic City, both of which would carry the Planet Hollywood name (Sterngold 1996b). Not to be outdone, the Rank Organisation, owner of the Hard Rock Cafe chain, is pursuing a partnership with Trump Hotels and Casino Resorts Inc., whereby the ailing Trump's Castle casino in Atlantic City will be converted to a rock and roll establishment which will carry the Hard Rock logo and include a Hard Rock Cafe restaurant and retail store (Orwall 1996c). This follows on from the favorable revenue figures generated by the Las Vegas Hard Rock casino-hotel built by Peter Morton, the firm's co-founder and Rank's former partner. Several of these projects are presently stalled due to unexpected events such as the Hilton takeover bid of ITT. The future, however, is likely to contain some version of these casinos as theme restaurants.

Casinos in family-oriented theme parks and attractions are a more uncertain proposition. As is often the case, the industry has awaited Disney's direction which up until now has been hesitant. Not that replacing the apples and

169

oranges on slot machines with Mickeys and Donalds isn't seen as an economically attractive expansion route. But, stung by protests from conservative pro-family groups over some of the films released by the company-owned Touchstone and Hollywood Pictures as well as over the issue of "Gay Days" at the theme parks, Disney publicly denies that it is contemplating entry into the gaming business, the possible exception being their planned cruise ship line. Nevertheless, industry rumors and speculation abound that Disney is looking for a fail-safe way of expanding into casinos. An industry newsletter, *Phil Havener's Gaming Hotline*, reported in April 1995 that Disney had taken an option to buy a 1,000 acre parcel of land west of the interstate highway that parallels the Strip in Las Vegas. But to date, nothing concrete has been announced. Similarly, industry analysts took an interest when Michael Eisner hired Stephen Bollenbach, an expert in hotel and casino financing, as chief financial officer of the Walt Disney Company (Johnston 1995). However, at the time Eisner denied that knowledge of the gambling business was a factor in the appointment, and in any case Bollenbach soon left to assume a senior position at Hilton Hotels.

Alternatively, casino owners could decide to risk walking the tightrope without a net by establishing UEDs without the gambling component. At first glance this doesn't seem a likely option, but the recent experience of Mirage's Treasure Island could suggest otherwise. At Treasure Island slightly more than half of total revenue is derived from non-gaming sources: hotel rooms (which charge market rates triple the usual Las Vegas casino rate), restaurants and entertainment (in particular, the Cirque du Soleil show and boutique.) Next door at the Mirage, the Siegfried and Roy magic show, still the hottest ticket in Las Vegas, grosses $250,000 per night. Still, Vegas entrepreneurs are wary of severing the umbilical cord to gambling which is still seen as their base revenue source.

In part, the cautious position adopted by casino owners reflects their mixed view of families as desirable client bases. A great amount has been written about the transformation of Las Vegas from an adult playground to a family theme park with gambling on the side. Literary critic Al Alvarez (1996), a big fan of Las Vegas, recalls that fifteen years ago Circus Circus was the only casino which made any pretense at catering for children by including a mezzanine crammed with carnival sideshows and video games. Alvarez recounts how his small daughter was taken to the Circus Circus by the mother of a friend she had met at a swimming pool. When the 9-year-old girls had exhausted their money at the arcade, they wandered off to find the mother and were promptly arrested by a security guard for violating a law which forbade minors to enter the gambling areas in casinos. The situation is very different today, as there is plenty for kids to do in Las Vegas – including two amusement parks attached to casino hotels. Still, it's not yet Disneyland. While Mirage has taken the lead by catering to families, its management has always been forthright in pointing out that they don't believe casinos are a suitable place for children. One continuing problem is that some parents leave their offspring to wander unsupervised while they gamble. The inherent dangers of this were recently highlighted when a 7-year-old girl was raped and strangled in the washroom of the Primadonna Casino; the girl was evidently amusing herself in the arcade section while her father gambled in the casino area.[18]

One of the first non-gaming entertainment complexes is already near completion along the Strip. Called The Showcase, it combines such standard UED components as a family entertainment center (the 47,000 square foot Sega Gameworks), several theme restaurants (Marvel Mania, Official All Star Cafe) and a United Artists eight screen multiplex movie theater with such custom features as a "World of Coca Cola" store fronted by a 100 foot high glass Coke bottle, and a whimsical 360 foot plaza landscaped with hedges, clipped cones and curved balls which will light up.

To a large degree, the future of the gaming industry depends on correctly identifying and catering to key markets. "High rollers," the traditional mother lode of Las Vegas casinos are unlikely to venture beyond the baccarat tables or their gratis luxury hotel suites. Slot-machine patrons, regarded as the bread and butter of casinos, are more likely to be lured away from gambling. A third group, tourists who are only incidentally interested in gambling, if at all, presently constitute only about 10 to 15 percent of the market. This group, however, are increasingly drawn to the city by attractions such as The Showcase and The Freemont Street Experience as well as by the themed hotels and show spectaculars.

Beyond Las Vegas, a testing ground for many of these new strategies may turn out to be Niagara Falls, Canada. Already a major international tourist attraction, in the late 1990s Niagara opened its first gambling casino a poker chip's toss from the American border. At present, Niagara Falls draws 14 million tourists a year as opposed to the 30 million who go to Las Vegas. With its spatial juxtaposition of great natural beauty and tacky entertainment (Tussaud's Wax Museum, Ripley's Believe It or Not), Niagara resembles a throwback to an earlier age, although its waterfront people mover and IMAX theater are beacons of twentieth-century technology. In the past, Niagara Falls has had several encounters with the world of themed entertainment, the most successful of which is the heavily promoted but seasonal Marine Land and Game Farm, a Sea World-style park developed by John Holer, a local entrepreneur from the former Yugoslavia. By contrast, Maple Leaf Village, a tourist shopping mall and amusement park housed in a mock-Tudor structure, went under financially and is now the site of a temporary gambling casino. Vedaland, a "New Age"-styled theme park sponsored by the Transcendental Meditation (TM) movement and pitched by magician and TM adherent Doug Henning, failed to get off the ground, despite considerable publicity. Now the $160 million Casino Niagara (temporary version) is here, complete with cascading waterfalls, Roman-style columns and a Hard Rock Cafe. Like Las Vegas, gambling and entertainment are coming together in new ways but questions abound. Questions such as: are vacationers to the Falls gamblers or do they constitute a separate market? Will gambling enhance tourism in the Niagara region or plunder the clientele for existing attractions? What will happen to the casino in the winter when the tourist trade usually drops off for the better part of eight months? And, more generically, outside the unique orbit of Nevada, do tourism and casino gambling represent a super synergy or are they fundamentally incompatible?

Figure 9.1 "Planet Hollywood goes global": themed entertainment as world-wide phenomenon.
Source: Ruth Hannigan.

9

LAND OF THE RISING FUN

Themed entertainment comes to
the Asia-Pacific Rim

Although the predicted cost of $700 million for the Kyongju World Tradition Folk Village in South Korea can't compare to the record $3 billion spent on Euro Disney, nevertheless it promises to be an ambitious undertaking. The village, scheduled to be opened in 1998, is to be situated on 1,000 acres, a three-hour drive south of Seoul; the project is an amalgam of cultural theming with high-tech entertainment. The focal point is an international folk village area divided into "cultural zones," each with its own type of merchandise, food and attractions. Helping to bring these cultural "experiences" alive will be attractions from two of America's best-known presenters of widescreen filmed entertainment, IMAX and Iwerks. Elsewhere in the park there will be a Flags of the Nations Plaza, complete with a casino, an entertainment/rental village inspired by Universal's CityWalk, three five-star hotels with a combined 800 rooms, condominium housing and Shilla Dynasty Town, an educational and recreational activities area (Zoltak, 1997b).

The Kyongju World Tradition Folk Village is just the latest in a rising tide of themed entertainment projects to be built or planned across the Asia-Pacific region. While some of these theme parks are located a considerable distance from existing cities, most are situated in urban areas, frequently capping the top floors of large multi-storey retail malls. With the exception of Japan, few of these themed developments are being developed by the big international players such as Disney, Universal and Six Flags. Instead, the majority are under-written by local or regional millionaires or corporate conglomerates and are designed and/or managed by North American architectural and design firms, notably Duell Corporation, Forrec, Landmark and International Theme Park Services. Unlike in Europe and America, financing has not been the major problem. Frank Stanek (1996), President of international new business development, Universal Studios Recreation Group, told an Urban Land Institute (ULI) seminar in 1996 that one large international pension fund he know of had allo-cated a billion dollars to the Asia market, of which 60 percent was to be placed in retail entertainment projects over the next eighteen months. Rather, the problem is more one of identifying projects that will work in a market which is quickly becoming flooded with new entertainment destinations.

Competition, however, is the nectar which sustains many economies in the Asia-Pacific region and the success of some of the leading theme parks and UEDs is a powerful aphrodisiac. Tokyo Disneyland, which opened in 1983, attracted 10 million visitors in its first year of operation and today boasts an annual attendance of 17.36 million (fiscal 1997). Canal City, Hakata, a 1.4 billion urban entertainment district in Fukwoka, Japan which opened in April 1996, had attracted 7–8 million visitors by the end of August that year. Built around a canal which functions as its main street, it includes a 1,200 seat live theater, a thirteen-screen AMC multiplex and a 55,000 square foot Sega arcade called Joypolis (Zoltak 1996d). Given these figures, it is no surprise that several additional mega-projects are slated for Japanese cities in the near future. Universal is undertaking a Japanese version of CityWalk near Osaka at a cost of over a billion dollars while the city of Kobe, devastated by an earthquake in 1995, is attempting to mark its rebirth with the opening in 1998 of CyberSeas, a mixed-use complex described as having "something of a Jules Verne meets Rube Goldberg look to it" (Traiman 1997: 16).

Challenging the Kyongju complex is Samsung Corporation's Everland, South Korea's premier theme park which is in the process of creating a 3,700 acre international resort town to add to the existing attractions: Festival World theme park, Caribbean Bay, a $120 million water park, and the Everland Raceway. The new resort will include 6,500 residential homes and apartments, three hotels, two golf courses, a mountain ski resort, an international convention center and a light-rail transportation link to downtown Seoul. Not to be outdone, Hyundai, another of Korea's large industrial corporations, has announced plans for Hyundai Sungwoo Leisuretown, a $200 million theme park, while a third *chaebol* (conglomerate), Daewoo, has engaged Duell Corporation, the designer of Everland as well as the Six Flags theme parks in the US, to develop a tourist site two and a half hours south of Seoul into a four-part attraction: an indoor waterpark, an outdoor waterpark, a Korean/Japanese-style spa and an enclosed entertainment retail center modeled on the Forum Shops in Las Vegas (Zoltak 1997a).

Despite its return to China, Hong Kong is by no means slowing the pace of its leisure development. Inspired by the success of its maritime-themed Ocean Park which attracted almost 3.6 million visitors in 1997, another maritime theme park is planned along with a virtual reality game park and a "snow dome" which would bring Arctic (or perhaps more appropriately Antarctic) weather to the Tropics ("Asians at play" 1996: 50).

Even in Vietnam, the newest Asian economy to attract a flood of foreign companies and capital, urban entertainment is set to land, specifically on the roof of the first mixed-use development in the original part of Ho Chi Minh City (formerly Saigon). Financed by JIN-WEN Enterprise, a consortium of Taiwanese companies active in real estate development and construction, and designed by a California-based consulting company, the entertainment complex is to include a theme park, a family entertainment center and, eventually, a five-star hotel. With the balance between the private and the public sector still in a state of flux in Vietnam, this $400 million project is by no means certain. However, the concept of "themed" projects is something which the country seems set to embrace in the near future.

The growth of themed entertainment on the Asia-Pacific Rim

To a considerable extent, the Asia-Pacific region in the 1990s can be compared to that of the affluent years of America in the 1950s. In both instances, you have an expanding economy, an increase in leisure time and a ballooning middle class with rising discretionary income. The recent and in some cases severe, economic woes that have impacted south-east Asia, Japan, Hong Kong and South Korea may temporarily stall and perhaps modify this so-called "Asian economic miracle," but it is unlikely that the desire for urban entertainment will disappear.

Over the last decade, most economies in the region have grown at a rate of 7–10 percent per year, more than twice that of Europe and North America. According to the "World Outlook" prepared by the *Economist* Intelligence Unit at the start of 1997, 40 percent of the twenty fastest growing countries are located in the Asia-Pacific region – Vietnam, Malaysia, Indonesia, South Korea, Thailand, Singapore, Philippines and Taiwan ("Emerging market indicators" 1997).

One offshoot of this has been the growth of a huge pool of middle-class consumers. By the dawn of the twenty-first century it has been estimated that the Asian middle class (excluding Japan) will exceed 500 million, rising to 800 million people by the year 2010. In Bangkok, for example, the middle class is estimated to make up 70 percent of the city's 10 million residents ("Thais eager to consume" 1996). While disposable incomes have not yet reached the level of Japan, nevertheless, they have reached new heights in Singapore, Bandor Seri, Begawan, Hong Kong, Taipei, Seoul and other Asian cities. By 1995, the average income (adjusted for purchasing power parity) in Malaysia had risen to US$10,000 (Wheeler 1996). Almost two-thirds of households in Petaling Jaya, near Kuala Lumpur, earn more than US$800 a month; with over a third bringing in more than US$1,200 per month (Naisbitt 1996: 89). Overall, more than half the total population of Asia will be able to afford consumer goods by the first part of the new millennium.

With rising incomes, the new middle class is primed to spend. High savings rates – up to 38 percent in some countries – mean that consumers have plenty of disposable income. Since most houses are limited in size and availability, people are propelled towards activities outside the home such as shopping, dining and movie-going. Many of the developing leisure products and services are foreign-supplied or inspired. One example of this is golf, which combines business and pleasure. In 1988, it was estimated that there were 1,582 golf courses in Japan catering to approximately 10 million golfers (see Rimmer 1992: 1621). More recently, the demand for new golf courses in developing countries in the region has been expanding rapidly. In the mid 1990s, for example, Thailand was one of the world's fastest growing golfing nations with Malaysia and Indonesia following close behind (Cohen 1995:1). In the Philippines, rising incomes and increased leisure time have led to a golf boom with a dozen courses scheduled to be built in 1996–97. Sensing a boom, a foursome of investors – property developers, hotel chains, commercial banks (Far East Bank, Solidbank, Metrobank, Philippine Commercial International), and even the military's pension fund – have ventured into golf and golf resorts ('In the Phillipines' 1996).

At the same time as the rise in income, the amount of spare leisure time of many Asian employees and managers has increased. In Japan, the five-day working week was officially implemented in 1989, but it was enforced only recently, thanks in part to a government campaign to encourage workers to take part in leisure activities on their days off. Elsewhere in Asia, Indonesia adopted the five-day week as late as 1995, and in China it became more widely accepted in 1994. Today, Asian workers still don't have as many paid holidays as their fellow employees in Europe and North America but in capital cities, such as Seoul, Bangkok, Hong Kong, Taipei and Singapore, holidays are on the increase as the number of working hours per year falls (Go 1997: 11).

One result of this has been a boom in foreign travel both abroad and within Asia. This propensity to travel is especially prevalent in Japan, South Korea, Malaysia and Taiwan which as a whole counted 26 million outbound travelers in 1995 (ibid.: 16). Much of this tourist market is intra-regional. In 1992, for example, over a quarter of the visitor arrivals in Indonesia were from neighboring Singapore, with just under quarter from Japan and Malaysia.

With money in their pockets and spare time to enjoy themselves away from home, many Asians have looked to more local attractions. Jettisoning the traditional Asian department stores, street-level retail and night markets, Asian consumers are embracing western retail formats, specialty boutiques, entertain-

Table 9.1 Travel propensity in eight Asian countries (figures for 1995)

Country	GNP (US$ billions)	Population (millions)	Potential travellers (millions)	Outbound travellers (millions)
Japan	4,255	124	62	14
South Korea	306	44	9	3
Malaysia	55	19	10	4
Taiwan	181	21	11	5
Thailand	79	59	9	2
China	547	1,200	12	4
India	272	860	9	2
Indonesia	120	189	9	1

Source: Go (1997): 16

ment concepts (movies, nightclubs, theme parks, interactive shopping experiences and water theme parks) and even discount retailing (Munkacy 1997a). Shopping malls, for example, have sprouted up everywhere, both in city centers and in the new suburbs. From 1993 to 1996, more than a dozen malls were built in Jakarta, Indonesia with an average size of 1 million square feet. Bangkok is now home to two of the world's largest shopping malls; one of them, the 5 million square foot Seacon Square, hosts 100–200,000 shoppers every week ("Thais eager to consume" 1996). Many of these malls have added mini-theme parks or family entertainment centers on their top levels or roofs in order to remain competitive in the face of a blitz of new mall construction.

Already we are seeing the leading edge of the American themed commercial culture coming ashore in Asia. There is a Nike store in Shanghai, twelve McDonald's restaurants in Beijing, and Hard Rock franchises in Singapore, Bangkok, Taipei, Jakarta and Kuala Lumpur (Naisbitt 1996: 110). Still, there are gaps to be filled in the provision of leisure facilities. Movie theaters, for example, are in relatively scarce supply given the number of potential customers. Thus, while Singapore with a population of 3.1 million has 107 cinemas (about one theater for each 29,000 residents), Bangkok with three times the population has more or less the same number of venues (one theater per 75,000 population) (see Table 9.2, p. 180). It is not surprising then that multiplex theaters have become a driving force throughout Asia in terms of meeting leisure demand. Also taking advantage of the opportunity are the reigning trinity of specialty, high-tech, giant screen movie firms. In 1995, IMAX's thirty-one theaters in the Asia-Pacific region brought in a quarter of its total gross revenue of $100 million (1996). Its rival, Iwerks Entertainment, had at least ten projects active in the Far East throughout 1996 worth more than $8 million including a giant screen theater in Bandung (Waddell 1996a) and six TurboRide theaters in China. A third firm, Showscan, has been contracted for the installation of a minimum of ten simulation theaters in Taiwan and six simulation attractions in Malaysia (Traiman 1996: 20).

The growth of the leisure entertainment industry along the Pacific Rim has also been propelled by the proclivity of its constituent nations to invest in neighboring economies. Malaysians, for example, invested $2 billion between 1990 and 1995 in fellow countries in the ASEAN trade bloc, most of it in Singapore, although $165 million found its way as far as the Philippines (Wheeler 1996). Increasingly, Asian investors have looked to the themed entertainment sector as an investment target. When Australia's Wonderland theme park was purchased in 1997 by Malaysian property giant Sunway City Berhad, owner of the Sunway Theme Park and the Sunway Lagoon resort in Java, some surprise was expressed in the business press. Yet, in recent years, the financial tentacles of Asian conglomerates have extended throughout the region and have frequently included resort and entertainment related projects.

As an example, consider the Lippo Group, a $12 billion Indonesian banking, real estate and insurance empire controlled by the ethnic Chinese Riady family.

Table 9.2 Movie theaters in capital cities in the Asia-Pacific region

City	Population	No. of cinemas	Population per cinema
Singapore	3,100,000	107	28,971
Taipei	2,653,000	78	34,012
Metro Manila	8,403,570	239	35,161
Jakarta	8,222,515	178	46,193
Kuala Lumpur	1,295,300	27	47,974
Tokyo	11,780,948	205	57,468
Bangkok	9,100,000	121	75,206
Seoul	10,925,000	132	82,765
Beijing	12,510,000	70	178,714

Source: Taken from "Special report cities," *Asiaweek*, 25 October 1996, p. 46

Estimated to be Indonesia's sixth largest conglomerate, it employs more than 25,000 workers across Asia in more than 100 companies (Mydans 1996). At home, one of its jewels is Lippo Village on the edge of Jakarta, a residential-commercial complex which includes golf courses, WalMart and J.C. Penney stores, a family entertainment center and a Mediterranean-themed food court. Outside the country, the Lippo Group have financial, insurance and real estate projects in Hong Kong, Singapore and China. Although it is currently sitting on the shelf, one project would see the Riady family invest $10 billion over ten years to develop a port, industrial park and resort complex complete with a golf course on Meizhou Island in the Fujian province on the Chinese mainland (Mydans 1996).

Another cross-border developer of entertainment projects is Hong Kong's Shaw Bros. Company, headed by the colorfully named entrepreneur "Run Run" Shaw. The Shaw Studios are recognized as the leading movie producers in Hong Kong, turning out a stream of highly popular action films, most of which are produced inexpensively and quickly. Shaw has plans to build a string of movie-based theme parks across Asia, beginning with a $200 million Shaw Studio Theme Park, Shenxhan in Indonesia, designed by Forrec and scheduled to open in 1999.

Theming Matilda: UED and casino development in Australia

Amusement parks in Australia can be traced back to the early part of the twentieth century, notably the Luna Park in Sydney and the one in Melbourne. However, the country's first home-grown theme park, Dreamworld, didn't open until 1981. Located on the Gold Coast south of Brisbane, in Coomera, Dreamworld was developed by local entrepreneur John Longhurst who hoped it would become Australia's answer to Disneyland. The story of Dreamland's construction is the stuff of Hollywood movies: Longhurst taught himself to operate a bulldozer and proceeded to spend twelve hours a day for two-and-a half years digging out an 800 meter waterway for a paddlewheel steamer, named *Captain Strut* ("Australia's first theme park" 1985). In 1996, Longhurst sold Dreamland to the Singapore shipping magnate, Kua Phek Long, for A$85 million. In keeping with the vision shared by many developers in the Asia-Pacific region, the new owner announced A$330 million of expansion plans which included a 450 room hotel–motel with ninety-two treehouses and a themed retail mall, as well as a A$250 million regional shopping center (O'Meara and Syvret 1997).

Australia's Wonderland, the second contemporary theme park to be built in the Antipodes, opened in Sydney's western suburbs in 1987. It was developed by Taft Broadcasting, an Ohio media conglomerate whose string of amusement parks once included the still thriving Canada's Wonderland near Toronto. In its early years, Australia's Wonderland was plagued by high costs and was open only during the summer months and on weekends in the spring and fall. Later, however, it achieved profitability and extended its opening times. As previously noted, the park was sold in 1997 for A$50 million (US$39 million) to Sunway City, one of Malaysia's most successful property developers whose portfolio of investment properties especially favors the leisure market (House 1997). Australia's Wonderland counted more than 1.35 million visitors in 1996, but its real attraction to Sunway was the surrounding 390 acres of park land, the largest single block of tourism-zoned land in the Sydney area (O'Brien 1997b). Sunway's expansion plans seem likely to mirror those of Kua Phek Long for Dreamland.

A third park, or to be more precise, a trio of parks – Sea World, Movie World and Wet 'n' Wild Waterpark – are the joint venture of American communications giant Warner Bros. and Village Roadshow, and are located in south-east Queensland in the Brisbane Gold Coast tourist corridor. Operating all year round, the two larger parks, Sea World and Movie World, attract approximately 1.4 million visitors annually while the waterpark admits 450,000 per year (O'Brien 1996f).

Unlike in Asian cities, Australian developers tend not to crown their shopping centers with entertainment and leisure attractions (although these have been incorporated into super regional and major regional centers). As shown below in Table 9.3, these types of shopping environments are concentrated in the states of New South Wales, Queensland and Victoria. In addition, there are themed centers – specialty shopping centers located primarily in tourist areas and which mainly comprise of specialty shops with food courts. Most of these (65 percent), as is to be expected, are located along the tourist corridor in Queensland.

The newest themed attraction in Australia is the A$80 million (US$66 million) Sega World in the Darling Harbour area of Sydney. A 10,000 square meter indoor center with six major attractions and 200 smaller rides, Sega World is housed in a distinctive glass-coned building on the eastern side of the harbor. Among its offerings are interactive rides, theme restaurants, interactive

Table 9.3 Distribution of shopping centers in Australia (by type)

State	City centre	Super regional	Major regional	Themed
New South Wales	43	3	11	5
Queensland	22	2	6	15
Victoria	17	2	7	3
South Australia	18	3	4	0
Western Australia	19	0	0	0
Total	119	10	28	23

Source: Property Council of Australia, 22 May 1996

retail stores and street theater. At the time of its opening in April 1997, the project was only 75 percent pre-leased; this percentage is even less if one doesn't include the Sega World tenancy itself (Jimenez 1997). This figure is low compared to some American projects; the Irvine Entertainment Center, for example, was 90 percent pre-leased.

Finally, it is important to note the experience of casinos in the Australian urban entertainment industry. When they were first introduced in the 1970s, Australian casinos were small facilities in remote locations which modeled themselves on the British, low-key club-style gambling establishments of the time. Furthermore, each had a monopoly in the state in which it was located. Since 1980, however, Australian casinos have adopted a more aggressively commercial approach, fashioned in part on the glitter, luxury and showmanship of the American prototype (McMillen 1996: 280). Presently, there are four major casinos – the Sydney Harbour Casino, the only legal casino in the state of New South Wales; the Crown Casino in Melbourne; and Jupiters in Brisbane and along the Gold Coast. In addition, a clutch of smaller casino-hotels – Townville, Breakwater, the Reef Casino in the northern Queensland resort of Cairns – operate in the tourist zone along the south-east coast. By American standards these casinos are not huge players. Revenue from Jupiter's Gold Coast, for example, was $154.6 million in the second half of 1996 with a 77.5 percent occupancy rate at the hotel. By way of comparison, the four riverboat gambling casinos in the St Louis, Missouri area together do more than $400 million in business per year (Jinker-Lloyd 1996: 60).

The Brisbane operation has shown even poorer results with figures for the second half of 1996 showing only a 52.6 percent hotel occupancy rate, up from a dismal 30.6 percent the previous half (O'Meara 1997). Worse yet has been the performance of the Reef Casino which opened in April 1996. Designed to attract "junket gamblers" – mostly Asian tourists combining beach and baccarat – the Reef Casino lost $4.7 million in 1996. While there are various possible explanations, a lower than expected number of repeat visitors was a major contributor. As one local Japanese tour operator told the *Far Eastern Economic*

Review, "only about 2% of the people who visit Cairns come back again because after you have visited the reef and the rain forests, there isn't much to do . . . which is why people are spending less time here" (Heazle 1996b: 72). This of course, is the nightmare scenario for anyone with a financial stake in the newly developing Fantasy City – that is that all their customers will be one-timers. Las Vegas casino owners seem to have overcome this by offering such a multitude and range of attractions that people feel they have something new to see each time. It is more difficult, however, to instantly create this critical mass in resort areas which are just beginning to become established.

Cultural theme parks and "reconstructed ethnicity"

In a 1994 Trend Report in the journal *Current Sociology*, Malaysian sociologist Raymond Lee (1994) has suggested that we may be witnessing the unfolding of a new paradigm in the industrializing countries of Asia which stresses ambivalence as the linchpin of development. By this Lee means that the progress of modernity, rather than constituting a straight path ahead, instead assumes a more complex form in which the global is tailored to the local and vice versa.

Nowhere is this more evident than in the culture industry. On the one hand, the penetration of multinational capitalism into Asian societies brings with it the complete package of western cultural forms – television, fast food chains, shopping malls, freeways, theme parks and sports entertainment – all of which signify instances of the good life (Lee 1994: 29). Yet, rather than completely undermine and replace local cultures, as might be expected, instead this seems to have resulted in the emergence of a new type of consciousness which is both particular and universal at the same time (ibid.: 27). Lee identifies this as part of the global trend towards "staged" and "reconstructed" authenticity (MacCannell 1976), wherein traditional crafts, dances, foods etc. are artificially preserved and reconstructed for the benefit of international leisure-seekers. Historical memory here is utilized primarily for sensory effect (Lee 1994: 28).

Such displays have been criticized on the grounds that they convey an unreal image of indigenous life, representing the dominant group's decision as to what is superficially interesting about the minority groups' cultures (Richter 1989: 186–8). This is of particular concern in multi-ethnic nations such as Indonesia, Malaysia and Singapore where political power is concentrated in the hands of a single ethno-religious group.

To a certain degree, the development of themed entertainment venues on the Asia-Pacific Rim validates Lee's observation. At the same time, as the American-created model of Fantasy City steamrolls across Asia, one also finds an increasing emphasis on "cultural theme parks" which attempt to revive elements of traditional culture for purposes of tourist gazing (Urry 1990). What Lee may have overlooked, however, is the extent to which this plays to local and regional consumers as well as to the flow of international pleasure-seekers.

There are two templates to consider here. First is the "buffet" model whereby the visitor is given a number of choices, some of which are rooted in global culture, while others are more concerned with replicating traditional ways. At the (soon to be opened) Kyongju World Tradition Folk Village, visitors will be able to choose from various "cultural zones" – South Pacific, European, Americana – as well as visit an educational and recreational center themed from Korean history. Already in operation is a park called "Seoulland," divided into five themed areas. Whereas most of the roller coasters and rides are located in "Tomorrow Land" and "Adventure Land," "Samchulli Land" appeals to the local Korean clientele, providing a variety of traditional Korean dishes, an outside shopping bazaar and a traditional crafts exhibit area (O'Brien 1996c: 27).

Second is the possibility of theming of a park around local elements and customs. An early example of this was a park conceived by Tien, the late wife of President Suharto of Indonesia, in 1971. Called Taman Mini Indonesia Indah, it reproduces in miniature the thousands of islands that make up the Indonesian archipelago and contains exhibits, somewhat static by today's standards, of the culture and daily life in various parts of the country. Another park with a long history is Singapore's Haw Par Villa (soon to be renamed Tiger Balm Gardens) which, in its present manifestation, bills itself as the only Chinese mythological theme park in the world, and as a place "where both Singaporeans and tourists can appreciate the Chinese culture and values" ("Asians at play" 1996).

In keeping with present-day trends in museums and other cultural institutions toward a greater sensitivity to indigenous people and their historical experience, several recent additions to the roster of theme parks are more explicit in stressing aboriginal themes. Balinesia, in Bali, Indonesia, is a $100 million cultural theme park project with plans to culturally link-up various Indonesian islands at the same time as providing rides for visitors accustomed to the high-tech fantasy experience. A second Balinese attraction, the Taman Festival Park, which was to be completed in July 1997, is currently on hold. While it now opens on a limited basis for weekend laser shows, it is still not quite finished – a casualty of the present uncertain financial situation in Indonesia. Incorporating local culture into the project required a great amount of research, notes Steve Moorhead of Forrec, the park designer: "We've had to invent it from a lot of different things we know" (Zoltak 1996c). Another proposed theme park, the Agro Tourism Resort in Penang, Malaysia, is to be a themed destination created around the cultural history of the country. Among other things, it will juxtapose a waterpark and a nature and wildlife preserve.

Perhaps the most integrity-soaked cultural theme park in the region is the Tjapukai Cultural Theme Park, in Cairns in the Queensland state, Australia. Light years away ideologically, if not geographically, from the Reef Casino, Tjapukai is partially owned by the local Aboriginal community. With the help of holographic and other state-of-the art technology, it attempts to provide an "authentic" introduction to the life, culture and language of the Tjapukai tribe of far north Queensland. In the "Creation Theatre," 3-D images and brightly painted dancers interact with one another in the presentation of a show about how Australian Aboriginals explain the beginnings of life. Outside, visitors venture into a traditional village where they can sample Aboriginal foods, learn about bush medicines, and receive lessons in boomerang throwing and didgeridoo playing (Heazle 1996a).

Tjapukai, however, is the exception rather than the rule, and the majority of the merchants of leisure in the Asia-Pacific region are primarily concerned with finding a formula that will be commercially successful. The precise nature of this formula is not yet clear. Chinese theme park developers, for example, don't appear to be certain how closely they should embrace Disney-style theming. The new theme parks which are set to open in the late part of the twentieth century, in the Chinese cities of Shenzhen, Shanghai and Guangzhou, are incorporating a sometimes eccentric cultural accommodation, with medieval knights and Wild West gunslingers alike delivering their lines in Mandarin Chinese (Reyes 1996). As Jeff McNair, president of Forrec, a Canadian planning and design firm which now does 40 percent of its business in Asia, notes: "they [prospective Chinese clients] have a hard time deciding what product will make sense. There's one set who wants to focus on the heritage and culture. Another set says forget that, let's do what works in North America. Nobody's done it right" (Muret 1996a: 39).

"Doing it right" in Asian countries involves taking into account a number of cultural differences for both developers and consumers. Unlike in American cities, the Asian middle class don't regard a trip into the central city as a safari into a zone of crime and danger. In fact, such leisure activities are normally undertaken in family groups rather than individually. One family event which is especially big and usually celebrated outside the home is a child's birthday party which may have three times the number of guests of an American party (Zoltak 1996b: 19). This necessitates a number of product and design changes. For example, wider walkways are required to provide room for three generations shopping together (Altoon 1997). Furthermore, unlike North American shoppers who prefer to circulate on only one or two levels, Asian consumers don't mind going up three or four storeys. As a result, entertainment centers can be profitably located on the top floors of retail entertainment malls.

At the same time there are a number of risk factors not evident in America. Retail location is governed by the practice of *feng shui*, a combination of architecture, metaphysics, science and parapsychology which aims to harmonize the placement of humanly constructed structures in nature. Failure to pay attention to the report of a *feng shui* expert when planning a project may result in a building being shunned by laborers, suppliers and customers (Munkacy 1997b). Throughout most of the Asia-Pacific Rim, the tendency is for independent merchants to own their own businesses and shops rather than to rent retail space (Altoon 1997). Where American-style retail relationships do exist, developers rarely provide tenant allowances. As a result, you need more capital and a higher return on rents to enter into joint ventures. Despite the considerable American content of these new urban entertainment destinations, then, they are by no means carbon copies.

Figure 10.1 "The city as entertainment": Downtown Toronto skyline and the former Greenwood Raceway.

Source: Michael Burns, courtesy of the Beach Metro Community News.

10

SAVED BY A MOUSE?

Urban entertainment and the future of cities

In his book *Edge City*, Washington journalist Joel Garreau (1991) proposes that the history of America constitutes a continuing attempt by utopian-minded pioneers to head out of the cities in order to create a new Eden on the physical edge of the landscape (the frontier). Here they would forge a "new restorative synthesis" by merging the best features of both urban and rural living: the machine and the garden. Contemporary "edge cities" – outer suburbs with their own corporate offices, shopping complexes and cultural centers – represent the most recent imprint of this dominant historical current. Unfortunately, Garreau fails to emphasize exactly what else underlies this century-long flight from the city proper: the desire for social class segregation. As historian Robert Fishman (1987: 119) has noted, unlike the rich who could securely barricade themselves wherever they wished, the middle class had more to lose if they were caught in a changing urban neighborhood engulfed by immigration. Remaining in an urban townhouse, he observes, represented a considerable economic and social risk for the American bourgeoisie after the mid-nineteenth century. Not only were their new working-class neighbors thought to be rowdy and given to bouts of public drunkenness but they were also suspected of harboring socialist and even anarchist political tendencies .[1]

As American cities swelled with the influx of immigrants in the late nineteenth and early twentieth centuries, a single-class residential district seemed incompatible with the urban core, so these were constructed instead at the periphery where distance served as an insulator (Fishman 1987: 119). The architects of these new middle-class suburbs were quite forthcoming about their intentions and strategies. In the 1860s, Frederick Law Olmsted, the designer of Central Park in New York, undertook a plan for the suburb of Riverside, Illinois, just outside Chicago, observing that prospective builders and buyers needed some assurance that "these districts not be bye and bye invaded by the desolation which thus far has invariably advanced before the progress of the town" (Schuyler 1986: 263). A half century later, his stepson John, also a landscape architect, justified the generous lot sizes in a fashionable Atlanta suburb on the grounds that "they mitigated against the likelihood of poor purchasers" (Goldfield 1989: 102). To ensure that undesirable land uses and residents would be kept out, these suburban neighborhoods were segregated along the lines of race, religion, ethnicity and economics. Thus, in Palos Verdes Estates outside Los Angeles, cost restrictions mandated minimum lot sizes, setback requirements and construction costs, and, if this wasn't enough, residential covenants attached to the deeds excluded African-Americans,[2] Asians and even Mexican-Americans who couldn't prove "pure" Spanish ancestry (Palen 1995: 51).

Much the same story applies to the gated communities of the 1990s which have grown in leaps and bounds, especially in Florida, California and the Pacific north-west. After interviewing a cross-section of these gated-community dwellers, planning professors Edward Blakely and Mary Gail Snyder concluded that residents above all sought a predictable, controlled environment with no surprises. "Fortress America," as they term it, is presented as a flight from chance, a safe, secure enclave in which people are protected from the "vagaries of existence . . . falling property values, vandalism, violence, even an unplanned conversation with a person unlike oneself" (Lears 1997: 9).

In *Fantasy City*, I have argued that this overriding desire of the American middle-class for predictability and security has for a long time spilled over into the domain of leisure and entertainment. During the "golden age" of public amusements (see Chapter 1), this was secured by a spate of restrictive laws and practices (e.g. separate entrances and seating) and by tight social control from amusement park police, theater ushers and others. After the Second World War when civil rights and other legislation swept away many of these protective devices, theme parks, sports arenas, stadiums and other entertainment venues were consciously situated beyond the geographic and financial reach of minorities and the poor in the exurban fringe or in rural counties. Despite a partial shift of amusement businesses back to the inner city, many of these same barriers are still in place in the 1990s.

Affordability is still one significant obstacle to wider accessibility. For example, at Sea World in San Diego, market research data from 1992 indicated the existence of an affluent (a third of those surveyed earned $50,000 a year or more) and educated (43 percent had a college degree or higher) customer base. Only 15 percent reported a family income of $15,000 or below. "Non-Anglos" constituted just 11 percent of customers (Davis 1997: 36–7). In her study, Susan Davis considers it likely that the admission price keeps poor people out of the park, but she also hypothesizes that Sea World deliberately and effectively exploits a long-standing connection between nature appreciation and middle-class self-improvement, constructing its "nature spectacles" with an eye to the educated, upwardly mobile and wealthy.

Geographic location continues to be another barrier to participation for poorer people in Fantasy City. Most of the major malls and theme parks are situated beyond the exurban fringe, making them difficult to reach without a car. In one tragic case, which was widely reported in the American media, Cynthia Wiggins, a young black single mother, was killed on her way to work at the upmarket Walden Galleria Mall in the suburbs adjacent to Buffalo, New York.

Although tour buses were allowed to enter the parking area, it appears city buses were not, and Wiggins was hit by a dump truck while attempting to cross a seven lane highway to reach the mall (Barnes 1996; Gottdiener 1997: 133–4).

Even within the boundaries of the central city, however, entertainment destinations can be surprisingly inaccessible to those who cannot drive there, as they are frequently located on the margins of docklands or former maritime ports. Philadelphia, Pennsylvania, is one such example. Between 1990 and 1995 fifteen new bars and restaurants opened along the city's waterfront boasting such exotic names as the Amazon Club, Katmandu, Egypt, Maui, Rock Lobster and Deco. The most ambitious of these is Dave & Busters, a 70,000 square foot entertainment and recreation complex for adults complete with a billiards room, two restaurants, two saloon-type bars, a midway, a high-tech video arcade and space for private dining and entertainment. These have been joined by an expanded seaport museum, an ice skating rink and a new Hyatt hotel. But, as a guest from the Philadelphia area pointed out to me, you can't reach the waterfront by public transit and the cab fare is too expensive for most people. Not surprisingly, this urban entertainment destination has become a popular preserve for the suburban middle class who drive in on weekends. The same dilemma is faced by those trying to reach The Docks, a trendy nightclub and leisure complex for young adults situated along the Toronto Harbor east of the downtown area. On one occasion, my wife and I attended a tourist bureau reception there after a lake cruise. Unable to secure a cab back, we started to walk but soon realized that this would require negotiating a battery of multi-level expressways on foot. Vanquished, we sought refuge in a no-frills supermarket warehouse en route and telephoned a friend to come and rescue us.

Furthermore, some critics have charged that the poor and disadvantaged in the postmodern American city not only find it difficult to access entertainment venues but these projects have, in fact, forced them out of spaces which they formerly occupied and utilized. In City of Quartz, Mike Davis' (1990) apocalyptic profile of contemporary Los Angeles, Davis concludes that what was once a genuine "democratic space" – free beaches, luxurious parks, "cruising strips" – is now extinct. Wealthy residents are increasingly retreating to defensible urban centers, notably the new corporate financial district, gentrified residential zones and luxury hotels, while the homeless and the working poor are sequestered in decaying neighborhoods studded with high-tech prisons and patrolled by police helicopters. Canadian architectural historian Trevor Boddy (1992) has coined the term "the analogous city" to describe a postmodern metropolis which is dominated by a controlled simulation. One leading aspect of this has been the emergence of new pedestrian systems – skyway pedestrian bridges, subterranean tunnels, glass walkways – which he identifies as having the same roots as the theme park and the festival market. These "surrogate streets" are insidious, Boddy claims, because they remove the last remaining vestiges of public life; imposing a kind of "virtual reality apartheid" in which the underclass is banished to the open streets while the white middle-class travel safely and separately. Sharon Zukin is barely more optimistic, arguing that in newer cities such as Los Angeles or San Antonio Texas, developments which attempt to reclaim the historic core, or more correctly, the "fictitious" historic core of the city for the middle classes serves to displace those who already live there from public spaces they once considered their own and to purge these landscapes of their authenticity (1995: 19–20). Zukin calls this marginalization of local people and cultures by a commercially driven, safe, middle-class culture "pacification by cappuccino" (ibid.: 28).

In short, issues of public (and private) space – who uses it, who feels welcome to use it, and who knows better than to try and use it – are as relevant for urban entertainment as we enter the new millennium as they were during the early decades of the twentieth century (Abelson 1996: 528). From the creation of a new public culture in turn-of-the-century cities through to the most recent ventures in building suburban shopping malls and exurban theme parks, downtown festival market places and themed destinations, we can identify a continual search for "riskless" mass entertainment which minimizes contact between rich and poor, blacks and whites, at the same time as it maximizes financial returns to a small cohort of developers and leisure merchants. According to Herbert Muschamp (1995b), this "business class city" is an attempt to reinscribe secure, middle-class values within the urban center. A kind of hybrid, urban–suburban ethos that "fuses suburban security and standardization with urban congestion and pizzazz", it offers the middle class a pleasant public setting where people can enjoy a public space without fear. But, observes Muschamp, the business class city threatens to remake the city into an invisible fortress where "rich and poor are still polarized but the gap between them is less conspicuous" (1995b: 38).

A second important feature in the evolution of Fantasy City is the identity of its gatekeepers; those people who decide what will be built, how it will look, where it will go and how it will be funded. During the "golden age," these gatekeepers were (at least initially) idiosyncratic and colorful individual investors and impresarios who built entertainment empires from scratch. Later, as the new corporate-industrial order in America flourished the entertainment business was underwritten by banks and investment houses and run according to more conventional business practices.

When city building resumed after the Second World War, the gatekeeper role expanded to include city politicians, planners and administrators who joined real estate developers in what came to be known as "public–private partnerships" (see Chapter 7). One reason for the involvement of the public sector was the rich flow of federal government funds – for urban renewal, highway construction, new residential housing – for which they acted as conduits. Despite its public face, however, most of this development continued to be carried out within a predominant "ideology of privatism" (Squires 1989: 4). Initially designed to encourage the development of low-cost residential housing, the urban renewal mandate was expanded to include non-residential projects, the rationale being that downtown commercial areas were under threat from the increasing popularity of suburban shopping centers. Soon, shopping malls, office buildings and convention centers rather than housing became the central focus of urban renewal projects and the downtown public–private partnerships which built them became skilled players in the game of grabbing massive public subsidies for private business development.

One of the legacies of these downtown revival efforts was the privatization of large tracts of land in or adjacent to the central business core. For example, Charles Center in Baltimore stretched over 33 acres; Government Center in Boston 44 acres; the Capital Mall in Sacramento, California 59 acres; and the Gateway Center in Minneapolis 72 acres (Frieden and Sagalyn 1989: 27). Later on, the "Rouseification" of waterfront areas in many American cities (see Chapter 3) further extended this privatizing of urban land and space, although nominally some of these festival market places were owned by publicly consti- tuted redevelopment agencies.

The differences between private and public space soon became apparent. While Red Cross blood donor clinics were permitted to set up shop inside new developments, groups which espoused a social or political cause were excluded. Political demonstrations were banned and strikers were not allowed access inside malls to picket stores where they were employed. Small vendors were kept out in favor of large, chain-store tenants. Curfews were imposed on those suspected of bringing trouble with them, notably teenagers. In the spirit of Disneyland, dress rules (e.g. shirts and shoes to be worn at all times) were declared. In addition, the corporate owners of these new landscapes of consumption increasingly began to take over the transitional spaces which buffered the inside from the outside. Boyer (1993: 119) notes how the festival market places, museum atriums and shops, corporate foyers, public art, 'gardens' and interior arcades in public places such as Battery Park City in Manhattan are in fact advertising sites linked to public relations campaigns in an attempt to humanize "public-spirited" super companies. This has had the effect of further blurring the boundaries between the public and the private realms.

In the most recent round of urban development in the 1990s, the private sector has continued to call the shots. To start with, decades of cutbacks in government grants and subsidies to museums, arts organizations and leisure venues has made it a necessity to bring in private partners. Furthermore, some of the larger private firms appeared to possess both sterling track records and ready access to capital. Disney's phenomenal success at creating walkable streets and pleasing public spaces in its theme parks at "precisely the same time when Americans were abandoning the city for their cars and suburban cul-de-sacs" (Pollan 1997: 58) seemed reason enough to give the company, and companies like it, license to direct future urban growth. Whereas others had failed, cities might just "be saved by a mouse" (Blake 1972: 24; Cited in Warren 1994: 94).

The private partners of the late 1990s are a mix of the old and the new. Some developers such as the Simons and the Ratners have simply carried on where they left off in the 1980s. Others such as TrizecHahn have reconfigured under new ownership. Once counted out, the Reichmanns are back pursuing urban entertainment projects in Toronto and New York under the auspices of their Heathcliffe Development Company. At the same time, the new players in this sector are the global entertainment companies – Disney, Universal, Sony, Rank – who are able to bring to the table an ability to exploit a wide range of brand synergies and roll outs.

While it's too early to sound the death knell for what remains of public space in the city, there are some disquieting indications that the Maginot Line has been breached in some new and unexpected ways. For example, today's leisure merchants have not hesitated to use trademark law to establish a monopoly over the right to reproduce and market visual images of their pleasure domes. In one case, a local Cleveland photographer was legally restrained from taking and selling postcard pictures of the exterior of the Rock and Roll Hall of Fame. Disney has a history of being reluctant to allow authors the right to reproduce photos of their theme parks, especially if these are thought to be in any way critical of the Disney organization (see Bryman 1995: ix). Disney World, Michael Sorkin quips, "is the first copyrighted urban environment in history, a Forbidden City for postmodernity" (1992: 206). It also signifies the triumph of market over place (see Zukin 1991), as brand identity and protection is extended from manufactured goods to the spaces and places of the city.

Furthermore, the corporate chains who own and operate sites and services within the theme park city have been attempting to colonize the transitional space between the interior and exterior of their facilities. Take for example, the case of "tailgating parties" which are a popular pastime at NFL games in such cities as Kansas City, Pittsburgh, Buffalo, San Diego and San Francisco. Tailgating fans arrive at the stadium at 9 a.m. on a Sunday, five hours before the game, and set up their barbeques. Some tailgating parties can become quite elaborate with square dancing and even tables set with china and candelabras. Many fans have been doing this for years and have turned it into a boisterous social event. Stadium managers don't usually discourage tailgating, although they often attempt to regulate it; at the Meadowlands in New Jersey, for example, "tailgating squads" patrol the parking lots and encourage people to take up only a single space. Some food concessionaires have sensed an opportunity and have set up barbeque tents and in some instances their own pre-game events. The best example of this is the Metrodome, the home of both the Minnesota Vikings of the NFL and Major League Baseball's Minnesota Twins. The Metrodome management spent $4.6 million constructing a new plaza which covers nearly a two-block area; it is equipped with permanent concessions and washrooms as well as interactive games and live bands booked by the Twins (Waddell 1996b: 33). Thus tailgating represents a terrain where public and private cultures potentially come into conflict. Under the rubric of improving the experience, some operators are clearly attempting to convert a form of grass-roots collective behavior into a commercial enterprise. Among other things, they have injected an element of stratification, introducing separate corporate party areas (Minneapolis), VIP tents and company parties (Kansas City). Not all fans have been receptive to this corporate tailgating but in some locations it seems to be gaining ground, thereby threatening to privatize and formalize an emergent local tradition.

A final feature of fantasy cities that should be noted is the nature of their "urban imaginary," that is, the set of meanings about the city that arise in a specific historical or cultural space (Guthreau et al. 1997). These meanings become transformed over time and are specifically reflected in changing architectural landscapes. In her study of tourist sites in Monterey, California, Martha Norkunas (1993) has demonstrated how canneries, which once processed fish, now display them as biological curiosities (the aquarium) or serve them up as leisure displays (hotels which offer diving experiences to tourists). Wright and Hutchison (1997) use the method of spatial semiotics to analyze the symbolic meaning of another cannery, the Cannery Restaurant in Newport Beach, California. In addition, they scrutinize the 94th Aero Squadron Restaurant of Long Beach, a themed eatery modeled on a First World War French farmhouse, similar to the type used by American soldiers. The former, they claim, aestheticizes work while the latter does the same for war. Yet, in its simulation of the work world the Cannery removes any possible image of industrial accidents, exploitation, pollution and class conflict, while the 94th Aero Squadron leaves out any images of death and destruction. Themed artifacts, they observe, are selected to create the theme but not "a theme that is too real" (1997: 207). As we saw in Chapter 8, once gambling interests took over in Gilpin County, Colorado, local landmarks were gutted inside and replaced by a contrived version of community history and culture which fit the casino-owners' fantasies of the Old West (Stokowksi 1996). What these examples have in common is a perceived loss of authenticity. That is, each suggests, more or less, that Fantasy City development is problematic because it transforms the meaning of a place from its original and genuine version to a commercial construction which tells a different story altogether.

Susan Fainstein (1994: 230–3) identifies and then proceeds to debunk two major assumptions which underlie this dismissal of contemporary redevelopment projects as inauthentic. First, that "authenticity" reigned in an earlier period of our history; and, second, that today's leisured landscapes are not "genuine" because they are unrelated to industrial production. The first assumption is nonsense, Fainstein argues, because most major structures in the western city since the Renaissance have been bastardized historical re-creations, often of Greek or Roman architecture. Even the most urbane and praiseworthy buildings have sustained the false front and a faulty imitation of times past. Much the same is true of the "golden age" of urban entertainment where the Hippodrome extravaganzas or the elaborate motion picture palaces almost always presented faux versions of past events or structures.

As for the second assumption, Fainstein argues that it is at odds with the reality of an economy that is increasingly organized around information flows, tourism and the consumption of services. The requirement that the genuine can only refer to craft workshops, steel mills and working maritime ports is nostalgia for a bygone era. While it is true, as Christine Boyer (1992) and Jon Goss (1996) have argued (see Chapter 3), that today's "experiential placemaking" rarely addresses the historical experience of the powerless who have built the city with their blood, sweat and tears, it is doubtful that this angle would play very successfully to touristic fantasy. After all, when we go to Caesar's Palace in Las Vegas, it is to imagine ourselves as sybarites at the Emperor's Court not as slaves rowing his galley ships.

Nevertheless, there are still some troubling aspects concerning the urban imaginary in the theme park city. Because the components of Fantasy City are largely standardized and follow the same modular configuration, most urban entertainment destinations lack distinctiveness thus reinforcing the "placelessness" which cultural geographer Ted Relph (1976) has pronounced the bane of contemporary cities. Indeed, this represents a good illustration of how the economics of development constrains and shapes the nature of the urban landscape. Since few companies have any sort of track record in entertainment retailing, developers invariably opt for the same short-list of tenants, each of whom has access to substantial lines of credit. What makes financial sense in the short term, however, may be disastrous five or ten years down the road. Little, it seems, has been learnt from the death of strip shopping centers and secondary malls built during the golden age of retail (1970–1989). Heralded at the time as being the future of shopping, their standardized design and mix of tenants resulted in a bland homogeneity, thereby opening the gates to challenges by big box power retailers, factory outlet malls and other new retailing concepts and formats. Might the same fate befall today's urban entertainment projects?

Furthermore, there is a danger that themed attractions and experiences will substitute for and challenge activities formerly associated with local communities. As I outlined in Chapter 4, the aggressive entry of theme parks and other entertainment centers into the holiday celebration market is one major example of this. For Hallowe'en 1997, for example, the MGM Grand hosted a special event where trick or treaters were invited to drop by and fill their sacks with goodies donated by local casinos. Disney has been especially adept at co-opting local experiences by providing a level of technology and service which is difficult to match. Some state fairs in the US have begun to experiment by including Disney attractions alongside the usual midways, agricultural exhibits and pie-eating contests. For the time being this is perceived as an attractive revenue booster with no negative effects. But for how long will Disney be content to remain a minor adjunct to the traditional fair activities? Likewise, how can American towns and cities match the lure of Disney's Wide World of Sports complex in Florida where amateur baseball championships are played out

196

in a lushly turfed, lemon-colored, 7,500 seat stadium and "even the losers get to go to Disney World" (Lipsyte 1997: 4)?

Looking ahead

What should we expect for the future of themed entertainment? As simulation and theming become more commonplace, it will become increasingly difficult to invent new and attractive products that will jointly meet escalating expectations for novel stimulation without increasing the corresponding levels of consumer risk. Not that we've reached that stage quite yet. IMAX's "Ridefilm" technology, for example, is genuinely unique and exciting, in the way that the first roller coaster must have been for amusement park patrons a century ago. Eventually, however, continued exposure may well lead to a profound sense of disappointment. Nigel Clark has termed this the "self-defeating nature of hyper-real simulation" and warns that it is only a matter of time before "sublimity cedes to banality" (1997: 85). This is less likely to occur in the handful of top venues, where the operators have the resources to constantly be on the cutting edge of new technologies, than in the thousands of regional family fun centers, theme restaurants and other attractions where the "real fake," as Ada Louise Huxtable (1997b: 2–1) has called it, is rarely witnessed.

Will the new entertainment economy, then, make twenty-first century cities more livable or will it further accelerate the fragmentation and loss of community which have been the hallmarks of recent urban history? Perhaps the best answer to this which I have seen is suggested in a review of two books, by historian Jackson Lears, on gated communities and neighborhood renewal. Lears comments that, "fruitopian communities" – restored urban areas organized around festival market places and the like – may be closer to stage sets than real streetscapes, but, "even a Fruitopian town is better than a placeless suburbia where there is no town to go to at all" (1997: 10). Nevertheless, Lears advances several guidelines for distinguishing between gentrification and revitalization. Is wealth being recreated in the community or is capital being drained away from local merchants and consumers and directed to distant corporate headquarters? Is the flight from chance which is so central to life in gated communities able to be reversed so as to recreate the possibility of safe, random encounters? Can post-industrial downtowns retain their distinctiveness even as they switch to providing services that could be found anywhere and everywhere? Lears' three questions apply equally well to the emerging Fantasy City which I have profiled in this book.

Regarding whether or not wealth is recreated, the answer seems to be a resounding "no." By and large, mega-projects such as downtown shopping malls, festival market places, new sports arenas and stadiums and urban entertainment centers are loss leaders in which intangible, image-related "spillovers" are expected to outweigh the actual economic benefits for the local community. Nowhere is this more obvious than in the case of Cleveland, Ohio. Along with

Baltimore, Cleveland has been celebrated as "a poster child of urban redevelopment" in the 1990s. With a revived entertainment district (Playhouse Square), a new sports complex (Gateway Center) and the high-profile Rock and Roll Hall of Fame, Cleveland bills itself as the "Comeback City": the premier tourist destination between New York and Chicago. While there is no doubt that the local growth machine in Cleveland has produced a miraculous turnaround in its reputation, critics have noted that the central city, by and large, remains impoverished, with 40 percent of Clevelanders, half of whom are black, trapped beneath the poverty line. This population has suffered the most due to deindustrialization, while enjoying few of the benefits of the sports and entertainment renaissance of the 1990s (Warford and Holly 1997: 218–19).

Fantasy City also stumbles on Lears' second test. As Paul Goldberger observes, the new urban paradigm which characterizes the theme park city "sanctions disengagement," denying the premise of the traditional city even as it professes to celebrate the virtues of urbanity" (1996: 137). In Chapter 4, I cited the relative frequency of casual, serendipitous encounters among visitors to Las Vegas. More typical, however, is the theme park model in which social interaction is restricted to those who accompany you on the trip. At Disney World, for example, most of the rides are intentionally designed to disallow seeing anyone, much less touching or talking to them; contact with fellow guests is "only minimally available and not at all desirable" (Kuenz 1993: 72). Certainly, it's nothing like walking down the street in my Toronto neighborhood where it's normal to encounter a familiar face. Such safe, pleasurable chance encounters also often occur at local leisure and entertainment venues in our neighborhood (the Fox, a second-run movie theater; the Beaches Arts Centre; the Easter Parade; the summer jazz festival; the Victoria Day fireworks extravaganza) but rarely do they happen at megaplexes, giant book, record and clothing stores or professional sporting events.

Finally, there's the question of local communities being able to retain their distinctiveness even as they embrace the fantasy entertainment components proffered by global entertainment companies. The situation here is a paradoxical one. As noted earlier in this chapter, the line-up of attractions at most themed destinations is highly uniform. Indeed, success in the theme park economy depends on being able to develop brand recognition both domestically and internationally. At the same time, villages, and especially towns and cities, are constantly scrambling to create distinctive entertainment identities, either by manipulating local history and culture or by producing "fantasies of a past that never was" (Hewison 1987: 10). In Harrisburg, Pennsylvania, for example, the present mayor, Mayor Reed, has already spent millions of dollars on historical objects which are intended to furnish a yet-to be-built Civil War Museum. Le Roy, New York has constructed its local identity and tourist appeal around its status as the place where "Jell-O" was invented.

In a newspaper interview, Lee Wagman, an executive with TrizecHahn, made the observation that the entertainment-based redevelopments which work are the ones that are "woven into the city's fabric," while the failures are those that become "stand-alone" islands which "don't evoke the locale's culture, history and identity" (Milner 1997b: B-1). In a similar vein, themed environment designer Bob Rogers (1996) cautions local entrepreneurs who may be tempted to rush in and embrace UEDs, to think carefully when creating a marketable identity. A classic mistake, he notes, is to engage in "cookbook thinking," putting a grab bag of discordant items (simulators, Wild West shoot-outs) next to one another without an attempt to create a unified meaning. The danger is that one of the big entertainment companies will subsequently step in with their branded characters and enormous film libraries and swallow you up. It is better, Rogers advises, to come up with an unique, community-based identity and to stay true to it. But how communities achieve this in an unforced and natural way is more difficult to divine, especially once you go beyond such cities as New York or San Francisco where strong historical identities have been at the forefront for a long time. Too often, an attempt to revitalize a town or neighborhood along historic lines results in falling into the "gentrification trap," whereby the original households are replaced and instead what is preserved and celebrated is the authenticity of the renovation (Ley 1996: 310).

Nearly seventy years ago, the pioneering urban sociologist Robert Park (1929), citing the German writer Von Ogden Vogt, distinguished between communities that are *descript* and those that are *nondescript*. The former, as epitomized by Oberammergau (known today as the site of the annual Passion Play), Bangkok and Oxford, are places of unity and charm where the common view is set forth "in laws, customs and the arts of life." In contrast, nondescript communities, although they may be of interest, lack an overriding sense of common purpose, mutual understanding or organized public opinion. As an example, he cited the Lower North Side of Chicago which at the time was in the process of evolution and lacked an identifiable collective bond. Nine years later, in the introduction to a book on ecological succession in Hawaii, Park (1938) noted the globalizing tendency of the modern world where European commerce and culture traveled along "a great ocean highway" that connects London, New York and San Francisco with Yokohama, Shanghai, Hongkong, Calcutta, Bombay and the Mediterranean. "A trip around the world in one of the seagoing hotels now in vogue" (i.e. ocean liners), he observed, "is now as much of an adventure as a bus trip up Fifth Avenue in New York or taking a stroll on Michigan Avenue in Chicago."

It seems to me that the Fantasy City I have tried to describe in this book, shares many of the same qualities of the globalizing, nondescript city as described by Park. Despite the new virtual technologies and clever simulations, the refurbished theaters and ballparks, Fantasy City lacks the social and aesthetic unity of the descript community. In addition, the great ocean highway identified by Park is now carrying an even greater volume of traffic, only this time the content is of American origin and even Bangkok has become a notable port of call.

During the same period as Park was writing about the nature of cities, another noted American sociologist, George Lundberg, and his colleagues reported the results of a detailed study of the leisure and recreational habits of a suburban community in Westchester County near New York. Lundberg noted that almost all the leisure and recreational pursuits cost money and had become explicitly organized, and thus regarded as "commodities to be purchased rather than experiences to be lived" (1934: 85). In Fantasy City, leisure and entertainment continue to be commodities but today lived experiences are also for sale, even if these are more often than not virtual rather than real. But whereas in Westchester County in the 1930s public entertainment (attendance as a spectator at sports, movies, theaters, fashion shows and amusement parks) fell into fourth place as a favored leisure activity behind eating, visiting and reading, today it is a major part of our lives with a strong "corporate existence" that was not evident in the earlier era.

All of the above should give us pause to consider whether this is the kind of leisure and the kind of city which we want for the first decades of the next millennium. As Susan Fainstein (1995: 136) has pointed out, "creating [entertainment] spaces that people enjoy, even if they do not faithfully reproduce the past and even if it makes some people feel like outcasts is not in itself so terrible" .Yet, at the same time, are we willing to give up the attempt to create a descript city in which the "dream of a public culture" (Zukin 1995: 294) flourishes? Are we prepared to overlook the cultural diversity in the community in favor of pre-packaged corporate entertainment destinations? Will there be room for leisure activities other than those which can be branded, licensed, franchised and rolled out on a global scale? And, finally, are we prepared to designate our inner cities no-go zones except for the heavily fortified themed attractions which welcome a constant flow of tourists embarked on leisure safaris into the depths of the postmodern metropolis?

NOTES

INTRODUCTION

1 For an opposing view, see the scathing review of Huxtable's book by architect and urban commentator Witold Rybczynski (1997) in the *New York Times Book Review*.

1 "AT PRICES ALL CAN AFFORD"

1 This account is based on the article "Big New Year's Fete at Times Square," *New York Times*, 1 January 1905, p.1.
2 See Jaher (1982); Couvares (1984).
3 In fact, it was Davis' extensive portfolio of commercial property which both allowed him to try out the nickelodeon idea in temporarily vacant storefronts and expand quickly when it began to take off beyond his initial expectations. See Musser (1990), p. 420.
4 Halsey, Stuart & Co. , "Prospectus," 27 May 1927. Reprinted in Balio (1976).
5 *Motion Picture World*, 1, no. 25 (August 1907), p. 391. Cited in Waller (1995), pp. 70–1.
6 "Management's proclamation to the public," *New York Times*, 9 April 1905.
7 "The reason why Balaban and Katz Theatres do not reserve seats." *Balaban & Katz Magazine* 1 (27 July 1925), p. 10. Cited in Nasaw (1993), p. 232.
8 This quote originally appeared in an article by the social reformer Julia Howe, "How the Fourth of July should be celebrated," *Forum* 15 (July 1893), p. 572. Cited in Rosenzweig (1983), p. 154.
9 As it was, Cobb had a near escape. Crowd members yanked the cable connecting the trolley to the electrical power source but a conductor reconnected it and the vehicle pulled away. See Kuklick (1991), pp. 31–2.
10 "Coney Island crowd huge, happy, orderly," *New York Times*, 31 May 1905, p. 7.
11 Slosson identified New York theatergoers as " that ordinary American crowd, the best natured, best dressed, best behaving crowd in the world." See Edwin E. Slosson, "The amusement business," *Independent* 59 (21 July 1904), p. 135. Cited in Nasaw (1993), p. 46.
12 *Lexington Herald* (28 November 1909), p. 7. Cited in Waller (1995), p. 81.
13 From 1890–1910 New York restaurateurs invested large sums in building, renovating and decorating lavish establishments in a faux style. John L. Murray's "Roman Gardens," for example, was designed to reflect the opulence of the ancient world with its Roman-style gardens and Egyptian- and Pompeii-style rooms. After hours, these restaurants became the haunt of wealthy society: sporting and club men who dined with actresses and showgirls over champagne and lobster suppers. See Erenberg (1991).

14 Gated communities are residential areas with restricted access and are designed to privatize normally public spaces. It is estimated that at least 3–4 million Americans live in these types of developments (see Blakely and Synder 1997).

2 DON'T GO OUT TONIGHT

1 "Astor roof N.Y passes: changed into offices," *Variety*, 28 June 1955, p. 2.
2 "More than twice as many pools," *The American City*, 78 (7) (July 1963), p. 28.
3 "In the swim of the backyard," *Life*, 18 July 1960, p. 64.
4 "The leisured masses," *Business Week*, 12 September 1953, pp. 142–52.
5 Darryl Zanuck, "Entertainment vs. recreation," *Hollywood Reporter*, 26 October 1953. Cited in Belton (1992), p. 77.
6 "The leisured masses," p. 150.
7 These figures are derived from the US Department of Commerce Social and Economic Statistics Administration, Bureau of Economic Analysis (Survey of Current Business). Cited in Jowett (1976), p 473.
8 "Drive-in theaters," *Dictionary of Twentieth Century Culture* (ed.) Karen L. Rood. Detroit: Gale Research Inc., 1994, p. 102.
9 According to Kerry Segrave (1992), author of what is probably the most complete history of drive-in theaters, in order for drive-ins to catch on, a country had to be wealthy, have a good deal of vacant, accessible, relatively cheap land, and possess a citizenry who widely owned and used their cars. This eliminated much of Europe and Japan where land was scarce and extremely expensive and the weather uncooperative (drive-in ventures in Britain, for example, failed in large part due to the climate). New Zealand never had drive-ins, primarily due to a twenty year moratorium on government approval. Australia first adopted drive-ins in 1954 and by 1957 nearly fifty had been built including a giant ozoner in Perth with a 120-foot screen and a 1,000 thousand car capacity. Despite its shorter six month season and a late start in Quebec due to clerical opposition, Canada reached a peak of 315 drive-ins in 1975, second only to the US.
10 For example, in early 1952 just 28 percent of drive-ins were owned by chains as against 46.8 percent of indoor theaters. However, the chains controlled more than half (54.7 percent) of the larger venues, that is, those with a capacity of more than 500 cars. See Segrave (1992), p. 75.
11 "Business bulletin," *Wall Street Journal*, 16 September 1965, p. 1.
12 "Education with fun and shivers: booming amusement parks spike bits of history with lots of excitement," *Life*, 1 August 1960, pp. 26–33.
13 "It's a new, brighter year for drive-ins," *Motion Picture Herald*, 20 May 1950, p. 3. Cited in Segrave (1992), p. 73.
14 "1 in 8 pic-goers went to drive-ins in July," *Variety*, 6 September 1950, p. 4. Cited in Segrave (1992), p. 145.
15 *Wall Street Journal*, 20 May 1965, p. 1.
16 Twenty years later, in the late 1990s, football appears poised to move back downtown from the suburbs; the Lions have proposed building a stadium alongside a new Tiger stadium for baseball in the Woodward Avenue corridor. See Suris and Blumenstein (1996).
17 "Detroit in Decline," *TIME*, 26 October 1961.
18 See: "Euclid Beach Park" and "The Euclid Beach Park Riot," in Van Tassel and Grabowski (1987), pp. 381–2; Bush (1983).
19 For an account of the final days of Olympic and Riverview parks see Adams (1991), pp. 66–73.
20 "Plan for Disneyland' (1965); Price (1995).

3 "CITIES ARE FUN"

1 It should be noted that Waterside represented Rouse's first project with the Enterprise Development Company (EDC), a new non-profit corporation which he founded after retiring from active day-to-day involvement in the Rouse Company. See "Norfolk and its waterfront: a timely partnership," *Center City Report* (International Downtown Executives Association), August 1983, pp. 1–2; 4.

2 This need not necessarily always be the case. In Bermuda's "Dockyard" complex, there is the usual retail line-up of a mini-mall, pushcarts, arts center, craft market and several theaters in addition to the Bermuda Maritime Museum. In one of the old buildings within the Museum yard can be found an emotionally moving exhibit showing the history of indentured laborers who toiled on the dockyard building in the nineteenth century, a fate worse than death according to one inmate whose thoughts have survived and are displayed in the exhibit.

3 Unfortunately, by the mid-1970s, armed with long-term tax abatement and tax exemption benefits from City Council, professional real estate developers had moved in to the district, eventually raising rents to a level which priced many artists out of the loft market. See Zukin (1982).

4 It is worth noting that an earlier (1972) bond issue which put all of the onus for financing on the city itself was canceled when only 18 percent of citizens expressed support in a pre-election poll. See "Super-cultural facility sparks redevelopment," *Center City Report* (International Downtown Executives Association), February 1981: pp. 9–11.

5 See: "Cleveland" in McNulty *et al.* (1986), pp. 83–5; "Playhouse Square" in Van Tassel and Grabowski (1987), pp. 771–2; Johannesen (1984); Miller and Wheeler (1990).

6 See Teaford (1990), p. 278. Illitch's plans for the surrounding area may have been overly ambitious, but the Fox has prospered. According to *Amusement Business* 1995–96 Mid-Year Report on the top grossing entertainment events in North America, an eight-show run of Andrew Lloyd Webber's show *Cats*, which ran at the Fox from April 16–21, 1996, grossed just under a million dollars, ranking it in the top twenty-five (*Amusement Business*, 17–23 June, 1996, p. 12).

7 "Property means development, livability," *Center City Report*, June 1981, pp. 1–3.

8 "Retail at the crossroads: how downtown can gain the retailing advantage," *Downtown Idea Exchange* 43, 4 (15 July 1996), pp. 1–3.

4 "SANITIZED RAZZMATAZZ"

1 The illusion of speed was accomplished here by four separate moving belts and screens arranged at slightly different heights and traveling at speeds ranging from 1,000 feet per minute (soil and rocks) to 16 feet per minute (remote backgrounds). The whole journey took forty-five minutes (De Vries 1971; Korol 1987).

2 According to the National Retail Federation, Hallowe'en generated $2.5 billion in sales in 1996, surpassing both Easter and Mother's Day. Hallowe'en has now become the leader in sales of candy ($900 million) and second in sales of home decorating goods behind Christmas (Cohen 1997; Steinhauer 1997).

5 SHOPERTAINMENT, EATERTAINMENT, EDUTAINMENT

1 It was recently announced that Royal Caribbean International is buying Celebrity Cruise Lines Inc. in a $1.3 billion cash and stock deal that will give the combined

company a fleet of more than 20 ships totalling more than 38,000 berths by the year 2000.

2 For details of NikeTown design and technology, I have drawn extensively on Creaux's (1997) profile in the trade periodical *TCI* (*Theatre Crafts International*).

3 This phrase seems to be universally loathed but it has somehow stuck, perhaps because it spells out, however, inelegantly, what is being conjoined here.

4 As Candace Slater (1995: 126) has pointed out, the compression of two words, rain and forest, into a single noun doubling as an adjective is a marketing strategy allowing it to be used to describe a host of products: Brazilian Rainforest gels, lotions and shampoos, Rainforest Crunch candy and, of course the Rainforest Cafe.

5 Given the bankruptcy of the Stratosphere Tower, it remains to be seen if this was a wise choice of venues after all.

6 Perelman's dealings with Earl have, in fact, been the subject of some controversy. In May, 1996, Christopher Connelly and Nancy Griffin, senior editors at a film magazine, *Premiere*, which was partly owned by Perelman, resigned rather than shelve a column, "California Suites" which was to examine the business dealings of actor Sylvester Stallone including his role in the Planet Hollywood chain. Recently, the Marvel company has itself been racked by problems with Perelman attempting to take it into bankruptcy in order to fend off a takeover by corporate investor Carl Icahn.

6 THE "WEENIE" AND THE "GENIE"

1 I will deal separately with the fifth category – public sector agencies – as part of my discussion of public–private partnerships in Chapter 7.

2 "The world according to Zell," *Urban Land* 53, September 1994: 25–9.

3 In 1995 J.P. Morgan & Co. Inc. assembled an in-house team of experts to provide paid advice to clients on the topic of risk management. The centerpiece of its approach has been the trademarked "Risk Metrics" system which provides methodologies for calculating the risks to which a company or financial institution is exposed (*Wall Street Journal*, 31 October 1995: 16).

4 *The Rockford Files* ran on NBC from 1974 to 1980 and then went on to become a hit in syndication. After determining that the show had pulled in more than $120 million for syndication, foreign and other subsidiary markets, the studio's accountants informed Garner that the official earnings were less than $1 million and his share amounted to not quite $250,000. Incensed, Garner sued and nearly a decade later settled out of court for a reported $5 million. See Prindle (1993: 23).

5 Not included here are Hilton, ITT, Mirage and the other major hotel and gaming companies, which I deal with separately in Chapter 7.

6 While two years may seem like a long time, in fact the original signed lease was for five years. At best when it closes in August 1997, the production will have only broken even. See Renzetti (1997).

7 "Walt and the golden mouse," *Forbes*, 15 February 1964: 38–9.

8 It is worth noting, however, that these robust sales figures are not uniform. Some units on the upper tier of CityWalk have evidently not performed as well, leaving a few unanticipated vacancies.

9 *Wall Street Journal*, 8 November 1994: A-1.

10 In its first six months of operation, the Sony–IMAX theater at Lincoln Square attracted more than 800,000 paying customers at $8 per ticket. See Gamerman (1995).

11 "Imax expands relationship with Sony," *TCI*, 29 May 1995: 15.

12 "Simon Property's purchase of DeBartolo creates real estate giant" *Financial Post*, 27 March 1996: 10.

13 Perhaps a glimpse of what is contained within this "black box" has been revealed in "Cafe-at-Play." With a patent application under consideration, the details of this project are still sketchy but it appears to be a unique juncture of location based entertainment and on-line computer technology, a combination which if successful would be the future of the new urban entertainment industry. Described as interactive, collaborative and multi-media, Cafe-at-Play is a joint venture of Simon's company, IMAX, and MRA, a leading urban entertainment consultant headed by former architect and urban designer Michael Rubin.

14 During the five-year recession in the commercial real estate market from 1990–95, the Rouse Company eschewed new development, including regional shopping malls, and concentrated instead on renovating and running its existing malls. See Haggerty (1995).

15 This term evidently originated from Walt Disney. Disney, it's alleged, got the idea for a visual attraction which pulls visitors toward it from his boyhood memory of luring a dog home by dragging a wiener on a string (Sharkey 1997: 8).

7 CALLING THE SHOTS

1 Ultimately none of these measures proved necessary since the Meadowlands project never got off the ground.

2 One notable exception to this is the erection of sports facilities, perhaps because these touch issues of community pride and identity in a way which is more powerful than for other types of entertainment and leisure facilities. In Denver, Colorado, for example, the public sector agreed to pay $156 million for the construction of "Mile High Stadium," a new baseball facility (Rosentraub 1997: 47).

3 Of the $74 million raised through the sale of PSLs, $26 million went to compensate the City of Anaheim with which the Rams still had continuing lease obligations; $13 million was earmarked for relocation expenses; $10 million went to the National Football League as part of the relocation penalties; $5 million was for a new practice facility; slightly less than $5 million was devoted to stadium improvements; $8 million covered the cost of settling a dispute over lease rights to the new stadium; and $6.5 million went to legal and advertising fees. All of this was in addition to the $700+ million promised by the City in order to build a new stadium, which, as Rosentraub (1997: 312–15) points out, would be used for only ten home games per year and which, due to an escape clause in the lease, could be abandoned as early as the year 2005.

4 Brad Segal, *Business Improvement Districts: A Tool for Economic Development*, International City/County Management Association, nd. Cited in *Downtown Idea Exchange*, June 1, 1997: 7.

5 The proposal to build the park is, in fact, associated with the Mashantucket Pequot tribe who operate the Foxwoods Resort Casino (see Chapter 8) and who own the land. According to one poll, 44 percent of residents in North Stonington oppose the project (McCormick 1997: 9).

6 Recently, the O'Malley ownership dynasty seems to have come to an end as the sale of the Dodgers to media mogul Rupert Murdoch has been announced. Murdoch evidently needed control of the team to give him access to the cable television broadcast rights for their home games. This is said to be part of a wider strategy for expanding into a national sports broadcaster.

8 GAMBLING ON FANTASY

1 This figure does not include the two documentaries made about Elvis, *Elvis – That's the Way It Is* (1970) and *Elvis on Tour* (1972).

2 It is worth noting that the two worlds have finally begun to move closer. For example, the popular rock group U2 recently launched their start of their world tour in Las Vegas.

3 Prior to 1969, the State of Nevada required all stockholders in a gambling business to be licensed. The new law waived this rule, requiring only major stockholders to be licensed.

4 Even today, whether an author uses the term "gambling" or "gaming" can act as a code to his/her support or opposition to the industry. For example, in a letter to *Urban Land*, a correspondent castigated William Katz (1996), an executive of Sun International (a resort and casino developer), for titling his article on the Mohegan Sun casino in Connecticut, "Mohegan Sun Theme Gaming." Within Chapter 8, I use both terms interchangeably, although I reserve the term "gaming" more for references to the industry itself.

5 Taxi drivers were said to have avoided the Stratosphere because it was difficult to find somewhere to turn around to head back along the Strip.

6 My discussion of the introduction of riverboat gambling in Iowa which follows is based on the account given in Goodman (1995).

7 "Daley outlines plan for Chicago's entertainment complex," News Release, Office of the Mayor, Chicago, 2 June 1993.

8 "Safe Bet or Risky Business?," A report on an all-day forum, 6 December 1993, on the pros and cons of riverboat gambling in Chicago. Sponsored by the Chicago Council on Urban Affairs. Chicago, 1994.

9 Summary of Chicago Entertainment Center Legislation, June, 1993.

10 The Cooper & Lybrand Consulting Group, *Report to the Ontario Casino Project*, Toronto, 12 August 1993, Figure 4.

11 However, in the fall of 1996 the Mohegan Pequots jumped on the gaming bandwagon, opening a 600,000 square foot casino ten miles away from Foxwoods.

12 Initially, the Pequots were unable to get conventional bank financing; as a result they turned to a casino operator in Malaysia who gave them a $55 million loan (Gregory 1992: 3).

13 In addition to contributing $500 million to the state between 1993 and 1997, the Pequots have also sponsored an $18 million waterfront rehabilitation program in nearby Norwich and given $5 million to the Mystic Marinelife Aquarium, $500,000 to the Hartford Ballet and $10 million to the Smithsonian Institution's Museum of the American Indian (K. McCormick 1997: 4).

14 One piece of advertising for the casino is a flyer titled, "Your Lucky Ticket to Casino Rama." Printed in English and Chinese, it promises Chinese-speaking hosts and dealers, and prints the number of a "Chinese Information Hotline."

15 In its first year of operation, revenue from the *Casino Queen* riverboat generated $10 million in taxes to the city and allowed property taxes to be reduced by 77 percent (Jinker-Lloyd 1996: 58).

16 It should be noted, however, that as a result of pressure from a coalition of community organizations in the mid-1980s, a small percentage (1.25 percent) of all gross receipts for gambling now goes by law to the New Jersey Casino Reinvestment Authority which uses half for housing-related projects and half for general community reinvestment.

17 CREN (Citizens' Research Education Network). *The Other Side of the Coin: A Casino's Impact in Hartford.* Hartford, CT: 16 December 1992.

18 "Youth is held in slaying of girl at Nevada casino," *New York Times*, 30 May 1997: A 12.

10 SAVED BY A MOUSE?

1 For example, Richard Sennett (1969) describes how a form of "moral panic" ensued among the burghers of the quiet middle-class Chicago neighborhood of Union Park in the wake of a bomb attack at a labor rally, followed by several high-profile break-ins and murders. Shocked Union Park residents demanded a garrison of police who would be engaged in constant surveillance and patrolling activities in order to make the community riot-proof and crime free.

2 In fact, this was quite common elsewhere. For example in Detroit in the 1940s deeds in every subdivision specified the exclusion of African-Americans (Sugrue 1996: 44).

BIBLIOGRAPHY

Abelson, E.S. (1996) "The city as playground: Culture, conflict and race," *American Quarterly* 48: 523–9.

Abu-Lughod, J.L. (1994) *From Urban Village to East Village, The Battle for New York's Lower East Side*, Oxford, England, and Cambridge, Mass.: Blackwell.

"A busted flush" (1997) *The Economist*, 25 January: 26–8.

Adams, J.A. (1991) *The American Amusement Park Industry: A History of Technology and Thrills*, Boston: Twayne Publishers.

Adler, J. (1995) "Theme cities," *Newsweek*, 11 September: 68–70.

Aguilar, L. (1995) "Developers chip away at opposition to mall," *Washington Post*, 28 September: MDM-1–2.

Allen. R.C. (1982) "Motion picture exhibition in Manhattan, 1906–1912: Beyond the nickleodeon," in G. Kindem (ed.), *The American Film Industry: The Business of Motion Pictures*, Carbondale and Edwardsville, IL: Southern Illinois University Press.

Altheide, D.L. (1997) "Media participation in everyday life," *Leisure Sciences* 19(1): 17–29.

Altoon, R.A. (1997) "Adapting the U.S. retail prototype to Asia," *Urban Land* (Asia Supplement), May: 29.

Alvarez, A. (1996) "Learning from Las Vegas," *The New York Review of Books*, 11 January: 15–16.

Alvarez, L. (1997) "For tribes, a call to action to get tax plan defeated," *New York Times*, 18 June: 1–14.

Angelo, B. (1996) "Hungry for theme dining," *TIME*, 22 July: 30–2.

"Asians at play: a good day out." (1996) *The Economist*, 21 December: 47–50.

Austin, B.A. (1985) "The development and decline of the drive-in movie theater," *Current Research in Film*, no. 1, Norwood, NJ: Ablex.

"Australia's first theme park Dreamworld" (1985) *Amusement Park Journal* 8(1): 17.

Baade, R.A. (1994) "Stadiums, professional sports, and economic development: assessing the reality," *Heartland Policy Study* 62: 28 March.

——(1996a) "Professional sports as catalysts for metropolitan development," *Journal of Urban Affairs* 18(1): 1–17.

——(1996b) "Stadium subsidies make little economic sense for cities: a rejoinder," *Journal of Urban Affairs* 18(1): 33–57.

——and Dye, R.F. (1988) "Sports stadiums and area development: a critical review," *Economic Development Quarterly* 2: 265–75.

——(1990) "The impact of stadiums and professional sports on metropolitan area development," *Growth and Change* 21: 1–14.

Balio, T. (ed.) (1976) *The American Film Industry*, Madison, WI: University of Wisconsin Press.

Barnes, E. (1996) "Can't get there from here," *TIME*, 19 February: 33.

Bator, J. (1992) "Ogden Corporation," in P. Kapos (ed.) *International Directory of Company Histories*, vol. 6, Detroit MI and London: St James Press.

"Beantown U.S.A" (1996) *The Economist*, 21 December: 25–7.

Beck, U. (1992) *Risk Society*, Beverley Hills, CA: Sage.

Beers, D. (1996) *Blue Sky Dream: A Memory of America's Fall From Grace*, New York: Doubleday.

Belton, J. (1992) *Widescreen Cinema*, Cambridge, Mass.: Harvard University Press.

Bermel, A. (1963) "How to treat the Broadway Malady of 1963," *Harper's Magazine* 27 (December): 56–62.

Berry, B. (1985) "Islands of renewal in seas of decay," in P.E. Peterson (ed.), *The New Urban Reality*, Washington, DC: Brookings Institution.

Beyard, M.D. and Rubin, M.S. (1995) "A new industry emerges," *Urban Land* (Supplement), August: 6–8.

Bibby, R. W. (1987) *Fragmented Gods: The Poverty and Potential of Religion in Canada*, Toronto: Irwin Publishing.

Blake, P. (1972) "Walt Disney World," *Architectural Forum* 136: 24–41.

Blakely, E.J. and Snyder, M.G. (1997) *Fortress America: Gated Communities in the United States*, Washington: Brookings Institution Press/Lincoln Institute of Land Policy.

Boddy, T. (1992) "Underground and overhead: Building the analogous city," in M. Sorkin (ed.), *Variations on a Theme Park*, New York: Hill & Wang.

Bourdieu, P. (1984) *Distinction*, trans. R. Nice, London: Routledge & Kegan Paul.

Boyer, M.C. (1992) "Cities for sale: merchandising history at South Street Seaport," in M. Sorkin (ed.), *Reflections on a Theme Park*, New York: Hill & Wang.

——(1993) "The city of illusion: New York's public places," in P. Knox (ed.), *The Restless Urban Landscape*, Englewood Cliffs, NJ: Prentice Hall.

Bradbury, K.L., Downs, A., and Small, K.A. (1981) "Forty theories of urban decline," *Urban Affairs Papers* 3(2): 13–20.

——(1982) *Urban Decline and the Future of American Cities*, Washington, DC: The Brookings Institution.

Brown, C. (1995) "Meat loaf and monkeys," *Forbes*, 23 October: 44–5.

Brown, J.R. and Laumer, M. (1995) "Comeback cities," *Urban Land* 54(8): 46–51; 83.

Bruni, F. (1996) "Tourists flood Harlem's churches," *New York Times*, 24 November: 24.

Bryman, A. (1995) *Disney and his Worlds*, London and New York: Routledge.

Buffman, Z. (1995) "Financing, partnership, and management arrangements," Urban Land Institute Professional Development Seminar on "Developing Urban Entertainment Destination Projects," New York, 17 March.

Bukowczyk, J.J. (1989) "Detroit: the birth, death and renaissance of an industrial city," in J.J. Bukowczyk and D. Aikenhead (with P. Slavchett) (eds), *Detroit Images: Photographs of the Renaissance City*, Detroit: Wayne State University Press.

Bush, L.O. (1983) "Euclid Beach Park: more than special," *Amusement Park Journal* 5(2&3): 26–8; 30–3.

Byrne, P. and Cadman, D. (1984) *Risk, Uncertainty and Decision-making in Property Development*, London and New York: E. and F.N. Spon.

Cashill, R. (1996a) "Jekyll & Hyde: Theatre vets cook up drop-dead Manhattan dining," *TCI(Theatre Crafts International)* 30(2): 44–7.

——(1996b) "Wynn goes Italian, Chuck goes Russian," *TCI*, May: 21.

Chauncey, Jnr, G. (1991) "The policed: Gay men's strategies of everyday resistance," in W. Taylor (ed.), *Inventing Times Square*, New York: Russell Sage Foundation.

Choldin, H.M. (1985) *Cities and Suburbs: An Introduction to Urban Sociology*, New York: McGraw Hill.

Christenson, J. (1997) "The greening of gambling's golden boy," *New York Times*, 6 July: 3–1, 9.

Christiansen, E. and Brinkerhoff-Jacobs, J. (1995) "Gaming and entertainment: An imperfect union?," *Cornell Hotel and Restaurant Quarterly* 36(2): 79–94.

City of Chicago (1986) *The Impact of a Major League Baseball Team on the Local Economy*, Department of Economic Development, April.

Clark, N. (1997) "Panic ecology: Nature in the age of superconductivity," *Theory, Culture & Society* 14: 77–96.

Clay, G. (1994) "Cultural arts district," in *Real Places: An Unconventional Guide to America's Generic Landscape*, Chicago: University of Chicago Press.

"Coffee, tea or Broadway" (1997) *New York Times*, 20 April: 3–2.

Cohen. A. (1997) "U.S. adults and Halloween amount to a question for the psychologists," *Globe & Mail*, 27 October: A–16.

Cohen, E. (1995) "Golf in Thailand: From sport to business," *Southeast Asia Journal of Social Science* 23(2): 1–17.

Cohen, N. (1998) "Property developers strive for brand recognition," *Financial Post*, 20 January: 19.

Cooper, R.R. (1996) "California Dreamin" (a review of D. Beers' *Blue Sky Dream*), *New York Times Book Review*, 27 October: 25.

Covell, J. (1996) "Hard Rock Cafe International," in T. Grant (ed.), *International Directory of Company Histories*, vol. 12, Detroit MI and London: St James Press.

Couvares, F.G. (1984) *The Remaking of Pittsburgh: Class and Culture in an Industrializing City – 1877–1919*, Albany, NY: State University of New York Press.

Craig, S. (1997) "TrizecHahn unleashes US$200 M genie at Las Vegas' Aladdin," *The Financial Post*, 21 March: 1.

Crawford, M. (1992) "The world in a shopping mall," in M. Sorkin (ed.), *Variations on a Theme Park*, New York: Hill & Wang.

Creaux, E. Lampert (1997) "Show business: New York's Niketown redefines the retail experience," *TCI (Theatre Crafts International)* 31(3): 36–9.

Cronon, W. (ed.) (1995) *Uncommon Ground: Rethinking the Human Place in Nature*, New York: W.W. Norton & Company.

Crooks, H. (1993) *Giants of Garbage: The Rise of the Global Waste Industry and the Politics of Pollution Control*, Toronto: James Lorimer & Company.

Damsell, K. (1997) "Eateries hope to serve steady diet of profit," *The Financial Post*, 22 August: 18.

Davis M, (1990) *City of Quartz*, London: Verso.

——(1995) "House of cards," *Sierra* 80(6): 37–41; 76.

Davis, S. (1995) "Touch the magic," in W. Cronon (ed.), *Uncommon Ground*, New York: W.W. Norton & Company.

——(1997) *Spectacular Nature: Corporate Culture and the Sea World Experience*, Berkeley and Los Angeles: University of California Press.

Dear, M. (1995) "Prolegomena to a postmodern urbanism," in P. Healey, S. Cameron, S. Daroudi, S. Graham and A. Madani-Pour (eds), *Managing Cities: The New Urban Context*, Chichester, West Sussex: John Wiley & Sons.

Demarest, M. (1981) "He digs downtown: for master planner James Rouse urban life is a festival," *TIME*, 24 August: 36–42.

De Vries, L. (1972) *Victorian Inventions*, New York: American Heritage Press.

Dickinson, G. (1997) "Memories for sale: Nostalgia and the construction of identity in Old Pasadena," *Quarterly Journal of Speech* 83: 1–27.

Dunlap, D. W. (1995) "Along Times Sq., signs of new life abound," *New York Times*, 30 April: 2–1.

"Emerging market indicators" (1997) *The Economist*, 25 January: 100.

Enchin, H. (1997) "Imax scores its biggest deal in 10-theatre sale to Regal," *Globe & Mail*, 25 June: 8.

Erenberg, L. (1991) "Impressions of Broadway nightlife," in W. Taylor (ed.), *Inventing Times Square*, New York: Russell Sage Foundation.

Erichetti, M. (1995) "Financing, partnership and management arrangements," Urban Land Institute Professional Development Seminar on "Developing Urban Entertainment Destination Projects," New York, 17 March.

Erickson, B. H. (1996) "Culture, class and connections," *American Journal of Sociology* 102: 217–51.

Euchner, C. (1993) *Playing the Field: Why Sports Teams Move and Cities Fight to Keep Them*, Baltimore, MD: John Hopkins University Press.

Evans, R. ((1997) "Ogden to bring wilderness indoors," *Amusement Business*, 10 March:1; 38.

Fabrikant, G. (1997) "Of all that he sells, he sells himself best," *New York Times*, 1 June: 3–1.

Fader, S. (1995) "Universal CityWalk," *Urban Land* (Supplement), August: 18–23.

Fainstein, S.S. (1994) *The City Builders: Property, Politics and Planning in London and New York*, Oxford, England and Cambridge, Mass.: Blackwell.

Farnham, A. (1992) "US suburbs under siege," *Fortune*, 28 December: 42–4.

Featherstone, M. (1995) *Globalization, Postmodernism and Identity*, London: Sage Publications.

Fine, S. (1989) *Violence in the Model City: The Cavanagh Administration, Race Relations and the Detroit Riot of 1967*, Ann Arbor: University of Michigan Press.

Firat, A.F. and Venkatesh, A. (1995) "Liberatory postmodernism and the re-enchantment of consumption," *Journal of Consumer Research* 22: 239–67.

Fishman, R. (1987) *Bourgeois Utopias: The Rise and Fall of Suburbia*, New York: Basic Books.

Fitzsimmons, D.S. (1995) "Planning and promotion: City reimaging in the 1980s and 1990s," in W.J.V. Neill, D.S. Fitzsimmons and B. Murtagh (eds), *Reimaging the Pariah City: Urban Development in Belfast and Detroit*, Aldershot: Avebury.

Fjellman, S.M. (1992) *Vinyl Leaves: Walt Disney World and America*, Boulder, CO: Westview Press.

Fleissing, W.B. (1984) "The Yerba Buena Center," in K.W. Green (ed.), *The City as Stage*, Washington DC: Partners for Livable Places.

Frankel, M. (1997) "Machinations," *New York Times Magazine*, 11 May: 24.

Freudenburg, W.R. (1992) "Addictive economies: Extractive industries and vulnerable localities in a changing world economy," *Rural Sociology* 57: 305–32.

Frieden, B.J. and Sagalyn, L.B. (1989) *Downtown, Inc.: How America Rebuilds Cities*, Cambridge, Mass.: MIT Press.

Friend, T. (1996) "Strug vaults straight into life of fame," *New York Times*, 6 September: B–17; 19.

Furie, P. (1991) "Irving Berlin: Troubador of Tin Pan Alley," in W. Taylor (ed.), *Inventing Times Square*, New York: Russell Sage Foundation.

Gabarine, R. (1997) "2d anchor begun in Trenton's revitalization plan," *New York Times*, 14 December: 11–17.

Gamerman, A. (1995) "Sony's new multiplex palace: cinema nostalgia," *Wall Street Journal*, 22 July: A–14.

Garreau, J. (1991) *Edge City: Life on the New Frontier*, New York: Doubleday.

Gelsi, S. (1997) "Sony's showcase at sea," *Brandweek*, 3 February: 20–1.

Gill, A. (1997) "Pop goes the highbrow cultural institution," *Globe & Mail*, 13 June: C–1, 2.

Glaser, J. (with A.A. Zenetou) (1996) *Museums: A Place to Work*, London and New York: Routledge/Smithsonian Institution.

Gleick, E. (1997) "Tower of psychobabble," *TIME*, 16 June: 59–61.

Glennie, P. and Thrift, N. (1996) "Consumption, shopping and gender," in N. Wrigley and M. Lowe (eds), *Retailing, Consumption and Capital: Towards the New Retail Geography*, Harlow, Essex: Longman Group Limited.

Go, F.M. (1997) "Asian and Australasian dimensions of global tourism development," in F.M. Go, and C.L. Jenkins (eds), *Tourism and Economic Development in Asia and Australasia*, London and Washington, DC: Cassell.

Goldberg, C. (1997) "Billionaire finances a vote about replacing stadium," *New York Times*, 25 May: 14.

Goldberger, P. (1996) "The rise of the private city," in J. Vitullo Martin (ed.), *Breaking Away: The Future of Cities*, New York: The Twentieth Century Fund.

——(1997) "The store strikes back," *New York Times Magazine*, 6 April: 45–9.

Goldfield, D. R. (1989) *Cotton Fields and Skyscrapers: Southern City and Region*, Baltimore: Johns Hopkins University Press.

Gomery, D. (1992) *Shared Pleasures: A History of Movie Presentation in the United States*, Madison, WI: University of Wisconsin Press.

Goodman, R. (1995) *The Luck Business: The Devastating Consequences and Broken Promises of America's Gambling Explosion*, New York: The Free Press.

Gordon, S. (1995) "Defining a concept, structuring a program and creating a development strategy," Urban Land Institute Professional Development Seminar on "Developing Urban Entertainment Destination Projects," New York, 16 March.

Gornto, M.M. (1981) "Festivals are effective promotion tools," *Center City Report* (International Downtown Executives Association), June: 10–11.

Goss, J. (1996) "Disquiet on the waterfront: Reflections on nostalgia and utopia in the urban archetypes of festival marketplaces," *Urban Geography* 17: 221–47.

Gottdiener, M. (1997) *The Theming of America: Dreams, Visions, and Commercial Spaces*, Boulder, CO.: Westview Press.

Graham, J. (1989) *Vegas: Live and In Person*, New York: Abbeville Press.

Gratz, R. Brandes (1989) *The Living City*, New York: Touchstone.

Gray, C. (1997) "When a big waterfall was a sign of Times Square," *New York Times*, 30 March: 9–5.

Green, K.W. (ed.) (1984) *The City as a Stage: Strategies for the Arts in Urban Economies*, Washington, DC: Partners for Livable Places.

Gregory, M. (1992) "Communities bet their bottom dollar," *Public Investment*, September: 1–4.

Griffin, N. and Masters, K. (1996) *Hit and Run: How Jon Peters and Peter Guber Took Sony for a Ride in Hollywood*, New York: Simon & Schuster.

Grinols, E. L. (1994) "Bluff or winning hand? Riverboat gambling and regional employment and unemployment," *Illinois Business Review*, Spring issue.

Grossman, J.R. (1989) *Land of Hope: Chicago, Black Southerners and the Great Migration*, Chicago: University of Chicago Press.

Grover, R., Weber, J. and Melcher, R.A. (1994) "The entertainment economy," *Business Week*, 14 March: 58–64.

Guthreau, C., Wissinger, B., Halling, M., Lawler, K., Vitale, A.S., Nerio, R., Halley, J., Greenberg, M., Baskerville, R. and Stack, R. (1997) "'Growth, decline and the American dream': Las Vegas, Coney Island and the urban imaginary." Paper presented to the Annual Meeting of the American Sociological Association, Toronto, 9 August.

Hackett, V. (1995a) "Financing urban entertainment destination projects" *Urban Land* (Supplement), August: 25–8.

——(1995b) "Financing, partnership and management arrangements," Urban Land Institute Professional Development Seminar on "Urban Entertainment Projects," New York, 17 March.

Hackett, V. (1996) "Greenwood theater opens in Tenn's River Bluff Landing complex," *Amusement Business*, 15–21 April: 15.

Haggerty, M. (1995) "Rouse remains bullish on big regional shopping centers," *Washington Post*, 27 February: WB–37.

Haley, A.J. and Truitt, L.J. (1995) "Riverboat gambling in Illinois," *Annals of Tourism Research* 22: 694–5.

Halliday, A. (1996) "Partnering for success," Urban Land Institute Professional Development Seminar on "Urban Entertainment Development: Lights, Camera and Now What?," New York, 3 June.

Handy, B. (1997) "Miracle on 42nd St," TIME, 7 April: 50–3.

Hannigan, J.A. (1995) "The postmodern city: a new urbanization?," *Current Sociology* 43(1): 151–217.

Harrison, J. (1997) "Museums and touristic expectations," *Annals of Tourism Research* 24(1): 23–40.

Hartman, C. (1973) *Yerba Buena: Land Grab and Community Resistance in San Francisco*, San Francisco: Glide Publications.

Harvard Business School (1984) "Cultural revitalization in six cities," in K.W. Green (ed.), *The City as a Stage*, Washington DC: Partners for Livable Places.

Harvey, D. (1991) "The urban face of capitalism," in J.F. Hunt (ed.), *Our Changing Cities*, Baltimore: The John Hopkins University Press.

Heazle, M. (1996a) "Digital didgeridoos," *Far Eastern Economic Review* 159 (30): 68.

—— (1996b) "Reef grief," *Far Eastern Economic Review* 159 (49): 72–3.

Herron, J. (1993) *After Culture: Detroit and the Humiliation of History*, Detroit: Wayne State University Press.

Hewison, R. (1987) *The Heritage Industry: Britain in a Climate of Decline*, London: Methuen.

Hillman, S. (1984) "Leveraging prosperity in Baltimore," in K.W. Green (ed.), *The City as Stage*, Washington DC: Partners for Livable Places.

Himmel, K. (1995) "Planning and design innovations," Urban Land Institute Professional Development Seminar on "Developing Urban Entertainment Destination Projects," New York, 16 March.

Hochschild, A.R. (1997) *The Time Bind: When Work Becomes Home and Home Becomes Work*, New York: Metropolitan Books/Harry Holt & Company.

House, K. (1997) "Wonderland sold to Malaysia," *Financial Review* (Australia), 1 April.

"How to remake a city" (1997) *The Economist*, 31 May– 6 June: 25–6.

Hughes, R. (1996) "The case for elitist do-gooders," *New Yorker*, 27 May: 32–4.

Huxtable, A. L. (1997a) *The Unreal America: Architecture and Illusion*, New York: The New Press.

——(1997b) "Living with the fake and liking it," *New York Times*, 30 March: 2–1; 40.

"Imax expands relationship with Sony," *TCI* (*Theatre Crafts International*) 29(5): 15.

"In the Philippines, golf is the only game in town" (1996) *Asiaweek*, 28 June: 54.

Iovine, J.V. (1997) "Show biz grows from seedling to cash crop," *New York Times*, 2 November: 1–1, 30.

Jaher, F.C. (1982) *The Urban Establishment: Upper Strata in Boston, New York, Charleston, Chicago and Los Angeles*, Urbana, IL: University of Illinois Press.

Jackson, K.T. (1985) *Crabgrass Frontier: The Suburbanization of the United States*, New York: Oxford University Press.

James, C. (1997) "A master of suspense, with a touch like Midas's," *New York Times*, 13 June: B–16.

Jaques, Jnr, C.J. (1981) "Theme Parks in the New York area," *Amusement Park Journal* 3 (January): 30–4.

——(1982) *Kennywood: Roller Coaster Capital of the World*, Vestal, NY: Vestal Press.

Jerde, J. (1995) "Casinos: Playing the urban entertainment card beyond Las Vegas," Urban Land Institute Professional Development Seminar on "Developing Urban Entertainment Projects: The Sequel," Beverly Hills, CA, 26 October.

Jimenez, C. (1997) "A virtual world open indoors," *Financial Review* (Australia): 19 March.

Jinker-Lloyd, A. (1996) "Gambling on economic development," *American City & County*, 111(8): 57–64.

Johannesen, E. (1984) "Cleveland's Circle and Square," in K.W. Green (ed.), *The City as a Stage*, Washington DC: Partners for Livable Places.

Johnson, G. (1996) "Dispute over Indian casinos in New Mexico produces quandary on law and politicians," *New York Times*, 18 August: 1–10.

Johnson, M.D. (1995) "Public/private partnership produces ice-skating rink," *Urban Land* 54(8): 14–16.

214

Johnston, D.C. (1995) "Disney names casino expert to a top post," *New York Times*, 5 April: C–6.

Jonas, S. and Nissenson, M.N. (1994) *Going Going Gone: Vanishing Americana*, San Francisco: Chronicle Books.

Jowett, G. (1976) *Film: The Democratic Art*, Boston: Little, Brown & Company.

Kakutani, M. (1996) "Slumming," *New York Times Magazine*, 26 May: 16.

Kaplan, D. (1997) "Music biz sees inspiration in experiential retailing," *Billboard*, 17 May: 1; 74.

Kasson, J.F. (1978) *Amusing the Millions: Coney Island at the Turn of the Century*, New York: Hill & Wang.

Katz, W. (1996) "Mohegan Sun: Theme gaming," *Urban Land* 55(8): 32–5.

Kaufman, J. (1996) "Fergie on her toes for another tour," *Wall Street Journal*, 19 November: A–20.

King, M.J. (1991) "Never Land or Tomorrowland?," *Museum* 169(1): 6–8.

Kornblum, W. and Williams, T. (1978) "Lifestyle, leisure, and community life," in D. Street and Associates (ed.), *Handbook of Contemporary Urban Life*, San Francisco: Jossey-Bass Publishers.

Korol, P. (1987) "Victorian ride simulators," *Amusement Park Journal* 9(4): 7–9.

Koselka, R. (1995) "Mergermania in medialand" (an interview with Michael J. Wolf), *Forbes*, 23 October: 252–9.

Kowinski, W. S. (1985) *The Malling of America*, New York: William Morris and Company.

Kuenz, J. (1993) "It's a small world after all: Disney and the pleasures of identification," *The South Atlantic Quarterly* 92(1): 63–88.

Kuklick, B. (1991) *To Every Thing a Season: Shibe Park and Urban Philadelphia, 1909–1976*, Princeton, NJ: Princeton University Press.

Kyriazi, G. (1976) *The Great American Amusement Park: A Pictorial History*, Seacaucus, NJ: Citadel Press.

Labalme, J. (1995) "Belly up on the Mississippi," *Southern Exposure*, Spring: 10.

Landler, M. (1994) "Are we having fun yet? Maybe too much," *Business Week*, 14 March: 66.

Landro, L. (1996) "Entertainment-industry outlook is a tearjerker," *Wall Street Journal*, 9 July: B–1; B–3.

Langdon, P. (1994) "Sprawl control," *Progressive Architecture*, 75 (November): 74–9.

Lash, S. and Urry, J. (1994) *Economies of Signs and Space*, London: Sage.

Law, C.M. (1992) "Urban tourism and its contribution to economic regeneration," *Urban Studies*, 29: 597–618.

——(1993) *Urban Tourism: Attracting Visitors to Large Cities*, New York and London: Mansell Publishing Limited.

Lawrence, J. C. (1992) "Geographical space, social space and the realm of the department store," *Urban History*, 19: 64–83.

Leach, W. (1991) "Brokers and the new corporate-industrial order," in W. Taylor (ed.), *Inventing Times Square*, New York: Russell Sage Foundation.

——(1993) *Land of Desire: Merchants, Power and the Rise of a New American Culture*, New York: Pantheon Books.

Lears, J. (1997) "No there there," *New York Times Book Review*, 28 December: 9–10.

Lee, R.L.M. (1994) "Modernization, postmodernism and the third world," *Current Sociology*, 42(2): 1–66.

Leonhardt, D. (1997) "Are pro sports conning our cities?" (review of Rosentraub 1997), *Business Week*, 3 March: 13.

Levine, J. (1995) "Hamburgers and tennis socks," *Forbes*, 20 November: 184–5.

Levine, M.V. (1987) "Downtown redevelopment as an urban growth strategy: a critical appraisal of the Baltimore Renaissance," *Journal of Urban Affairs*, 9(2): 103–23.

——(1989) "The politics of partnership: Urban redevelopment since 1945," in G.D. Squires (ed.), *Unequal Partnerships: The Political Economy of Urban Redevelopment in Postwar America*, New Brunswick, NJ: Rutgers University Press.

Levy, D. (1996) "Panel oks Yerba Buena Gardens retail complex,"*San Francisco Chronicle*, 7 February: A–15.

Ley, D. (1996) *The New Middle Class and the Remaking of the Central City*, Oxford and New York: Oxford University Press.

Lipsyte, R. (1997) "Wish upon a star, then be one," *New York Times*, 27 July: 8–1, 4.

Lockwood, C. (1994) "Edge cities on the brink," *Wall Street Journal*, 21 December: A–14.

Logan, J.R. and Molotch, H.L. (1987) *Urban Fortunes: The Political Economy of Place*, Berkeley and Los Angeles: University of California Press.

Lorimer, J. (1978) *The Developers*, Toronto: James Lorimer & Company.

Lundberg, G.A., Komarowsky, M. and McInerny, M.A. (1934) *Leisure: A Suburban Study* (Reprint New York: Agathon Press, Inc., 1969), New York: Columbia University Press.

MacBride, P. (1995) "The world of entertainment destination projects," Urban Land Institute Professional Development Seminar on "Urban Entertainment Destination Projects," New York, 16 March.

MacCannell, D. (1976) *The Tourist: A New Theory of the Leisure Class*, New York: Schocken.

McCormick, J.T. (1996) "Bringing retail back to downtown Norfolk," *Urban Land* 55(5): 10–11.

McCormick, K. (1997) "In the clutch of casinos," *Planning* 63(6): 4–9.

McCormick, M. (1997) "Viacom's flagship store opens," *Billboard*, 7 June: 67–8.

McCoy, B.H. (1994) "The creative destruction of real estate capital markets," *Urban Land* 53 (6): 19–22.

Macdonald, G. (1995) "Gretsky plans rink chain," *Financial Post*, 8 August: 1–2.

Macdonald, S. (1996) "Theorizing museums: An introduction," in S. Macdonald and G. Fyfe (eds), *Theorizing Museums*, Oxford, England and Cambridge, Mass. : Blackwell Publishers/The Sociological Review.

McLaughlin, G. (1996) "Peter's priciples," *Financial Post*, 21 December: 8.

McMillen, J. (1996) "From glamour to grind: The globalisation of casinos," in J. McMillen (ed.), *Gambling Cultures: Studies in History and Interpretation*, London and New York: Routledge.

McNamara, B. (1991) "The entertainment district at the end of the 1930s," in W. Taylor (ed.), *Inventing Times Square*, New York: Russell Sage Foundation.

McNulty, R.H., Penne, R.L., Jacobson, D.R. and Partners for Livable Places (1986) *The Return of the Livable City: Learning from America's Best*, Washington, DC: Acropolis Books Ltd.

Maffesoli, M. (1996) *The Time of the Tribes: The Decline of Individualism in Mass Society*, London: Sage.

Maffi, M. (1994) "The other side of the coin: Culture in Loisaida," in J.L. Abu-Lughod (ed.), *From Urban Village to East Village*, Oxford, England and Cambridge, Mass.: Blackwell.

Magyar, L.F. (1997) "Back to the future: A Century of Selling," (boxed insert) in "The store strikes back," *New York Times Magazine*, 6 April: 45–9.

Marcy, L.B. (1994) "The evolution of Walt Disney World," *Urban Land*, October: 36–41; 84.

Marks, P. (1997) "Climbing tooth and claw to the top of the heap," *New York Times*, 15 June: 2–4, 30.

Martin, D. (1996) "Amazing! Odd! Incredible! 2 sideshows on 1 street!," *New York Times*, 2 June: 1–17.

Melvin, M.K. (1996a) "Ogden IFC to manage Sydney venue," *Amusement Business*, 23 September: 1, 11.

—— (1996b) "Massachusetts Spookyworld Park adds $600,000 worth of scary stuff," *Amusement Business*, 7 October: 11.

——(1996c) "Six Flags studying potential Conn. site," *Amusement Business*, 11 November: 51.

—— (1996d) "Madison Scare Garden frightens nearly 48,000, grosses $743,270," *Amusement Business*, 18 November: 7.

—— (1997) "MADhattan re-creates the New York experience," *Amusement Business*, 31 March: 5.

Merritt, R. (1976) "Nickelodeon theatres 1905–1914: Building an audience for the movies," in T. Balio (ed.), *The American Film Industry*, Madison WI: University of Wisconsin Press.

Miles, S. (1996) "The cultural capital of consumption: understanding 'postmodern' identities in a cultural context," *Culture & Psychology* 2: 139–58.

Miller, C. Poh, and Wheeler, R. (1990) *Cleveland: A Concise History, 1796–1990*, Bloomington and Indianapolis: Indiana University Press.

Millspaugh, M. (1995) "Urban revitalization: A public perspective on entertainment destinations," Urban Land Institute Professional Development Seminar on "Developing Urban Entertainment Destination Projects," New York, 16 March.

Milner, B. (1997a) "New York developer eyes Toronto site: Millennium has designs on land adjacent to Eaton Centre," *Globe & Mail*, 10 June: A–1.

——(1997b) "Play centres dress up downtowns," *Globe & Mail*, 15 September: B–1.

Molotch, H. (1996) "LA as a design product: How art works in a regional economy," in A.J. Scott and E.W. Soja (eds) *The City: Los Angeles and Urban Theory at the End of the Twentieth Century*, Berkeley and Los Angeles: University of California Press.

"More than just cafes, Rank plans to expand Hard Rock" (1996) *New York Times*, 9 August: C–4.

Morgenson, G. (1993) "The fall of the mall," *Forbes*, 24 May: 106–12.

Morris, K. (1997) "REITS are going like a house afire," *Business Week*, 2 June: 122–3.

Morris, M. (1988) "Things to do with shopping centres," *Culture Studies*, WP 1 Centre for Twentieth Century Studies, University of Wisconsin-Milwaukee, 1:2.

Munkacy, K. (1997a) "East meets West in retail development," *Urban Land* (Asia Supplement), May: 28–30.

——(1997b) "Feng Shui," *Urban Land* (Asia Supplement), May: 30.

Muret, D. (1996a) "Both established and emerging markets have something to offer," *Amusement Business*, 5–11 August: 38–9.

——(1996b) "The name is the game," *Amusement Business*, June 24: 19.

——(1997a) "Interactive Viacom Entertainment Store merges six of its most popular brands," *Amusement Business*, 9 June: 5.

——(1997b) "Ogden enters FEC industry with 'Enchanted' purchase," *Amusement Business*, 24 November: 1, 26.

Muschamp, H. (1995a) "A flare for fantasy: 'Miami Vice' meets 42nd Street," *New York Times*, 21 May: 2–1, 27.

——(1995b) "Remodeling New York for the bourgeoisie," *New York Times*, 24 September: 2–1, 38.

Musser, C. (1990) *The Emergence of Cinema: The American Screen to 1907*, New York: Charles Scribner's Sons.

Mydans, S. (1996) "Clan tied to American donations created in Indonesian empire," *New York Times*, 20 October: 1–6.

Myers, D.W. (1995) "Gaming bug spreads across country," *Urban Land* 54(8): 55.

Naisbitt, J. (1996) *Megatrends Asia*, New York: Simon & Schuster.

Nasaw, D. (1993) *Going Out: The Rise and Fall of Public Amusements*, New York: Harper-Collins.

Newborne, E. (1997) "This exhibit is brought to you by . . . ," *Business Week*, 10 November: 91, 94.

"New construction, parks & attractions: a partial list of proposed projects in the Far East," *Amusement Business*, 5–11 August: 22, 36.

"Next step: The space station" (1997) *The E Zone* 1(5): 4.

Noll, R.G. (1974) "Attendance and price setting," in R.G. Noll (ed.), *Government and the Sports Business*, Washington, DC: Brookings Institution.

Norkunas, M.K. (1993) *The Politics of Public Memory: Tourism, History, and Ethnicity in Montery, California*, Albany, NY: State University of New York Press.

Nye, R.B. (1981) "Eight ways of looking at an amusement park," *Journal of Popular Culture*, 15: 63–75.

O'Brien, T. (1996a) "Themed eateries thriving on crowds of others, but how long will it last," *Amusement Business*, 4 March ; 2–3; 38.

——(1996b) "Themed eateries hit big time," *Amusement Business*, 13 May: 15–16.

——(1996c) "With three amusement parks, Seoul has arrived," *Amusement Business*, 5 August: 24–7.

——(1996d) "Universal-Fla.: Buy Halloween tix early or risk being left in the dark," *Amusement Business*, 30 September: 6.

——(1996e) "Six Flags to build up at home before going abroad," *Amusement Business*, 7 October: 3.

——(1996f) "Warner's Australian parks gain momentum," *Amusement Business*, 9 December: 1, 16.

——(1997a) "Kennedy Space Center Visitor center predicts 10% increase in attendance," *Amusement Business*, 31 March: 34.

——(1997b) "Australia" s Wonderland sold for $39 mil," *Amusement Business*, 14 April: 22.

——(1997c) "Parks using Halloween events to score up shoulder season business," *Amusement Business*, 27 October: 5: 17.

——(1998) "Ogden Entertainment moving into entertainment product ownership," *Amusement Business*, 12 January: 17.

O'Connor, J. and Wynne, D. (1993) *From the Margins to the Centre: Cultural Production and Consumption in the Post-Industrial City*, Manchester: Manchester Institute for Popular Culture (*Working Papers in Popular Cultural Studies*, no. 7).

Oertley, K. (1996) "I theme, you theme, we all theme," *Amusement Business*, 8–14 April: 2.

O'Meara, M. (1997) "Table has turned for Jupiters," *Financial Review* (Australia), 6 February.

——and Syvret, S. (1997) "Park operators are head over heals with their results," *Financial Review* (Australia), 31 January.

Orwall, B. (1996a) "Hard Rock Cafe empire to be reunited as Morton plans to sell his half to Rank," *Wall Street Journal*, 10 June: B–8.

——(1996b) "Gambling industry hopes to hit jackpot through consolidation," *Wall Street Journal*, 10 June: A–1,10.

——(1996c) "Rank Organisation and Trump Hotels to develop Hard Rock Cafe at casinos," *Wall Street Journal*, 3 October: A–4.

——(1996d) "Roller-coaster ride of Stratosphere Corp. is a tale of Las Vegas," *Wall Street Journal*, 27 October: A–1,6.

——and Pope, K. (1997) "Disney, ABC promised 'synergy' in merger; so what happened?," *Wall Street Journal*, 16 May: A–1, 9.

"Outlet center opens near 6 Flags Park," (1997) *New York Times*, 4 May: 9–1.

Pacelle, M. and King, T.R. (1996) "MCA picks Loews as partner in plan for Florida hotels to challenge Disney," *Wall Street Journal*, 3 May: B–12.

Pagano, M.A. and Bowman A. (1995) *Cityscapes and Capital*, Baltimore and London: The John Hopkins University Press.

Palen, J.J. (1992) *The Urban World* (4th edition), New York: McGraw-Hill, Inc.

——(1995) *The Suburbs*, New York: McGraw-Hill, Inc.

Panek, R. (1997) "Superstore inflation," *New York Times Magazine*, 6 April: 66–74.

Park, R. (1929) "Introduction" to H. M. Zorbaugh, *The Gold Coast and the Slum*, Chicago: University of Chicago Press.

——(1938) "Introduction" to A.W. Lind, *An Island Community: Ecological Succession in Hawaii*, Chicago: University of Chicago Press.

Peiss, K. (1986) *Working Women and Leisure in Turn-of-the-Century New York*, Philadelphia: Temple University Press.

Perez-Pena, R. (1997) "Economists dispute value of spending for stadiums," *New York Times*, 3 August: 29, 31.

Perez-Rivas, M. (1996) "Duncan and 'Dream' developers disagree on what went wrong," *Washington Post*, 14 November: E–9.

——and Pressler, M.W. (1996) "County Executive says developers lack funds," *Washington Post*, 13 November: A–1.

Peter, J. (1967) "A LOOK report on suburban USA," *LOOK Magazine*, 16 May: 28–9.

"Plan for Disneyland in downtown St. Louis is said to be canceled: Civic officials state Disney firm has dropped project" (1965) *Wall Street Journal*, 9 July: 13.

"Planet Hollywood and AMC in venture" (1997) *New York Times*, 25 July: C–5.

Pollack, A. (1996) "Remaking Sony, bit by bit," *New York Times*, 19 May: 3–1: 10–11.

Pollack, K. (1996) "A tribe that's raking it in," *U.S. News & World Report*, 15 January: 59.

Pollan, M. (1997) "Town-building is no Mickey Mouse operation," *New York Times*, 16 May: 28–9.

Popenoe, D. (1977) *The Suburban Environment: Sweden and the United States*, Chicago: University of Chicago Press.

Postman, N. (1985) *Amusing Ourselves to Death*, New York: Viking.

——(1991) "Love your machines," *Museum* 169(1): 9.

Pressler, M. W. (1995) "Developers want help in Silver Spring Mall," *Washington Post*, 9 September: 1–2.

——(1996) "Md. mall fails to find financing: American Dream firm hires New York bank to recruit investors," *Washington Post*, 12 November: A–1.

"Presto! A David Copperfield magic restaurant" (1997) *New York Times*, 13 July: 9–1.

Price, B. (1995) "Defining a concept, structuring a program, and creating a development strategy," Urban Land Institute Seminar on Developing Urban Entertainment Destination Projects, New York, March 16.

Price, J.S. (1962) *The Off-Broadway Theater*, New York: The Scarecrow Press, Inc.

Prindle, D.F. (1993) *Risky Business: The Political Economy of Hollywood*, Boulder, CO: Westview Press.

Provost, G. (1994) *High Stakes: Inside the New Las Vegas*, New York: Truman Talley Books/Dutton.

Purcell, K. (1997) "Review of Gottdiener (1997)," *Community and Urban Sociology Section Newsletter* (American Sociological Association) 25(3): 12.

Purdy, M. (1997) "Disney to turn Manhattan Goofy," *New York Times*, 13 June: A–15.

Reardon, K.M. (1997) "State and local revitalization efforts in East St. Louis, Illinois," in D. Wilson (ed.), "Globalization and the Changing U.S. City," *Annals* 551 (May): 235–47.

Reekie, G. (1992) "Changes in the Adamless Eden: The spatial and sexual transformation of a Brisbane department store 1930–90," in R. Shields (ed.), *Lifestyle Shopping: The Subject of Consumption*, London and New York: Routledge.

Register, Jnr, W.W. (1991) "New York's gigantic toy," in W. Taylor (ed.), *Inventing Times Square*, New York: Russell Sage Foundation.

Reinhard, R.T. (1984) "Synergistic environment spours Richmond's growth," *Center City report* (International Downtown Executives Association), April: 1–2; 6.

Relph, E. (1976) *Place and Placelessness*, London: Pion Ltd.

Renzetti, E. (1997) "Monster musicals take to the road," *Globe & Mail*, 3 May: C–10.

Reyes, A. (1996) "Taking China for a ride: a Hong Kong group wants to be like Disney," *Asiaweek*, 30 August: 49.

Rice, V. (1996) "Casino ready to roll Dec. 9," *The Standard* (St Catherines-Niagara), 14 November: A–1,3.

Richter, L. K. (1989) *The Politics of Tourism in Asia*, Honolulu: University of Hawaii Press.

Riess, S.A. (1989) *City Games: The Evolution of American Urban Society and the Rise of Sports*, Urbana and Chicago: University of Illinois Press.

Rimmer, P.J. (1992) "Japan's resort archipelago: Creating regions of fun, pleasure, relaxation and recreation," *Environment and Planning "A"* 24: 1599–1625.

Ritzer, G. (1993) *The McDonaldization of Society*, Thousand Oaks, CA: Pine Forge Press.

Roberts, S.M. and Schein, R.H. (1993) "The entrepreneurial city: Fabricating urban development in Syracuse, New York," *Professional Geographer* 45(1): 21–33.

Robertson, K.A. (1995) "Downtown redevelopment strategies in the United States: An end-of-the-century assessment," *Journal of the American Planning Association* 61(4): 429–37.

Robinett, J. and Camp, D. (1997) "Urban entertainment centers signal an emerging trend," *Urban Land* (Europe Supplement), March: 20–2.

Rogers, B. (1996) "Emerging projects, financing deals and technology: an update," Urban Land Institute Professional Seminar on "Urban Entertainment Development: Lights, Camera, and Now What?," New York, 3–4 June.

Rohde, D. (1997) "Revival of the 'Crown Jewel' of Brooklyn is stalled again," *New York Times*, 22 June: B–10.

Rojek, C. (1993) *Ways of Escape: Modern Transformations in Leisure and Travel*, Basingstoke: Macmillan.

Rood, K.L. (1994) *Dictionary of Twentieth Century Culture*, Detroit: Gale Research Inc.

Rosentraub, M.S. (1996) "Does the emperor have new clothes? A reply to Robert A. Baade," *Journal of Urban Affairs* 18(1): 23–31.

——(1997) *Major League Losers: The Real Cost of Sports and Who's Paying For It*, New York: Basic Books.

Rosenzweig, R. (1983) *Eight Hours For What We Will: Workers and Leisure in an Industrial City, 1870–1920*, Cambridge, England: Cambridge University Press.

——and Blackmar, E. (1992) *The Park and the People: A History of Central Park*, Ithaca, NY: Cornell University Press.

Roth, M. (1976) "Going downtown to suburbia," *Chicago* 25 (August), 114; 177.

Rouse, J.W. (1984) "The case for vision," in P.R. Porter and D.C. Sweet (eds), *Rebuilding America's Cities: Roads to Recovery*, New Brunswick, NJ: Center for Urban Policy Research.

Rowe, P.G. (1991) *Making a Middle Landscape*, Cambridge, Mass.: The MIT Press.

Ruben, P.L. (1987) "Randall Duell – pioneering park design," *Amusement Park Journal* 9(3): 8–10.

Rubin, C. (1996) "Partnering for success," Urban Land Institute Professional Development Seminar on "Urban Entertainment Development: Lights, Camera and Now What?" New York, 3 June.

Rubin, M. (1995) "The world of entertainment destination projects," Urban Land Institute Professional Development Seminar on "Developing Urban Destination Projects," New York, 16 March.

——and Gorman, R.J (1993) "Reinventing leisure," *Urban Land*, February: 26–32.

Rubin, M., Gorman, R.J., and Lawry, M.H. (1994) "Entertainment returns to Gotham," *Urban Land* 53(8): 59–65.

Rybczynski, W. (1996) "Tomorrowland," *The New Yorker*, 22 July: 36–9.

—— (1997) "Review of Huxtable (1997b), *New York Times Book Review*, 6 April: 13.

Sagalyn, L.B. (1997)"Negotiating for public benefits: the bargaining calculus of public–private development," *Urban Studies* 34: 1955–70.

Savage, M. and Warde, A. (1993) *Urban Sociology, Capitalism And Modernity*, Basingstoke: Macmillan.

Schmidt, L.E. (1995) *Consumer Rites: The Buying and Selling of American Holidays*, Princeton, NJ: Princeton University Press.

Schor, J.B. (1991) *The Overworked American: The Unexpected Decline in Leisure*, New York: Basic Books.

Schuyler, D. (1986) *The New Urban Landscape: The Redefinition of City Form in Nineteenth Century America*, Baltimore: John Hopkins University Press.

Segrave, K. (1992) *Drive-In Theaters: A History from Their Inception in 1933*, Jefferson, NC: McFarland & Company, Inc.

Selhot, L. (1995) "Penn's Landing: Philadelphia's birthplace reborn," *Urban Land* 54 (10): 47–50.

Sennett, R. (1969) "Middle class families and urban violence: the experience of a Chicago community in the nineteenth century," in S. Thernstrom and R. Sennett (eds), *Nineteenth Century Cities: Essays in New Urban History*, New Haven: Yale University Press.

Serino, J. (1996) "Signature entertainment gaining ground in urban development field," *Amusement Business*, 8–14 July: 26, 28.

Serrano, B. (1996) "Anaheim beckons Seahawks owner," *Seattle Times*, 7 February.

Shapiro, J. (with T.M. Ito, P. Loeb, K. Pollack and G. Cohen) (1996) "America's gambling fever," *U.S. News & World Report*, 15 January: 52–61.

Sharkey, N. (1997) "The learning vacation produced by Disney," *New York Times*, 1 June: 5–8,9, 28.

Shields, R. (1989) "Social spatialization and the built environment: the West Edmonton Mall," *Environment and Planning D: Society and Space* 7: 147–64.

Short, J.R. (1996) *The Urban Order: An Introduction to Cities, Culture and Power*, Cambridge Mass. and Oxford: Blackwell.

Shropshire, K.L. (1995) *The Sports Franchise Game: Cities in Pursuit of Sports Franchises, Stadiums and Arenas*, Philadelphia: University of Pennsylvania Press.

Siegel, L.C. (1996) "The changing face of value retail," *Urban Land* 55(5): 29–32; 58–9.

Sigafoos, R.A. (1962) "What is happening to the downtown business district?," *Western City Magazine*, June: 25–6.

Simon Property's purchase of DeBartalo creates real estate giant," *Financial Post*, 27 March: 10.

Slater, C. (1995) "Amazonia as Edenic narrative," in W. Cronon (ed.), *Uncommon Ground*, New York: W.W. Norton & Company.

Smith, M.P. (1979) *The City and Social Theory*, New York: St Martin's Press.

Smith, N., Duncan, B. and Reid, L. (1994) "From disinvestment to re-investment: mapping the urban frontier in the Lower East Side," in J.L. Abu-Lughod (ed.), *From Urban Village to East Village*, Oxford, England and Cambridge Mass.: Blackwell.

Snyder, R.W. (1989) *The Voice of the City: Vaudeville and Popular Culture in New York*, New York: Oxford University Press.

Soja, E. (1989) *Postmodern Geographies*, New York: Verso.

Sorkin, M. (ed.) (1992a) *Variations on a Theme Park: The New American City and the End of Public Space*, New York: Hill & Wang.

——(1992b) "See you in Disneyland," in M. Sorkin (ed.), *Variations on a Theme Park*, New York: Hill & Wang.

Squires, G.D. (1989) "Public–private partnerships: Who gets what and why," in G.D. Squires (ed.) *Unequal Partnerships: The Political Economy of Urban Redevelopment in Postwar America*, New Brunswick, NJ and London: Rutgers University Press.

Stagg, J. (1968) *The Brothers Shubert*, New York: Random House.

Stanek, F. (1996) "The international dimension," Urban Land Institute Professional Development Seminar on "Urban Entertainment: Development: Lights, Camera, and Now What?," New York, 3–4 June.

" Stars draw throng to the Planet," (1997) *The Vancouver Sun*, March 17: A–1, 6

Steinhauer, J. (1997) "Halloween buying: How sweet it is," *New York Times*, 2 November: 4–2.

Stern, J.D. (1995) "An amusement park moves downtown," *Urban Land*, 54 (8): 13–14.

Sterngold, J. (1996a) "20 years after Howard Hughes died, his empire ends," *New York Times*, 23 February: C–4.

——(1996b) "ITT and Planet Hollywood to develop casinos," *New York Times*, 28 June: C–6.

Storm, J. (1995) "Urban entertainment centers – enhancing value in high-density commercial areas," Urban Land Institute Fall Meeting, Philadelphia, November.

Stokowski, P. (1996) *Riches and Regrets: Betting on Gambling in Two Colorado Mountain Towns*, Niwot, CO: University Press of Colorado.

Sugrue, T.J. (1996) *The Origins of the Urban Crisis: Race and Inequality in Postwar Detroit*, Princeton, NJ: Princeton University Press.

Surface, M. (1983) "Recollections of Pacific Ocean Park," *Amusement Park Journal* 5(1): 41–3.

Suris, O. and Blumenstein, R. (1996) "Lions and Tigers help Detroit roar back to life, " *Wall Street Journal*, 21 August: A–2.

Takiff, J. (1995) "A tough new competitor in the arena," *Philadelphia Daily News*, 31 May: 22.

Talmadge, E. (1996) "Japanese get away to theme parks," *Globe & Mail*, 24 December: B–5.

Tarlow, P.E. and Muesham, M.J. (1996) "Lessons from the Mississippi casino-gaming experience," *Annals of Tourism Research*, 23: 709–10.

Taylor, W.R. (1988) "The launching of a commercial culture: New York City 1860–1930," in J. H. Mollenkopf (ed.), *Power, Culture and Place: Essays on New York City*, New York: Russell Sage Foundation.

——(1991a) *Inventing Times Square: Commerce and Culture at the Crossroads of the World*, New York: Russell Sage Foundation.

——(1991b) "Broadway: the place that words built," in W. Taylor (ed.), *Inventing Times Square*.

"TEA forms Eastern U.S. chapters," *TCI (Theatre Crafts International)* 31(4), April: 23.

Teaford, J.C. (1990) *The Rough Road to Renaissance: Urban Revitalization in America, 1940–1985*, Baltimore: Johns Hopkins University Press.

"Thais eager to consumer," (1996) *Financial Post*, 3 December: 15.

"The world according to Zell," (1994) *Urban Land* 53(9): 25–9.

Thrift, N. (1993) "An urban impasse," *Theory, Culture & Society* 10: 229–38.

Tippit, S. (1996) "Mickey" s megastore," *The Financial Post*, 5 October: 12.

Traiman, S. (1996) "Staying busy is theme for TEA members," *Amusement Business*, 5–11 August: 20–1.

——(1997) "Industry observers agree: unprecedented growth a central theme in the Pacific Rim," *Amusement Business*, 24 February: 15–16.

Travis, D.J. (1981) *An Autobiography of Black Chicago*, Chicago: Urban Research Institute, Inc.

Urry, J. (1990) *The Tourist Gaze*, London: Sage.

Van Hoogstraten, N. (1991) *Lost Broadway Theatres*, New York: Princeton Architectural Press.

Van Tassel, D.D. and Grabowski, J.J. (1987) *The Encyclopedia of Cleveland History*, Bloomington and Indianapolis: Indiana University Press.

Vander Doelen, C. (1996) "Niagara falls for casino fever," *Windsor Star*, 14 November: A–1, 5.

Veblen, T. (1925) *The Theory of the Leisure Class*, London: Allen & Unwin.

Verhovek, S.H. (1996) "Using ghouls to get to God," *New York Times*, 27 October: 4–1, 3.

Vogel, H.L. (1986) *Entertainment Industry Economics: A Guide for Financial Analysis*, Cambridge: Cambridge University Press.

Waddell, R. (1996a) "Hi-tech attractions highly successful," *Amusement Business*, 5–11 August: 32.

——(1996b) "Better to embrace tailgating than fight tailgating," *Amusement Business*, 13 May: 31–3.

——(1997) "Pittsburgh proposal pegged at $1.5 billion," *Amusement Business*, 9 June: 1;13.

Walker, W. (1997) "Ontario hooked on casino cash," *Toronto Star*, 2 March: WS-3.

Waller, G.A. (1995) *Main Street Amusements: Movies and Commercial Entertainment in a Southern City, 1896–1930*, Washington and London: Smithsonian Institution Press.

"Walt and the golden mouse" (1964) *Forbes*, 15 February: 38–9.

Ward, R. (1984) "Riverfront renaissance meshes old and new," *Center City Report* (International Downtown Executives Association), June: 1–2; 6.

Warford, B. and Holly, B. (1997) "The rise and fall of Cleveland," in D. Wilson (ed.) "Globalization and changing US city," *The Annals of American Academy of Political and Social Science*, 551(5): 208–21.

Warner, S.B. (1968) *The Private City: Philadelphia in Three Periods of its Growth*, Philadelphia: University of Pennsylvania Press.

Warren, S. (1993) "This heaven gives me migraines: The problems and promise of landscapes of leisure," in J. Duncan and D. Ley (eds), *Place/Culture/Representation*, London and New York: Routledge.

——(1994) "Disneyfication of the metropolis: Popular resistance in Seattle," *Journal of Urban Affairs*, 16: 89–107.

Washington, F. (1928) "Recreational facilities for the negro," *American Academy of Political and Social Science, Annals* CXXXX (November).

Weathersby, Jnr. W. (1994) "Las Vegas: Architecture 94," *TCI* (*Theatre Crafts International*) 28(5): 24.

"Hawaii Theater Center revived in Honolulu," (1996) *TCI* 30(7): 10–11.

Weinstein, R.M. (1992) "Disneyland and Coney Island: Reflections on the evolution of the modern amusement park," *Journal of Popular Culture* 26: 131–64.

Weisbrod, C. (1995) "Urban revitalization: a public perspective on entertainment destinations," Urban Land Institute Professional Development Seminar on "Developing Urban Entertainment Destination Projects," New York, 16 March.

Welsh, M. (1996) "Casino countdown," *Toronto Star*, 28 July: WS1, 2.

Wendt, L. and Kogan, H. (1948) *Bet A Million! The Story of John W. Gates* (Reprint New York: Arno Press, 1981), Indianapolis, IN: Bobbs Merrill.

"West Side Yankees" (1996) *New York Times*, 7 April: 4–10.

Wetmore, R. and Sause, H. (1995) "Striking a public/private deal," *Urban Land*, 54(1): 25–8.

Wheeler, C. (1996) "Nation faithful to its vision," *Financial Post*, 9 November: 39.

Whitt, J.A. (1988) "The role of the performing arts in urban competition and growth," in S. Cummings (ed.), *Business Elites & Urban Development: Case Studies & Critical Perspectives*, Albany, NY: SUNY Press.

Widick, B.J. (1989) *Detroit: City of Race and Class Violence*, Detroit: Wayne State University Press.

Wilson, A. (1991) *The Culture of Nature: North American Landscapes From Disney to the Exxon Valdez*, Toronto: Between the Lines.

Wilson, E. (1991) *The Sphinx and the City*, London: Virago.

Wirth, C.L. (1963) "Park visitors increase," *The American City* (September): 24.

Wolfram, J. (1997) "CultureBoom," *The E Zone* 1(5): 6.

Wong, T. (1997) "Officials hail rail lands plan: it's a major vote of confidence in Toronto, mayor says," *Toronto Star*, 26 March: A–5.

Wood, R.C. (1958) *Suburbia: Its People and Their Politics*, Boston: Houghton Mifflin.

Woodbridge, S. (1994) "Yerba Buena Gardens opens in San Francisco," *Progressive Architecture* 75(1): 21.

Woodford, A.M. (1977) *Detroit: American Urban Renaissance*, Tulsa, Oklahoma: Continental Heritage Press.

Wright, T. and Hutchison, R. (1997) "Socio-spatial reproduction, marketing culture, and the built environment," *Research in Urban Sociology*, 4: 187–214.

Wynne, D. (1992) "Cultural quarters," in D. Wynne (ed.), *The Cultural Industry: The Arts in Urban Regeneration*, Aldershot: Avebury.

Young, C. and Wheeler, L. (1994) *Hard Stuff: The Autobiography of Mayor Coleman Young*, New York: Viking.

Zoltak, J. (1996a) "Tavares on Disney's sports plans, future of industry," *Amusement Business*, 24 June: 3.

——(1996b) "Guerilla marketing tactics work for FECs," *Amusement Business*, 5 August: 18–19.

——(1996c) "Indonesian park set to open in '97," *Amusement Business*, 7 October: 9.

——(1996d) "New urban center in Japan draws 7 mil-plus," *Amusement Business*, 7 October: 23.

——(1997a) "Korean corporations eye more park development," *Amusement Business*, 24 February: 18.

——(1997b) "$700 mil S. Korean center targets fall '98 opening," *Amusement Business*, 12 May: 28, 30.

——(1997c) "Sports, trade shows & education on forefront of theming trends," *Amusement Business*, 9 June: 17–18; 25–6.

Zukin, S. (1982) *Loft Living: Culture and Capital in Urban Change*, Baltimore and New York: The John Hopkins University Press.

——(1991) *Landscapes of Power: From Detroit to Disney World*, Berkeley and Los Angeles: University of California Press.

——(1995)*The Cultures of Cities*, Cambridge, Mass.: Blackwell.

NAME INDEX

SUBJECT INDEX